Richard Brinsley Sheridan, James P. Browne

The Works of Richard Brinsley Sheridan

Vol. I

Richard Brinsley Sheridan, James P. Browne

The Works of Richard Brinsley Sheridan
Vol. I

ISBN/EAN: 9783337055462

Printed in Europe, USA, Canada, Australia, Japan

Cover: Foto ©ninafisch / pixelio.de

More available books at **www.hansebooks.com**

THE WORKS

OF

RICHARD BRINSLEY SHERIDAN,

With a Memoir

BY

JAMES P. BROWNE, M.D.

CONTAINING EXTRACTS FROM THE LIFE

BY

THOMAS MOORE.

IN TWO VOLUMES.

VOL. I.

LONDON:
BICKERS & SON, 1, LEICESTER SQUARE.
1884.

CONTENTS OF VOL. I.

	PAGE
MEMOIR OF THE LIFE OF THE RIGHT HON. RICHARD BRINSLEY SHERIDAN	i
THE RIVALS: A COMEDY.	
Preface	xlvii
Prologue	1
Prologue, spoken on the Tenth Night	3
Epilogue	5
Dramatis Personæ	7
ST. PATRICK'S DAY; OR, THE SCHEMING LIEUTENANT. A FARCE	109
Dramatis Personæ	111
THE DUENNA: A COMIC OPERA	143
Dramatis Personæ	145
A TRIP TO SCARBOROUGH: A COMEDY	217
Dramatis Personæ	219
Prologue	221

A MEMOIR OF THE LIFE OF THE RIGHT HONOURABLE RICHARD BRINSLEY SHERIDAN.

Richard Brinsley Sheridan was born in September, 1751, at No. 12, Dorset Street, Dublin. His father, Thomas Sheridan, was, as an actor, second only to Garrick. He was the author of an excellent pronouncing dictionary and prosodial grammar, with other useful works on education. His mother was a woman of superior abilities as a novelist and dramatic writer. At the age of seven, Sheridan, with his elder brother, Charles, was placed under the tuition of Mr. Samuel Whyte, of Grafton Street, Dublin, with whom he stayed one year, and during that time he evinced not the slightest spark of that 'fire of Apollo' which in the days of his maturity shone forth with such warmth and brilliancy. Indeed, he was looked upon as a dull and unpromising boy.

In the year 1762, Richard was sent to Harrow, where he remained till his eighteenth year, under the care of Dr. Sumner and of Dr. Samuel Parr, who manifested all through life a strong friendship for Sheridan. 'At Harrow,' says Moore, 'Richard was remarkable only as a very idle, careless, but, at the same time, engaging boy, who contrived to win the affection and even admiration of the whole school, both masters and pupils, by the mere charm of his frank and genial manners, and by the occasional gleams of superior intellect which broke through all the indolence and indifference of his character.'

On leaving Harrow, his education was conducted at home (in London), under the care of his father and of Mr. Lewis Kerr. Still the same indolence in the regular pursuit of study, which signalized him at Harrow, was characteristic even under the eye of his father. But his faculty of acquiring, with little or no exertion, the substantial elements of knowledge, especially as they serve to shed light upon conduct and manners in social life, was early displayed by him. And an ample endowment of the faculty of language enabled him to translate, in conjunction with his schoolfellow Halhed, the seventh 'Idyll' and many of the lesser poems of Theocritus. In the year 1770, when Sheridan was residing with his family at Bath, and Halhed was pursuing his course of studies at Oxford, they entered into a literary companionship, the result of which was a variety of works, of which none but their translation of 'Aristœnetus' ever saw the light.

'There is something,' says Mr. Moore, 'in the alliance between these boys peculiarly interesting. Their united ages, as Halhed boasts in one of his letters, did not amount to thirty-eight. They were both abounding in wit and spirits, and as sanguine as the consciousness of talent and youth could make them; both inspired with a taste for pleasure, and thrown upon their own resources for the means of gratifying it; both carelessly embarking, without rivalry or reserve, their venture of fame in the same bottom, and both, as

Halhed discovered at last, passionately in love with the same woman.' In his allusion to their epistolary correspondence, Moore says:—'There is in the letters of Mr. Halhed a fresh youthfulness of style, and an unaffected vivacity of thought, which I question whether even his witty correspondent could have surpassed.'

A play, in three acts, called 'Jupiter,' was their first joint production. In 1770, Sheridan's family came to reside at Bath, and there became intimately acquainted with Mr. Linley, the eminent musician, whose daughter, then but sixteen years old, was an accomplished public singer, and the charm of all society. Both Charles Sheridan and Halhed were desperately in love with her, and confided their passion to Richard, little suspecting to find in him a rival; for so cleverly did he conduct his courtship, that his own admiration of his fair young friend escaped the notice even of his brother. The subsequent disappointment of these young men was deeply felt by the elder Sheridan; but it would seem to have blighted for ever the happiness of poor Halhed, as the following extract from Moore's 'Life of Sheridan' would imply:—

> 'My life has lost its aim!—that fatal fair
> Was all its object, all its hope or care:
> She was the goal, to which my course was bent,
> Where every wish, where every thought was sent;
> A secret influence darted from her eyes,—
> Each look, attraction, and herself the prize.
> Concentred there, I lived for her alone;
> To make her glad and to be blest was one.'

The epistle from which these lines are extracted was written by Halhed to his friend Sheridan, whose conduct in keeping him in the dark, respecting his own attachment to the lady, was reprehensible; as at that very time poor Halhed was sending him most impassioned letters, in order that he should forward, as a friend, his pretensions to the hand and heart of the fair enchantress. But he never received any reply in Sheridan's letter to these inquiries, though the latter said he had done so in a letter that must have miscarried. It is not, perhaps, a dereliction of charity to suppose that the disconsolate lover was doubtful of the existence of such a letter; but still the following lines from the epistle quoted above, show the sad but friendly spirit in which he took his leave of his cherished literary associate:—

'Adieu, my friend—nor blame this sad adieu,
Though sorrow guides my pen, it blames not you.
Forget me—'tis my pray'r; nor seek to know
The fate of him whose portion must be woe,
Till the cold earth outstretch her friendly arms,
And death convince me that he *can* have charms.'

The conquests of this charming girl were not confined to youthful poets; for one of her enthusiastic admirers had already approached the 'down hill of life.' This was Mr. Long, a gentleman of large fortune, who proposed marriage to her; but she, unaffected by the prospect of the immediate possession of opulence, refused his proposal, by saying that such a marriage could never lead to happiness. Nevertheless this good man, though no doubt chagrined at this disappointment, settled upon her the sum of three thousand pounds.

A formidable opponent to Sheridan's hopes soon arose in the person of Mr. Mathews, a man of large fortune and accomplished manners, who succeeded in making a deep impression on the heart of this highly-gifted maiden of sixteen; but she, becoming aware of the wickedness of his designs, confided her troubles to Richard, who, knowing Mathews to be a married man, persuaded Miss Linley to leave Bath, and accompanied her to London, and thence to France, where he suggested to her the propriety of being married as soon as possible, as she could not, after elopement, again appear in England but as his wife. 'He was, therefore,' he said, 'resolved to deposit her in a convent, till she had consented, by the ceremony of a marriage, to confirm to him that right of protecting her which he had now but temporarily assumed.' It did not, we may suppose, require much eloquence to convince her heart of the truth of this reasoning; and, accordingly, at a little village not far from Calais, they were married about the latter end of March, 1772, by a priest well known for his services on such occasions. On their arrival at Lisle she consented to retire to an apartment in a convent until such time as Sheridan was in a position to support her as his acknowledged wife. But this plan was frustrated by the arrival of her father, who had just found his daughter ill at the house of Dr. and Mrs. Dolman, of York, who were then living at Lisle. Sheridan soon managed to reconcile Mr. Linley to his daughter without informing him of their marriage; but the latter insisted on her immediately accompanying him to England, that he might by her services be enabled to fulfil certain engagements which he had entered into. This being agreed to, on condition that she should resume her retirement at Lisle when she had completed her engagement with her father, they all set out for England.

For his signal success in this romantic affair Sheridan had to encounter the angry remonstrances of his brother, and the contemptuous accusations of

Mathews, who vowed vengeance against him. The result of this was an advertisement in the *Bath Chronicle*, in which the character of Sheridan was grossly vilified. It runs thus—

'Wednesday, April 8th, 1772.

'Mr. Richard S— having attempted, in a letter, left behind him for that purpose, to account for his scandalous method of running away from this place, by insinuations derogating from my character, and that of a young lady, innocent as far as relates to *me* or *my* knowledge; since which he has neither taken notice of my letters, or even informed his own family of the place where he has hid himself, I can no longer think he deserves the treatment of a gentleman, and therefore shall trouble myself no further about him, than in the public method to post him as a L— and a S—.'

On seeing this notice, Sheridan vowed that on his arrival in London he would not sleep until he had made Mathews retract it; and he kept his word. The retractation which he was compelled to give at the point of the sword of his triumphant adversary, after having begged for his life, runs thus—

'Being convinced that the expressions I made use of to Mr. Sheridan's disadvantage were the effects of passion and misrepresentation, I retract what I have said to his disadvantage, and particularly beg pardon for my advertisement in the *Bath Chronicle*.

'THOMAS MATHEWS.'

So much did Mathews's reputation for courage suffer by his conduct in that affair, that he was persuaded by a friend to allow him to be the bearer of a challenge to Sheridan, which was instantly accepted. A fight took place, in which the swords of the combatants were broken; and when both of them in the struggle fell to the ground, they, in all the ferocity of rage, hacked each other till Sheridan, who was undermost, received a severe wound. The seconds, upon seeing this, cried out to him to ask for his life, but that he refused to do with the passionate instinct of unsubdued intrepidity. They were then separated. Sheridan, whose wound caused his friends much uneasiness, was soon restored to health by the skill of his medical attendants. It may be observed here that Mr. Paumier, Sheridan's second on that occasion, was totally unfit, either in feeling or presence of mind, for the delicate and important duty which he had undertaken to perform, and that Sheridan himself was very ill-prepared to enter the lists as a combatant, he having sat up (it is said by Mathews himself, in a bantering tone) the whole of the previous night. The news of this sad catastrophe had reached Oxford during the performance of the concert in which Miss Linley was engaged, but she was kept in ignorance of it by her father, who knew that the intelligence would totally disqualify her from appearing. And her distracted exclamation—'My Husband! My Husband!'—when, on her return to Bath, the misfortune was cautiously revealed to her by Mr. Panton, a clergyman, showed that Mr. Linley's judicious foresight on that occasion was well founded. During the first paroxysm of her grief she insisted upon seeing him, and 'upon her right as his wife to be near him, and watch over him day and night.' To avert the mischief which this untimely avowal was sure to create in the minds of old Mr. Sheridan and Mr.

Linley, it was resolved to attribute the untimely exclamation to the distracted state of her mind. But though this device tended to weaken or even efface the conviction of the parents as to the fact of a marriage having taken place, it yet could not remove their suspicion that such would undoubtedly be the result of this mutual attachment.

As soon as Sheridan was sufficiently recovered, his father, with the view of weaning him from the unfortunate associations connected with Bath, sent him to spend some months, in retirement, at Waltham Abbey, in Essex, under the care of his particular friends, Mr. and Mrs. Parker, of Farm Hill. Notwithstanding the painful mental disquietude under which he was then suffering, on account of his compulsory separation from the object dearest to his heart, he devoted himself to literary pursuits for the sake of diverting his thoughts from those sources of his present unhappiness.

But his mind, while at Waltham Abbey, was not entirely occupied with those early literary attempts; for his separation from his wife caused him great unhappiness. Of the state of despondency to which even his hopeful disposition was then almost forced to succumb, there remains abundant evidence in letters written at the time by Sheridan to a friend who remained faithfully attached to him through life. But so careful was he not to divulge the secret of his marriage, that he let fall no hint of it.

Not only was Sheridan doomed to endure in silence the pangs of separation, but he was harassed by rumours of the admiration paid by persons of fortune and rank to Miss Linley, whose marriage was, as yet, an impenetrable secret, and whose services, as a public singer, were still under the command of her father, who, no doubt, felt that the pecuniary interests of his family would be seriously interfered with, and the high prospects of his daughter marred by a marriage with a seemingly reckless young man, who had no other mode of subsistence than the exercise of his talents, which were of a kind that probably did not seem to him likely to lead on to fortune. He, therefore, kept the strictest watch over her conduct, and to such an extent was his vigilance carried that she was unable to convey to Sheridan any intimation of her state of mind. But though Mr. Linley took care to prevent their having a meeting, he could not hinder Sheridan from seeing his daughter at Covent Garden Theatre, where she was then charming the people with her delightful voice. But still he was precluded from any opportunity of conversing with her, except in the garb of a hackney-coachman, which he is said to have assumed for the purpose of speaking to her, while he was seemingly driving but an ordinary fare. At length, Mr. Linley finding it useless to persist in keeping the young couple any longer apart, consented to their being married; and, accordingly, their wedding took place, by licence, on the 13th of April, 1773.

A short time before his marriage Sheridan had entered his name as a student in the Middle Temple; but, to a mind constituted like his, it was scarcely to be expected that the dry technicalities of the law would afford a pleasurable intellectual pursuit. And though his talents were such as would enable him to become eminent in that profession, it is not at all likely that he would patiently and assiduously follow a line of study which was sure to be looked upon by him as an irksome task; and irksomeness is in all things antagonistic to industry. Neither was he influenced by a thirst for gold. Indeed, every act of his life showed how unfit he was for the careful accumulation of property. Desultoriness was an essential characteristic of his mind. But yet he was a zealous and keen observer of everything connected with the affairs of life; and the extraordinary quickness of his perception, and the acuteness of his discernment, rendered the acquisition of such knowledge so like an act of intuition, and his mode of pursuing it apparently so careless and devoid of attention, that he incurred the imputation of being an idle man. So strongly impressed were his most intimate friends with his want of assiduity, that his brother-in-law, Mr. Tickle, in allusion to it, has left prefixed to a copy of 'The Rivals,' which belonged to him, and which fell into the possession of Mr. Moore, a humorous dedication, to which he subscribes the name of Sheridan himself. He calls it a 'Dedication to Idleness.' In this address the successful author of 'The Rivals,' in a spirit of playful irony, is made to offer up at the shrine of that deluding goddess his grateful acknowledgments for the benefits she had conferred upon him. Yet, 'There was a time,' he says—'though it is so long ago that I now scarcely remember it, and cannot mention it without compunction—but there was a time when the importunity of parents, and the example of a few injudicious young men of my acquaintance, had almost prevailed on me to thwart my genius, and prostitute my abilities by an application to serious pursuits. And if you had not opened my eyes to the absurdity and profligacy of such a perversion of the best gifts of nature, I am by no means clear that I might not have been a wealthy merchant or an eminent lawyer at this very moment.' The narrow limits assigned to this sketch forbids that the whole of this dedication, which is given by Moore, should be quoted here; but a portion of the concluding sentence is so characteristic that its omission would detract from the truthfulness of the portrait. It runs thus: 'If I were to say here all that I think of your excellences, I might be suspected of flattery; but I beg leave to refer you for the test of my sincerity to the constant tenor of my life and actions.' . . .

But yet activity was an essential quality of Sheridan's intellect. This is fully shown by the existence of numerous pamphlets, found in a fragmentary state among his papers by Moore, and which must have been written, he says, between 1769 and 1774.

The early bias of Sheridan's mind to politics is strongly evinced in those essays. Amongst them there is a letter to the Duke of Grafton, written in a lively tone of sarcastic irony. In allusion to a passage in this letter Moore says: 'There is a clearness of thought and style here very remarkable in so young a writer.' It may be interesting to quote a part of this paragraph. It is as follows:—

'By pursuing the methods which they propose, viz., chopping off his head, I allow the impression would be stronger at first; but we should consider how soon that wears off. If, indeed, his crimes were of such a nature as to entitle his head to a place on Temple Bar, I should allow some weight to their argument. But, in the present case, we should reflect how apt mankind are to relent after they have inflicted punishment; so that, perhaps, the same men who would have detested the noble lord, while alive and in prosperity, pointing him as a scarecrow to their children, might, after being witnesses to the miserable fate that had overtaken him, begin in their hearts to pity him; and, from the fickleness so common to human nature, perhaps, by way of compensation, acquit him of part of his crimes; insinuate that he was dealt hardly with, and thus, by the remembrance of their compassion on this occasion, be led to show more indulgence to any future offender in the same circumstances.'

In a letter, ' dated 1770, addressed to " Novus," some writer in Woodfall's *Public Advertiser*, and appearing to be one of a series to the same correspondent,' there is a passage which Moore gives as a specimen of Sheridan's acuteness in criticising the absurd style of his adversary:—' You leave it rather dubious whether you were most pleased with the glorious opposition to Charles I., or the dangerous designs of that monarch, which you emphatically call " the arbitrary projects of a Stuart's nature." What do you mean by a man's *nature?* A man's natural disposition may urge him to the commission of some actions; Nature may instigate and encourage; but I believe you are the first that ever made her a projector.'

Surely in making this metaphysical distinction, Sheridan was guilty of an oversight; since the paramount natural disposition of man, in regard to his moral and intellectual attributes, can stimulate to action only those dispositions and talents which are capable of acting and of projecting; and as these talents and dispositions are the most subtile and refined and influential ingredients in the compound called human nature, it follows, of necessity, that Nature must be a projector of a certain line of conduct as well as a stimulator to the performance of it.

Among these papers were found, by Moore, essays for newspapers, and fragments of periodical papers, one of which was named ' The Dramatic Censor,' which was an indication of his early predilection for dramatic literature.

The first essay in this line that saw the light was the comedy of 'The Rivals.' It was brought out at Covent Garden, on the 17th of January, 1775, under the management of Mr. Harris, whose high opinion of its merits gave sanguine hopes of its success. But these hopes were marred, for the instant, by the bad acting of Mr. Lee on the first night of its performance. The substitution of Mr. Clinch, however, for Mr. Lee, in *Sir Lucius O'Trigger*, raised it, to use Moore's words, ' at once into that high region of public favour, where it has continued to float so buoyantly and gracefully ever since.' In Bath, Southampton, and elsewhere, it was, at the same time, received with rapturous applause, according to Miss Linley's letters to her sister, Mrs. Sheridan, whose talents were so highly thought of by her family, that not only her sister, but her father, felt assured that the Epilogue to 'The Rivals' was written by her. With regard to this fond but erroneous conjecture, Moore says: ' This statement respecting the Epilogue would, if true, deprive Sheridan of one of the fairest leaves of his poetic crown.' And with regard to the play itself, he says: ' With much less wit, it exhibits, perhaps, more humour than " The School for Scandal," and the dialogue, though by no means so pointed and sparkling, is, in this respect, more natural, as coming nearer the current coin of ordinary conversation; whereas the circulating medium of " The School for Scandal " is diamonds. The characters of " The Rivals," on the contrary, are *not* such as occur commonly in the world; and instead of producing striking effects with natural and obvious materials, which is the great art and difficulty of a painter of human life, he has here overcharged most of his persons with whims and absurdities, for which the circumstances they are engaged in afford but a very disproportionate vent. Accordingly, for our insight into their characters, we are indebted rather to their confessions than their actions. *Lydia Languish*, in proclaiming the extravagance of her own romantic notions, prepares us for events much more ludicrous and eccentric than those in which the plot allows her to be concerned; and the young lady herself is scarcely more disappointed than we are, at the tameness with which her amour concludes. Among the various ingredients supposed to be mixed up in the composition of *Sir Lucius O'Trigger*, his love of fighting is the only one whose flavour is very strongly brought out; and the wayward captious jealousy of *Falkland*, though so highly coloured in his own representation of it, is productive of no incident answerable to such an announcement; the imposture which he practises upon *Julia* being, perhaps, weakened in its effect, by our recollection of the same device in the " Nut-brown Maid " and " Peregrine Pickle." '

The character of *Sir Anthony Absolute* is, perhaps, the best sustained and most natural of any, and the scenes between him and *Captain Absolute* are richly, genuinely dramatic. His surprise at the apathy with which his son receives the glowing picture which he draws of the charms of his destined bride, and the effect of the question, ' And which is to be mine, sir— the niece or the aunt?' are in the purest style of humour. *Mrs. Malaprop's* mistakes, in what she herself calls ' orthodoxy,' have been often objected to as improbable for a woman in her rank of life; but though some of them, it must be owned, are extravagant and farcical, they are almost all amusing; and the luckiness of her simile, ' as headstrong as an *allegory* on the banks of the Nile,' will be acknowledged as long as there are writers to be run away with by the wilfulness of this truly 'head-strong' species of composition.

'Of the faults both in his witty and serious styles —the occasional efforts of the one, and the too frequent false finery of the other,' continues Moore, 'some examples may be cited from the dialogue of this play. Among the former kind is the following elaborate conceit:—

'"*Falk.* Has Lydia changed her mind? I should have thought her duty and inclination would now have pointed to the same object.

'"*Abs.* Ay, just as the eyes of a person who squints; when her love eye was fixed on me, t'other —her eye of duty—was finely obliqued: but when duty bade her point that the same way, off turned t'other on a swivel, and secured its retreat with a frown."

'This, though ingenious, is far too laboured; and of that false taste by which, sometimes, in his graver style, he was seduced into the display of second-rate ornament, the following speeches of Julia afford specimens:—

'" Then, on the bosom of your wedded Julia, you may lull your keen regret to slumbering; while virtuous love, with a cherub's hand, shall smooth the brow of upbraiding thought, and pluck the thorn from compunction."

'Again, " When hearts deserving happiness would unite their fortunes, virtue would crown them with an unfading garland of modest, hurtless flowers; but ill-judging passion will force the gaudier rose into the wreath, whose thorn offends them when its leaves are dropt."

'But notwithstanding such blemishes,' he continues,

'and it is easy for the microscopic eye of criticism to discover gaps and inequalities in the finest edge of genius, this play, from the liveliness of its plot, the variety and whimsicality of its characters, and the exquisite humour of its dialogue, is one of the most amusing in the whole range of the drama; and even without the aid of its more splendid successor, " The School for Scandal," would have placed Sheridan in the first rank of comic writers.'

Sheridan's next production was a farce, called 'St. Patrick's Day; or, the Scheming Lieutenant.' It was written to show how grateful he was to Clinch, whose acting contributed to rectify the unfavourable opinion respecting the merit of 'The Rivals,' which the bad acting of Mr. Lee had created. Success attended the acting of this play; for 'laughter,' Moore says, 'the great end of farce, is abundantly achieved by it.'

At the close of 1775 was produced 'The Duenna,' an opera, which he composed in the summer of that year.

Harris, the manager of Covent Garden Theatre, urged Sheridan to write to Mr. Linley, then at Bath, to come and 'put them in the right way as to the music' of this opera; and Sheridan, in his letter to Linley, says that Mr. Harris 'was extravagantly sanguine of the success of the plot and dialogue of the " Duenna."'

The able assistance thus called forth was available in due time, and the piece, thus carefully prepared, was received by the public with most remarkable success.

So distrustful was the anxious manager of the ability of any one connected with the theatre to do justice to the music, on this occasion, that Sheridan's own pressing letter to Linley was backed by his wife; for Moore says, 'On the opposite side of this letter is written, in Mrs. Sheridan's handwriting—

'" Dearest Father,

'" I shall have no spirits or hopes of the opera, unless we see you.

'" Eliza Ann Sheridan."'

'The Duenna,' says Moore, 'is one of the very few operas in our language which combines the merits of legitimate comedy with the attractions of poetry and song. The wit of the dialogue, except in one or two instances, is of that accessible kind which lies near the surface, which is produced without effort, and may be enjoyed without wonder.'

As to the lyric portion of 'The Duenna,' it would not be doing justice to Sheridan's genius if Moore's opinion regarding it was left unnoticed, notwithstanding the narrow space necessarily allotted to this memoir.

'Though some of the poetry of this opera is not much above that ordinary kind, to which music is so often doomed to be wedded—making up by her own sweetness for the dulness of her helpmate—by far the greater number of the songs are full of beauty, and some of them may rank among the best models of lyric writing. The verses, "Had I a heart for falsehood framed," notwithstanding the stiffness of this word "framed," and one or two other slight blemishes, are not unworthy of living in recollection with the matchless air to which they are adapted.'*

There is another song, less known, from being connected with less popular music, which, for deep impassioned feeling and natural eloquence, has not,

* Molly Asthore.

perhaps, its rival, through the whole range of lyric poetry. As these verses, though contained in the common editions of 'The Duenna,' are not to be found in the opera as printed in the British Theatre, and still more strangely are omitted in the late collection of Mr. Sheridan's works, I should feel myself abundantly authorized in citing them here, even if their beauty were not a sufficient excuse for recalling them, under any circumstances, to the recollection of the reader:—

' Ah, cruel maid, how hast thou changed
    The temper of my mind!
My heart, by thee from love estranged,
    Becomes like thee unkind.
By fortune favoured, clear in fame,
    I once ambitious was;
And friends I had who fanned the flame,
    And gave my youth applause.

' But now my weakness all accuse,
    Yet vain their taunts on me;
Friends, fortune, fame itself I'd lose,
    To gain one smile from thee.
And only thou shouldst not despise
    My weakness or my woe;
If I am mad in others' eyes,
    'Tis thou hast made me so.

NOTE.—As this edition of Sheridan's works is professedly a reprint of the collection of his works, alluded to by Moore, it is necessary to cite a note which he has appended to his allusion, respecting the absence of this song from that collection.

' For this edition of his works I am no further responsible than in having communicated to it a few prefatory pages, to account and apologise to the public for the delay of the Life.'

'But days, like this, with doubting curst,
   I will not long endure—
Am I disdained—I know the worst,
   And likewise know my cure.
If false, her vows she dare renounce,
   That instant ends my pain;
For, oh! the heart must break at once
   That cannot hate again.'

'It is impossible to believe,' says Moore, 'that such verses as these had no deeper inspiration than the imaginary loves of an opera. They bear, burnt into every line, the marks of personal feeling, and must have been thrown off in one of those passionate moods of the heart, with which the poet's own youthful love had made him acquainted, and under the impression and vivid recollection of which these lines were written.'

Moore felt convinced of the correctness of this conjecture when he discovered that a poem, written by Sheridan in 1773, and addressed to his wife, was, he says, 'again despoiled of some of its lines for an Epilogue, which he began a few years after upon a very different subject.'

Moore's brief but brilliant comment upon this conduct of Sheridan is so characteristic of the author of the 'Irish Melodies,' that its insertion here cannot fail to be agreeable.

'There is something, it must be owned, not very sentimental in this conversion of the poetry of affection to other and less sacred uses; as if, like the ornaments of a passing pageant, it might be broken up after the show was over, and applied to more useful purposes. That the young poet should be guilty of such sacrilege to Love, and thus steal back his golden offerings from the altar, to melt them down into utensils of worldly display, can only be excused by that demand upon the riches of his fancy, which the rapidity of his present career in the service of the Dramatic Muse occasioned.'

In justice to the literary fame of Sheridan, it will be well to give Moore's concluding remarks respecting this famous opera.

'Among literary piracies or impostures, there are few more audacious than the Dublin edition of "The Duenna," in which, though the songs are given accurately, an entirely new dialogue is substituted for that of Sheridan, and his gold, as in the barter of Glaucus, exchanged for such copper as the following:

'"*Duen.* Well, sir, I don't want to stay in your house; but I must go and lock up my wardrobe.

'"*Isaac.* Your wardrobe! when you came into my house you could carry your wardrobe in your combcase, you could, you old dragon."'

The next specimen, which is longer and even coarser, need not be repeated here. 'These jokes,' says Moore, 'I need not add, are all the gratuitous contributions of the editor.'

At Christmas time, in the year 1775, during the triumphant success of 'The Duenna,' Sheridan entered into negotiations for the purchase of the moiety of the patent of Drury Lane Theatre, held by Garrick, who was then about to retire from the stage. The motive for his retirement is thus alluded to by Moore: 'He was then in the sixtieth year of his age, and might possibly have been influenced by the natural feeling, so beautifully expressed for a great actor of our own time by our greatest living writer:—

'" Higher duties crave
Some space between the theatre and the grave;

That, like the Roman in the Capitol,
I may adjust my mantle ere it fall." [*]

In the month of June following, the transfer of Garrick's share in Drury Lane Theatre took place. His moiety, amounting to 35,000*l.*, was divided into three parts; one of which fell to the lot of Sheridan; the second, which was of equal value, fell to Mr. Linley's share; and Dr. Ford became owner of the largest part, which cost him 15,000*l.*

An alteration of Vanbrugh's comedy, 'The Relapse,' entitled 'A Trip to Scarborough,' was the next production of Sheridan's dramatic ability. It was brought out by the new manager in February, 1777. It is evident that Moore did not think much of this effort of Sheridan's genius; for he says—

'In reading the original play, we are struck with surprise that Sheridan should ever have hoped to be able to defecate such dialogue, and at the same time leave any of the wit, whose whole spirit is in the lees, behind. The very life of such characters as *Berinthia* is their licentiousness, and it is with them, as with objects that are luminous from putrescence, to remove their taint is to extinguish their light. If Sheridan, indeed, had substituted some of his own wit for that which he took away, the inanition which followed the operation would have been much less sensibly felt. But to be so liberal of a treasure so precious, and for the enrichment of the work of another, could hardly have been expected from him. Besides, it may be doubted whether the subject had not yielded its utmost to Vanbrugh, and whether,

---

[*] 'Kemble's Farewell Address, on taking leave of the Edinburgh stage, written by Sir Walter Scott.'

even in the hands of Sheridan, it could have been brought to bear a second crop of wit.'

Though Sheridan was now fully engaged in the management of the theatre, he found time to write some verses to his wife, who was then at Bath, on a visit to her father and mother. Each of these stanzas, while it describes the presence of some charming harbinger of Spring, ends with *'tis not Spring*. Two or three of these I would fain give here to render clear the love-sick poet's train of thought:

> ' Sweet tutress of music and love,
>   Sweet bird, if 'tis thee that I hear,
> Why left you so early the grove,
>   To lavish your melody here?
> Cease, then, mistaken thus to sing,
> Sweet nightingale! it *is* not *Spring*.

> ' Yet the lily has drank of the show'r,
>   And the rose 'gins to peep on the day;
> And yon bee seems to search for a flower,
>   As busy as if it were May:
> In vain, thou senseless, flutt'ring thing,
> My heart informs me *'tis not Spring*.

' May poised her roseate wings, for she had heard
   The mourner, as she pass'd the vales along;
And, silencing her own indignant bird,
   She thus reproved poor Sylvio's song.

> ' How false is the sight of a lover!
> How ready his spleen to discover
>   What reason would never allow!
> Why, Sylvio, my sunshine and showers,
> My blossoms, my birds, and my flow'rs,
>   Were never more perfect than now.

Pardon (said Sylvio, with a gushing tear),
'Tis Spring, sweet nymph; *but Laura is not here.*'

Moore says he quotes those verses to Laura, from which the foregoing extracts have been made; 'less from their own peculiar merit, than as a proof how little Sheridan's heart had yet lost of those first feelings of love and gallantry, which too often expire in matrimony, as faith and hope do in heaven, and from the same causes :

'One lost in certainty, and one in joy.'

Along with these verses Sheridan sent an account of an entertainment, at which were assembled some of the most charming women of the aristocratic world; and though the marked attention paid to himself by these leaders of fashion in the highest circle of society must have been extremely gratifying to his comparatively humble, but devotedly fond 'Laura,' yet in her reply she seemingly indulges in a strain of what Moore calls 'poetical jealousy,' mingled with 'generous compliments to some of the most brilliant among his new fashionable friends.'[*]

'Though her verses,' says Moore, 'are of that kind which we read more with interest than with admiration, they have quite enough of talent for the gentle themes to which she aspired; and there is, besides, a charm about them, as coming from Mrs. Sheridan, to which far better poetry could not pretend.'

The presence of a few of the concluding stanzas of this poem, here, will be interesting, as they manifest the gentle, unselfish, and faithfully affectionate

---

[*] These were the Duchess of Devonshire, the Duchess of Rutland, the Countess of Jersey, Lady Craven (afterwards Margravine of Anspach), and Mrs. (afterwards Lady) Crewe.

disposition of the admirable woman, for whose sake Sheridan exposed himself to so many perils. They are as follows:—

'But where does Laura pass her lonely hours?
   Does she still haunt the grot and willow-tree?
Shall Sylvio, from his wreath of various flowers,
   Neglect to cull one simple sweet for thee?

'"Ah Laura, no," the constant Sylvio cries,
   "For thee a never-fading wreath I'll twine;
Though bright the rose, its bloom too swiftly flies,
   No emblem meet for love so true as mine.

'"For thee, my love, the myrtle, ever green,
   Shall every year its blossoms sweet disclose;
Which, when our spring of youth no more is seen,
   Shall still appear more lovely than the rose."

'"Forgive, dear youth," the happy Laura said;
   "Forgive each doubt, each fondly anxious fear,
Which from my heart for ever now is fled:
   Thy love and truth, thus tried, are doubly dear.

'"With pain I marked the various passions rise,
   When beauty so divine before thee moved;
With trembling doubt beheld thy wandering eyes,
   For still I feared; alas! because I loved.

'"Each anxious doubt shall Laura now forego;
   No more regret those joys so lately known;
Conscious that tho' thy breast to *all* may glow,
   Thy faithful *heart* shall beat for *her* alone.

'"Then, Sylvio, seize again thy tuneful lyre,
   Nor yet sweet Beauty's power forbear to praise;
Again let charms divine thy strains inspire,
   And Laura's voice shall aid the poet's lays.'"

The sagacity of Sheridan, as a minute observer of manners, and his singular dramatic skill in delineating them, was shown to great advantage in 'The Rivals' and 'The Duenna;' but still he had not reached that height of excellence to which his literary ambition soared, until he came forward with his comedy of 'The School for Scandal,' which both Byron and Moore looked upon as the best comedy in the English language; and to show Garrick's opinion of its merits, Moore quotes the following note, which, to use that poet's own words, 'will be read with interest by all those for whom the great names of the Drama have any charm:—

'Mr. Garrick's best wishes and compliments to Mr. Sheridan.

'How is the Saint to-day? A gentleman who is as mad as myself about ye School remarked, that the characters on the stage at ye falling of the screen stand too long before they speak. I thought so too ye first night; he said it was the same on ye 2nd, and was remark'd by others; tho' they should be astonish'd, and a little petrify'd, yet it may be carried to too great a length. All praise at Lord Lucan's last night.'

And Murphy, in his Life of Garrick, as quoted by Moore, tells us, 'that Mr. Garrick attended the rehearsals, and was never known on any former occasion to be more anxious for a favourite piece. He was proud of the new manager, and in a triumphant manner boasted of the genius to whom he had consigned the conduct of the theatre.'

Deep and unchangeable was Sheridan's gratitude to Garrick for the admiration and even homage that was so willingly and gracefully bestowed upon the brilliant offspring of his own dramatic genius by the acknowledged prince of dramatic actors. And the beauty of the strain in which this gratitude was publicly displayed will be acknowledged by all who have read his Monody on Garrick. So great, indeed, was the mutual regard of these two remarkable men of genius, that the poet had the sad privilege of following, as chief mourner, the consummate actor to his last resting place in Westminster Abbey, where he lies in Poets' Corner, at the foot of Shakespeare's statue, which the suggestive mind of his friend Edmund Burke remarked was pointing to the grave where the great actor of his works was laid. 'This hint,' says Moore, 'did not fall idly on the ear of Sheridan, as the following *fixation* of the thought, in the verses which he afterwards wrote, proved:—

'The throng that mourn'd as their dead favourite passed,
The grac'd respect that claimed him to the last;
While Shakespeare's image, from its hallow'd base,
Seem'd to prescribe the grave, and point the place.'

'This Monody,' continues Moore, 'which was the longest flight ever sustained by its author in verse, is more remarkable for refinement and elegance than for either novelty of thought or depth of sentiment. There is, however, a fine burst of poetical eloquence in the lines beginning "Superior hopes the poet's bosom fire;" and this passage, accordingly, as being the best in the poem, was, by the gossiping critics of the day, attributed to Tickell—from the same laudable motives that had induced them to attribute Tickell's bad farce to Sheridan. There is no end to the variety of these small missiles of malice with which the Gullivers of the world of literature are assailed by the Lilliputians around them.'

The 'School for Scandal' was represented, for the first time, on the 1st of May, 1777, and its success was so great that, through the season, the receipts at the theatre amounted to far more than the sum taken when 'Hamlet' or 'Macbeth' was performed. Even on the nights when the king went to the theatre the receipts did not exceed those on which it was thronged to see Sheridan's comedy, even in the absence of such potent attraction. Nor was this rare success ephemeral, for Moore found in the treasurer's notice of the receipts in 1779 the following remark:—'"School for Scandal" damped the new pieces;' and its performance was attended with the same success through the years 1780 and 1781. These facts are attested by extracts, given by Moore, from an account in the handwriting of Mrs. Sheridan, of which the following are a part:—

'1778. Jan. 3	Macbeth—Queen Mab	.	£212	19 0
,, 7	School for Scandal—Comus		292	16 0
,, 9	Do. —Padlock		281	6 0
Mar. 14	Do. —Deserter		263	18 6
,, 16	Venice Preserved — Belphegor (new) . .	.	195	3 6
,, 17	Hamlet—Belphegor.	.	160	19 0
,, 19	School for Scandal—Belphegor . . .	.	261	10 0

'The beauties of this comedy,' says Moore, 'are so universally known and felt that criticism may be spared the trouble of dwelling upon them very minutely. With but little interest in the plot, with no very profound or ingenious development of character, and with a group of personages, not one of whom has any legitimate claims upon either our affection or esteem, it yet, by the admirable skill with which its materials are managed—the happy contrivance of the situations, at once both natural and striking; the fine feeling of the ridiculous that smiles throughout; and that perpetual play of wit which never tires, but seems, like running water, to be kept fresh by its own flow—by all this general animation and effect, combined with a finish of the details almost faultless, it unites the suffrages at once of the refined and the simple, and is not less successful in ministering to the natural enjoyment of the latter, than in satisfying and delighting the most fastidious tastes among the former. And this is the triumph of true genius in all the arts—whether in painting, sculpture, music, or literature—those works which have pleased the greatest number of people of all classes, for the longest space of time, may, without hesitation, be pronounced the best; and, however mediocrity may enshrine itself in the admiration of the select few, the palm of excellence can only be awarded by the many.'

The originality of 'The School for Scandal' has been impugned by critics, who assert that the characters of *Blifill* and *Tom Jones* have suggested those of *Joseph* and *Charles Surface*. But as hypocritical selfishness and reckless generosity are the offspring of human nature itself, and offer striking instances of contrast of character, it is not to be supposed that a genius so observant of the peculiar idiosyncrasies of mankind as Sheridan, could fail to use them as powerful auxiliaries in the delineation of humorous conduct, without subjecting himself to the imputation of being a copyist. Neither is he to be looked upon, in Moore's opinion, as at all indebted to Molière. But with regard to Wycherley, to whose works it is said Sheridan was indebted for important suggestions, he says, 'There is, however, a scene in "The Plain

Dealer" (Act II.), where *Nevil* and *Olivia* attack the characters of the persons with whom *Nevil* had dined, of which it is difficult to believe that Mr. Sheridan was ignorant, as it seems to contain much of that *Hyle*, or First Matter, out of which his own more perfect creations were formed.'

Moore further says, that 'in Congreve's " Double Dealer," too (Act III., Scene 10), there is much which may, at least, have mixed itself with the recollections of Sheridan, and influenced the course of his fancy; it being often found that the images with which the memory is furnished, like those pictures hung up before the eyes of pregnant women at Sparta, produce insensibly a likeness to themselves in the offspring which the imagination brings forth. The admirable drollery in Congreve about *Lady Froth's* verses on her coachman:—

'" For as the sun shines every day,
So of our coachman I may say—"

is by no means unlikely to have suggested the doggerel of *Sir Benjamin Backbite;* and the scandalous conversation in this scene, though far inferior in delicacy and ingenuity to that of Sheridan, has somewhat, as the reader will see, of a parental resemblance to it.'

' Next to creation,' says Moore, ' the reproduction, in a new and more perfect form, of materials already existing, or the full development of thoughts that had but half blown in the hands of others, are the noblest miracles for which we look at the hands of genius. It is not my intention, therefore, to defend Mr. Sheridan from this kind of plagiarism, of which he was guilty in common with the rest of his fellow-descendants from Prometheus, who all steal the spark wherever they can find it. But the instances just alleged of his obligations to others are too questionable and trivial to be taken into any serious account. .... It is in the manner of transferring them to canvas that the difference—that the whole difference—between the master and the copyist lies; and *Charles* and *Joseph* would, no doubt, have been what they are if *Tom Jones* had never existed.'

The dramatic genius of Sheridan was next devoted to the production of 'The Critic,' which is so admirable an instance of his wit and humour, that it was capable of sustaining him in that high position in the Temple of Fame as a dramatic writer, to which the unrivalled excellence of the ' School for Scandal' had at once raised him, when he was but twenty-six years of age. He was only twenty when the idea of a 'Rehearsal' struck him, and it was a character in a joint humorous composition of his school-fellow Halhed and himself, as has been before suggested, that was the prototype of *Puff*. In the construction of this farce, he is likely to have availed himself of some hints from *Bayes*, in 'The Rehearsal,' by the Duke of Buckingham; and that he is indebted to Fielding for points of humour, which 'Pasquin,' with its fine vein of pleasantry, and one or two more of the rapidly constructed dramas of that great original genius could have supplied him with, there is reason for thinking. These are ' The Author's Farce,' and ' The Historical Register.' But, notwithstanding the early successful career of 'Pasquin,' Moore says, ' It was reserved for Sheridan to give vitality to this form of dramatic humour, and to invest even his satirical portraits—as in the instance of *Sir Fretful Plagiary*, which, it is well known, was designed for Cumberland—with a genuine character, which, without weakening the particular resemblance, makes them representatives for ever of the whole class to which the original belonged. *Bayes*, on the contrary, is a caricature; made up of little personal peculiarities, which may amuse as long as reference can be had to the prototype; but, like those supplemental features furnished from the living subject by Taliacotius, fall lifeless the moment the individual that supplied them is defunct.'

The 'Critic' was the last of the original dramatic compositions of Sheridan. But there were found among his papers fragments of three other plays: one of them founded on 'The Vicar of Wakefield;' another called 'The Foresters,' which is of a wild character; and the third, under the name of 'Affectation.'

His intention was not to make this contemplated comedy the vehicle of satire upon the folly attendant upon affectation of mere outward deportment; for by a memorandum, which Moore found written on the inside of the cover of a book, it is obvious that he meant to trace this selfish folly to its various recesses in the human mind. The contents of the memorandum are as follows:—

'Affectation of Business.
" of Accomplishments.
" of Love of Letters and Wit.
" " Music.
" of Intrigue.
" of Sensibility.
" of Vivacity.
" of Silence and Importance.
" of Modesty.
" of Profligacy.
" of Moroseness.'

It is to be regretted that he did not proceed with

his projected comedy, the subject of which was capable of affording a wide scope for the exercise of his singularly observant and perspicacious intellect. But it was left in so crude a state that it does not exhibit even the semblance of a plot; still it is easy to discern, even in the desultory state of the dialogue, that it bears the impress of the genius of the author of the 'School for Scandal.'

Along with these interesting dramatic fragments were others of poems, which were, perhaps, of earlier date; and these are very instructive, as they are striking examples of what persevering industry can accomplish in imparting a facility of literary composition, especially in rhythmical numbers; for these poetic fragments afford evidence of the difficulty which Sheridan had to encounter in giving grace of form to the emanations of his brilliant fancy. Some of his ideas are written down in prose; others in couplets; a proof that the author of the beautiful lyrics in 'The Duenna' was not so spontaneously capable of—

'Lisping in numbers, for the numbers came'—

as the author of 'The Rape of the Lock,' and of 'Heloisa to Abelard.'

With regard to this drawback upon the rapid outpouring of Sheridan's ideas, the following passage from Moore affords a striking example:—'The birth of his prose being, as we have already seen, so difficult, it may be imagined how painful was the travail of his verse. Indeed, the number of tasks which he left unfinished are all so many proofs of that despair of perfection, which those best qualified to attain it are always the most likely to feel.' Here it may be noted that a relatively defective faculty, under the assiduous promptings of a vigorous and tasteful understanding, and a disposition warmly desirous of fame, may, by judicious *exercise*, cause a comparatively weak faculty of the mind, such as this, for instance, to bloom into such a degree of ripeness as will enable its discriminating and *painstaking* possessor to raise it to the standard of power necessary for its amalgamation in harmonious and, therefore, effective proportion with his other talents which happen to be instinctively more powerful. Such was the happy result of the like indefatigable assiduity in Sheridan's case; for, in the opinion of Moore, he became a master of pure idiomatic English: a fact attested in his dramas, and also in his speeches.

In the year 1778 Sheridan's financial ability procured the means of purchasing Mr. Lacey's moiety of the shares in Drury Lane Theatre, which amounted to 45,000*l.* He subsequently bought Dr. Ford's part, which cost 17,000*l.*; while Mr. Linley still held his shares, which were worth a like sum. Sheridan now became reconciled to his father, and his increased power in the directing of the affairs of the theatre enabled him to make his father manager.

But though the theatre must have engrossed much of his attention, he ceased to charm the public any more with any original comedy or opera. And this cessation from a fascinating pursuit, which obtained for him such transcendent fame, and considerable pecuniary resources, was caused partly by the fact of his being endowed with talents which led him to take, as has been before observed, an ardent interest in politics, and which the agitated state of affairs both at home and in our American colonies at that time, was likely to enhance in one of such soaring ambition and hopeful self-reliance as Mr. Sheridan. An instance of his fitness for becoming a prominent actor in such a sphere of duty, so complicated and so changeful, was found among his papers, and it was written while he was preparing the 'Critic' for representation, and 'The School for Scandal' was in the zenith of its popularity. This was an 'Essay on Absenteeism,' in which he displays much acuteness as a political economist, and a compassionate spirit, as well as a patriotic attachment to his country; a characteristic which marked his political career all through life.

An opening to this new field for the exercise of his talents was afforded by the general election of 1780, when he was returned for the borough of Stafford. Though he felt his way for a considerable time, as a silent member, he, in due course, gave proofs of his capacity for brilliant and effective oratory; and this was wonderfully evinced on the trial of Warren Hastings. Another opportunity was afforded, by the illness of the King, for the exercise of his political talents. This was the Regency Question, which took place in 1788.

The next great subject which called forth the attention of Sheridan was the French Revolution, in 1790, during the debate on the Army Estimates.

On the 28th of June, 1792, Sheridan was afflicted by a heartrending misfortune; for at five o'clock that morning his beautiful and accomplished wife died; and his demeanour on the sad occasion proved the unabated intensity of his first love. 'The interview between him and the dear angel,' says a lady, who was present, 'was afflicting and heartbreaking to the greatest degree imaginable. I was afraid she would have sunk under the cruel agitation—she said it was indeed too much for her. She gave some kind injunction to each of them' (her family from Bath), 'and said everything she could to comfort them under this severe trial . . . Sheridan and I sat up all that night with her; indeed, he had done so for several nights before, and never left her one moment that could be avoided.'

'Dr. Bain,' says Moore, 'fully concurs with the writer of these letters in bearing testimony to the tenderness and affection that Sheridan evinced on this occasion: it was,' he says, 'quite "the devotedness of a lover."' 'The following note, addressed to him after the sad event was over, does honour alike to the writer and the receiver:—

'" My dear Sir,

I must request your acceptance of the enclosed for your professional attendance. For the kind and friendly attentions, which have accompanied your efforts, I must remain your debtor. The recollection of them will live in my mind with the memory of the dear object, whose sufferings you soothed, and whose heart was grateful for it.

Believe me,
Dear Sir,
Very sincerely yours,
R. B. SHERIDAN."'

The same friendly attendant on Mrs. Sheridan says, 'I have observed in general that this affliction has made a wonderful alteration in the expression of his countenance and in his manners.' And Moore says, 'I have heard a noble friend say that, happening about this time to sleep in the room next to him, he could plainly hear him sobbing throughout the greater part of the night.'

Sheridan's only source of comfort now lay in the almost constant presence of his two children—and their marked resemblance to their mother seemed to render his anxiety regarding them more intense—for, this lady says, 'It is impossible for any man to be more devotedly attached to his children than he is.'

During the session of 1792 Mr. Sheridan ceased to attend the House of Commons. The death of his wife—the 'St. Celia' of Sir Joshua Reynolds, and the one who appeared like an angel to the musician, Mr. Jackson, whenever he accompanied her on the piano, while she was singing—caused him the deepest sadness, and unfitted him for awhile for the political duties which his distinguished position imposed upon him. Moreover, the condemnation of the theatre, which was deemed by the surveyors incapable of repair, demanded all the energy and financial ingenuity he possessed, in order to make amends for the ruin that had thus overtaken him, should it prove to be irreparable. He succeeded in his efforts, and Drury Lane Theatre was rebuilt, at a cost which was double the amount of the original estimate; and thus was absorbed the money that was to defray the liabilities of the theatre. The necessity of employing the Opera Houses, and afterwards the Haymarket Theatre, added to the embarrassments of Sheridan, and his own thoughtless extravagance in maintaining three establishments augmented his pecuniary necessities.

In 1795, Sheridan married Miss Ogle, daughter of the Dean of Winchester. She was a young and accomplished girl, ardently devoted to him, though his age far exceeded that of Byron, when he deemed himself fallen into the 'sear and yellow leaf,' when he wrote 'The Flowers and Fruits of Love are gone.' Sheridan's spirits, on the contrary, were, on that happy occasion, remarkable for their buoyant vivacity.

On the introduction, in 1795, of the Treason and Sedition Bills, Sheridan spoke with great boldness;

and the Suspension of the Habeas Corpus Act was vigorously and perseveringly opposed by him. On the settlement of the Prince of Wales's debts, on the occasion of his marriage, he took an active part, and was more in the confidence of the Prince than any one of his party.

The Shakespeare forgeries, which were then brought forward, and the genuineness of which his friend, Dr. Parr, had espoused, were to all appearance, though he had misgivings, imposed upon Sheridan as the true works of the greatest of dramatic writers; for the play of 'Vortigern' was produced at Drury Lane Theatre, at considerable cost, but without success. It is strange that, according to the testimony of Boaden and Kemble, Sheridan evinced a want of enthusiasm for Shakespeare.

This anomaly in the legitimate working of a poetic mind is manifested, also, in the fact, that Sheridan appeared to be devoid of a sense of the beautiful in natural scenery. It would be, perhaps, easier to show cause for the latter instance of deficiency of taste than for that exhibited in regard to the former. But this is not the place for such an inquiry.

His conduct on the breaking out of the Mutiny of the Nore, 1797, was admirable. When his party held aloof and seemed apathetic, he without delay went to Mr. Dundas, and said: 'My advice is that you cut the buoys on the river, send Sir Charles Grey down to the coast, and set a price on Parker's head. If the Administration take this advice instantly, they will save the country; if not, they will lose it; and, on their refusal, I will impeach them in the House of Commons this very evening.' This signal triumph of true patriotism over the binding spirit of party added greatly to the already well-deserved popularity of Sheridan; and should have secured him in the days of his misfortune, sickness, and sorrow, the aid which his patriotism had entitled him to.

In 1798, he brought out 'The Stranger,' a German drama, which was translated by Mr. Thompson, but greatly altered and improved by Sheridan; if not entirely written by him, as he, himself, told his friend, Mr. Rogers, was the case.

'Among the political events of this year,' says Moore, 'the rebellion of Ireland holds a memorable and fearful pre-eminence. Sheridan's speech in the debate on that occasion was truthful, loyal, and such as became a man whose instincts inspired him with love of his native land, a sentiment extolled by Homer and many of our greatest poets as being an indispensable ingredient in the composition of a superior nature. He described it as the angry outburst of human beings crushed by the unrelenting severity of penal laws.

During this session he particularly distinguished himself by his speech on the Assessed Taxes Bill.

In May, 1799, Mr. Sheridan brought out 'Pizarro,' a version of the German play by Kotsebue, which was mainly sustained by the fine acting of John Kemble, as *Rolla*.

In this year he spoke against the legislative union with Ireland.

In the absence of Mr. Fox, he spoke frequently on the French Revolutionary War. In allusion to the Jacobins he said:—

'I do think, sir, Jacobin principles never existed much in this country; and, even admitting they had, I say they have been found so hostile to true liberty, that in proportion as we love it (and whatever may be said, I must still consider liberty an inestimable blessing), we must hate and detest these principles. But, more, I do not think they even exist in France. They have there died the best of all deaths; a death I am more pleased to see than if it had been effected by foreign force—they have stung themselves to death, and died by their own poison.'

His popularity was much enhanced at this time by his speech on the overtures for a maritime truce. After enumerating the glories achieved under the naval flag of England in the most spirit-stirring language, he concludes thus:—

'If our flag is to be insulted, let us nail it to the topmast of the nation; there let it fly while we shed the last drop of our blood in protecting it, and let it be degraded only when the nation itself is overwhelmed."

In 1804, the Prince of Wales, on the death of Lord Eliot, bestowed upon Sheridan the Receivership of the Duchy of Cornwall, ' as a trifling proof of that sincere friendship His Royal Highness had always professed and felt for him for a long series of years;' and, His Royal Highness added, in the same message, ' I wish to God it was better worth your acceptance.' Sheridan refused to accept office at this time, but when the Fox and Grenville administration took place, in 1806, he became Treasurer of the Navy—a place for which his negligent and unpunctual habits in matters of business totally unfitted him. But though he refused it in his earlier and more hopeful days, his embarrassed circumstances caused him at this juncture to accept it. But even this place, so far below what his high position in the Whig party seemed, at one time, to entitle him, he lost on the death of Mr. Fox.

Never after this did any opportunity offer for his

political advancement. It should be stated that during this period he took an active part in the Regency question; and on the Catholic question his conduct was cordial and patriotic.

On the 24th of February, 1809, when Mr. Ponsonby brought on his motion relative to the conduct of the war in Spain, Sheridan was in his place, when the House was illumined by a light which was caused by the burning of Drury Lane Theatre. An adjournment of the debate was proposed, but Sheridan, whose all was at stake, calmly said, that 'whatever might be the extent of the private calamity, he hoped it would not interfere with the public business of the country.' He then left the House, and proceeding to Drury Lane, witnessed, with a fortitude which strongly interested all who observed him, the entire destruction of his property.

The theatre was, however, rebuilt at vast cost by subscription; but, though he still possessed some interest in the property, he was deprived of all control in the management and disposal of the funds, which fell into the hands of a committee, at the head of which was Mr. Whitbread, whose firmness and attention were a strong contrast to the careless want of punctuality of Sheridan.

From this moment his misfortunes accumulated, until he was thrown as a helpless wreck upon 'the bleak shore of life;' not, indeed, bereft of a few devoted friends, who adhered to him to the last; but who were powerless to provide for him a genial harbour to shelter him from the pitiless storm of creditors by which he was assailed, even up to the last moment of his existence.

His own extravagant mode of living, into which he was led by the wonderful success of the theatre, may afford some excuse for uncalculating squandering of money. But if such extravagance, in the days of his theatrical prosperity, exempt him from the charge of moral carelessness, he cannot be freed from the imputation of being a singularly improvident man. Still it cannot be supposed that he was unscrupulous, when it is a fact that, after the payment of his chief liabilities, he died owing no more than five thousand five hundred pounds.

In January, 1816, this highly-gifted man fell sick, and in the following summer, his stomach being unable to retain any sustenance, he died, in a state of great emaciation, on the 7th of July, 1816, in the 65th year of his age. But this happy release from bodily pain did not take place until after he had been subjected to the most cruel treatment at the hands of the case-hardened myrmidons of the law, and their heartless employers. Even the bed-room of the unhappy man was invaded by the former with the intention of taking him to a spunging-house or prison. But this purpose was stopped by the physician then in attendance, Dr. Bain, who warned the bailiff that, if Mr. Sheridan died on the way, he would be answerable for his death.

He was buried, with great pomp, in Westminster Abbey, and his resting place is marked by this modest inscription:—

'RICHARD BRINSLEY SHERIDAN,

Born 1751,

Died 7th July, 1816.

This marble is the tribute of an attached friend,

PETER MOORE.'

EXTRACT FROM THE MONODY ON SHERIDAN BY BYRON.

'But should there be to whom the fatal blight
Of failing Wisdom yields a base delight,
Men who exult when minds of heavenly tone
Jar in the music which was born their own;
Still let them pause—Ah! little do they know
That what to them seem'd Vice might be but Woe
Hard is his fate on whom the Public gaze
Is fix'd for ever, to detract or praise;
Repose denies her requiem to his name,
And Folly loves the martyrdom of Fame.
The secret enemy, whose sleepless eye
Stands sentinel—accuser—judge—and spy,
The foe—the fool—the jealous—and the vain—
The envious who but breathe in others' pain;
Behold the host! delighting to deprave,
Who track the steps of Glory to the Grave,
Watch every fault, that daring Genius owes
Half to the ardour which its birth bestows,
Distort the truth, accumulate the lie,
And pile the Pyramid of Calumny!
These are his portion; but if join'd to these
Gaunt Poverty should league with deep Disease;
If the high spirit must forget to soar,
And stoop to strive with Misery at the door,
To soothe Indignity, and face to face
Meet sordid Rage, and wrestle with Disgrace,
To find in Hope but the renew'd caress,
The serpent-fold of further Faithlessness—

If such may be the ills which men assail,
What marvel if at last the mightiest fail?
Breasts to whom all the strength of feeling given
Bears hearts electric—charged with fire from Heaven,
Black with the rude collision, inly torn,
By clouds surrounded, and on whirlwinds borne,
Driven o'er the lowering atmosphere that nurst
Thoughts which have turn'd to thunder,—scorch, and burst.'

THE RIVALS:

A COMEDY.

FIRST ACTED AT COVENT GARDEN THEATRE ON TUESDAY, THE 17TH OF JANUARY, 1775.

PREFACE.

A PREFACE to a play seems generally to be considered as a kind of closet-prologue, in which—if his piece has been successful—the author solicits that indulgence from the reader which he had before experienced from the audience; but as the scope and immediate object of a play is to please a mixed assembly in *representation* (whose judgment in the theatre at least is decisive), its degree of reputation is usually as determined as public, before it can be prepared for the cooler tribunal of the study. Thus any further solicitude on the part of the writer becomes unnecessary at least, if not an intrusion: and if the piece has been condemned in the performance, I fear an address to the closet, like an appeal to posterity, is constantly regarded as the procrastination of a suit from a consciousness of the weakness of the cause. From these considerations, the following comedy would certainly have been submitted to the reader, without any further introduction than what it had in the representation, but that its success has probably been founded on a circumstance which the author is informed has not before attended a theatrical trial, and which consequently ought not to pass unnoticed.

I need scarcely add, that the circumstance alluded to was the withdrawing of the piece, to remove those imperfections in the first representation which were too obvious to escape reprehension, and too numerous to admit of a hasty correction. There are few writers, I believe, who, even in the fullest consciousness of error, do not wish to palliate the faults which they acknowledge; and, however trifling the performance, to second their confession of its deficiencies, by whatever plea seems least disgraceful to their ability. In the present instance, it cannot be said to amount either to candour or modesty in me, to acknowledge an extreme inexperience and want of judgment on matters, in which, without guidance from practice, or spur from success, a young man should scarcely boast of being an adept. If it be said, that under such disadvantages no one should attempt to write a play, I must beg leave to dissent from the position, while the first point of experience that I have gained on the subject is, a knowledge of the candour and judgment with which an impartial public distinguishes between the errors of inexperience and incapacity, and the indulgence which it shows even to a disposition to remedy the defects of either.

It were unnecessary to enter into any further extenuation of what was thought exceptional in this play, but that it has been said, that the managers should have prevented some of the defects before its appearance to the public; and in particular the uncommon length of the piece as represented the first night. It were an ill return for the most liberal and gentlemanly conduct on their side, to suffer any censure to rest where none was deserved. Hurry in writing has long been exploded, as an excuse for an author; however, in the dramatic line, it may happen that both an author and a manager may wish to fill a chasm in the entertainment of the public with a hastiness not altogether culpable. The season was advanced when I first put the play into Mr. Harris's hands: it was at that time at least double the length of any acting comedy. I profited by his judgment and experience in the curtailing of it, till, I believe, his feeling for the vanity of a young author got the better of his desire for correctness, and he left many excrescences remaining, because he had assisted in pruning so many more. Hence, though I was not uninformed that the acts were still too long, I flattered myself that, after the first trial, I might with safer judgment proceed to remove what should appear to have been most dissatisfactory. Many other errors there were, which might in part have arisen from my being by no means conversant with plays in general, either in reading or at the theatre. Yet I own that, in one respect, I did not regret my ignorance; for as my first wish in attempting a play was to avoid every appearance of plagiary, I thought I should stand a better chance of effecting this from being in a walk which I had not frequented, and where, consequently, the progress of invention was less likely to be interrupted by starts of recollection; for on subjects on which the mind has been much informed, invention is slow in exerting itself. Faded ideas float in the fancy like half-forgotten dreams; and the imagination in its fullest enjoyments becomes suspicious of its offspring, and doubts whether it has created or adopted.

With regard to some particular passages which on the first night's representation seemed generally disliked, I confess, that if I felt any emotion of surprise at the disapprobation, it was not that they were disapproved of, but that I had not before perceived that they deserved it. As some part of the attack on the piece was begun too early to pass for the sentence of *judgment*, which is ever tardy in condemning, it has been suggested to me, that much of the disapprobation must have arisen from virulence of malice, rather than severity of criticism; but as I was more apprehensive of there being just grounds to excite the latter than conscious of having deserved the former, I continue not to believe that probable, which I am sure must have been unprovoked. However, if it was so, and I could even mark the quarter from whence it came, it would be ungenerous to retort; for no passion suffers more than malice from disappointment. For my own part, I see no reason why the author of a play should not regard a first night's audience as a candid and judicious friend attending, in behalf of the public, at his last rehearsal. If he can dispense with flattery, he is sure at least of sincerity, and even though the annotation be rude, he may rely upon the justness of the comment. Considered in this light, that audience, whose *fiat* is essential to the poet's claim, whether his object be fame or profit, has surely a right to expect some deference to its opinion, from principles of politeness at least, if not from gratitude.

As for the little puny critics, who scatter their peevish strictures in private circles, and scribble at every author who has the eminence of being unconnected with them, as they are usually spleen-swoln from a vain idea of increasing their consequence, there will always be found a petulance and illiberality in their remarks, which should place them as far beneath the notice of a gentleman, as their original dulness had sunk them from the level of the most unsuccessful author.

It is not without pleasure that I catch at an opportunity of justifying myself from the charge of intending any national reflection in the character of Sir Lucius O'Trigger. If any gentlemen opposed the piece from that idea, I thank them sincerely for their opposition; and if the condemnation of this comedy (however misconceived the provocation) could have added one spark to the decaying flame of national attachment to the country supposed to be reflected on, I should have been happy in its fate; and might with truth have boasted, that it had done more real service in its failure, than the successful morality of a thousand stage-novels will ever effect.

It is usual, I believe, to thank the performers in a new play, for the exertion of their several abilities. But where (as in this instance) their merit has been so striking and uncontroverted, as to call for the warmest and truest applause from a number of judicious audiences, the poet's after-praise comes like the feeble acclamation of a child to close the shouts of a multitude. The conduct, however, of the principals in a theatre cannot be so apparent to the puplic. I think it therefore but justice to declare, that from this theatre (the only one I can speak of from experience) those writers who wish to try the dramatic line will meet with that candour and liberal attention, which are generally allowed to be better calculated to lead genius into excellence, than either the precepts of judgment, or the guidance of experience.

THE AUTHOR.

PROLOGUE.

BY THE AUTHOR. SPOKEN BY MR. WOODWARD AND MR. QUICK.

Enter Serjeant-at-Law, and Attorney following, and giving a paper.

Serj. WHAT's here! a vile cramp hand! I cannot see
Without my spectacles.
 Att.   He means his fee.
Nay, Mr. Serjeant, good sir, try again. [*Gives money.*
 Serj. The scrawl improves! [*more*] O come, 'tis pretty
   plain.
Hey! how's this? Dibble!—sure it cannot be!
A poet's brief! a poet and a fee!
 Att. Yes, sir! though *you* without reward, I know,
Would gladly plead the Muse's cause.
 Serj.   So! So!
 Att. And if the fee offends, your wroth should fall
On me.
 Serj. Dear Dibble, no offence at all.
 Att. Some sons of Phœbus in the courts we meet,
 Serj. And fifty sons of Phœbus in the Fleet!
 Att. Nor pleads he worse, who with a decent sprig
Of bays adorns his legal waste of wig.
 Serj. Full-bottom'd heroes thus, on signs, unfurl
A leaf of laurel in a grove of curl!
Yet tell your client, that, in adverse days,
This wig is warmer than a bush of bays.
 Att. Do you, then, sir, my client's place supply,
Profuse of robe, and prodigal of tie.
Do you, with all those blushing powers of face,
And wonted bashful hesitating grace,
Rise in the court, and flourish on the case. [*Exit.*

Serj. For practice then suppose—this brief will show it—
Me, Serjeant Woodward, counsel for the poet.
Used to the ground, I know 'tis hard to deal
With this dread *court*, from whence there's *no appeal;*
No *tricking* here, to blunt the edge of *law,*
Or, damn'd in *equity,* escape by *flaw:*
But *judgment* given, *your sentence* must remain;
No *writ of error* lies—to *Drury Lane!*

Yet when so kind you seem, 'tis past dispute
We gain some favour, if not *costs of suit.*
No spleen is here! I see no hoarded fury;
I think I never faced a milder jury!
Sad else our plight! where frowns are transportation,
A hiss the gallows, and a groan damnation!
But such the public candour, without fear
My client waves all *right of challenge* here.
No newsman from *our* session is dismiss'd,
Nor wit nor critic *we* scratch off the list;
His faults can never hurt another's ease,
His crime, at worst, a *bad attempt* to please:
Thus, all respecting, he appeals to all,
And by the general voice will *stand* or *fall.*

The play being withdrawn after the first night's representation, upon its second appearance the lines from 'Hey! how's this?' to 'no offence at all,' were omitted, and the following inserted:

'How's this! the poet's brief *again!* O ho!
'Cast, I suppose?
  '*Att.*   O pardon me. No—no.
'We found the court, o'erlooking stricter laws,
'*Indulgent* to the *merits* of the cause;
'By *judges* mild, unused to harsh denial,
'A rule was granted for *another trial.*
  '*Serj.* Then hark'ee, Dibble, did you *mend* your *pleadings;*
'*Errors,* no few, we've *found* in our *proceedings.*
  '*Att.* Come, courage, sir, we did *amend* our *plea,*
'Hence your *new brief,* and this *refreshing fee.*'

PROLOGUE.

BY THE AUTHOR. SPOKEN ON THE TENTH NIGHT, BY MRS. BULKLEY.

GRANTED our cause, our suit and trial o'er,
The worthy Serjeant need appear no more:
In pleasing I a different client choose,
He served the Poet—I would serve the Muse:
Like him, I'll try to merit your applause,
A female counsel in a female's cause.
   Look on this form,* where Humour, quaint and sly,
Dimples the cheek, and points the beaming eye;
Where gay Invention seems to boast its wiles
In amorous hint, and half-triumphant smiles;
While her light mask or covers Satire's strokes,
Or hides the conscious blush her wit provokes.
Look on her well. Does she seem form'd to teach?
Should you *expect* to hear this lady preach?
Is grey experience suited to her youth?
Do solemn sentiments become that mouth?
Bid her be grave, those lips should rebel prove
To every theme that slanders mirth or love.
   Yet thus adorn'd with every graceful art
To charm the fancy and yet reach the heart;
Must we displace her? And instead advance
The Goddess of the woful countenance—
The sentimental Muse! Her emblems view,
The Pilgrim's Progress, and a sprig of rue!
View her—too chaste to look like flesh and blood—
Primly portray'd on emblematic wood!

* Pointing to the figure of Comedy.

There fix'd in usurpation should she stand,
She'll snatch the dagger from her sister's hand:
And having made her vot'ries *weep a flood*,
Good heaven! she'll end her comedies in blood.
Bid Harry Woodward break poor Dunstal's crown!
Imprison Quick, and knock Ned Shuter down;
While sad Barsanti, weeping o'er the scene,
Shall stab herself, or poison Mrs. Green.

 Such dire encroachments to prevent in time,
Demands the critic's voice, the poet's rhyme.
Can our light scenes add strength to holy laws!
Such puny patronage but hurts the cause:
Fair Virtue scorns our feeble aid to ask;
And moral Truth disdains the trickster's mask.
For here their fav'rite stands,° whose brow, severe
And sad, claims Youth's respect, and Pity's tear;
Who, when oppress'd by foes her worth creates,
Can point a poniard at the Guilt she hates.

     ° Pointing to Tragedy.

EPILOGUE.

BY THE AUTHOR. SPOKEN BY MRS BULKLEY.

LADIES, for *you*, I heard our poet say,
He'd try to coax some *moral* from his play:
'One moral's plain,' cried I, 'without more fuss;
'Man's social happiness all rests on us:
'Through all the drama, whether d—n'd or not,
'*Love* gilds the *scene*, and *women* guide the *plot*.
'From every rank obedience is our due—
'D'ye doubt? The world's great stage shall prove it true.'
    The Cit, well skill'd to shun domestic strife,
Will sup abroad; but first, he'll ask his *wife:*
John Trot, his friend, for once will do the same,
But then—he'll just *step home to tell his dame.*
    The *surly Squire* at noon resolves to rule,
And half the day—Zounds! Madam is a fool!
Convinced at night, the vanquish'd victor says,
Ah, Kate! *you women have such coaxing ways!*
    The *jolly Toper* chides each tardy blade,
Till reeling Bacchus calls on Love for aid:
Then with each toast he sees fair bumpers swim,
And kisses Chloe on the sparkling brim!
    Nay, I have heard that Statesmen, great and wise,
Will *sometimes* counsel with a lady's eyes;
The servile suitors watch her various face,
She smiles preferment, or she frowns disgrace,
Curtsies a pension here—there nods a place.

Nor with less awe, in scenes of humbler life,
Is *view'd* the *mistress*, or is *heard* the *wife*.
The poorest Peasant of the poorest soil,
The child of poverty, and heir to toil,
Early from radiant Love's impartial light
Steals one small spark to cheer his world of night:
Dear spark! that oft through winter's chilling woes
Is all the warmth his little cottage knows!

The wand'ring *Tar*, who not for *years* has press'd
The widow'd partner of his *day* of rest,
On the cold deck, far from her arms removed,
Still hums the ditty which his Susan loved;
And while around the cadence rude is blown,
The boatswain whistles in a softer tone.

The *Soldier*, fairly proud of wounds and toil,
Pants for the *triumph* of his Nancy's smile;
But ere the battle should he list' her cries,
The lover trembles—and the hero dies!
That heart, by war and honour steel'd to fear,
Droops on a sigh, and sickens at a tear!

But ye more cautious, ye nice-judging few,
Who give to Beauty only Beauty's due,
Though friends to Love—*ye* view with deep regret
Our conquests marr'd, our triumphs incomplete,
Till polish'd Wit more lasting charms disclose,
And Judgment fix the darts which Beauty throws!
In female breasts did sense and merit rule,
The lover's mind would ask no other school;
Shamed into sense, the scholars of our eyes,
Our beaux from *gallantry* would soon be wise;
Would gladly light, their homage to improve,
The lamp of Knowledge at the torch of Love!

DRAMATIS PERSONÆ,

AS ORIGINALLY ACTED AT COVENT GARDEN THEATRE IN 1775.

Sir Anthony Absolute . . Mr. Shuter.
Captain Absolute . . . Mr. Woodward.
Faulkland . . . . . Mr. Lewis.
Acres . . . . Mr. Quick.
Sir Lucius O'Trigger . . Mr. Lee.[o]
Fag . . . . Mr. Lee Lewis.
David . . . . Mr. Dunstal.
Coachman . . . . . Mr. Fearon.

Mrs. Malaprop . . . . Mrs. Green.
Lydia Languish . . . . Miss Barsanti.
Julia . . . . Mrs. Bulkley.
Lucy . . . . Mrs. Lessingham.

Maid, Boy, Servants, &c.

Scene—Bath.

Time of Action—Five Hours.

[o] Afterwards by Mr. Clinch.

THE RIVALS.

ACT I.—SCENE I.

A Street in BATH.

COACHMAN *crosses the stage.* Enter FAG, *looking after him.*

Fag. WHAT! Thomas! Sure 'tis he? What! Thomas! Thomas!

Coach. Hey! Odd's life! Mr. Fag! Give us your hand, my old fellow-servant.

Fag. Excuse my glove, Thomas. I'm devilish glad to see you, my lad: why, my prince of charioteers, you look as hearty! But who the deuce thought of seeing you in Bath?

Coach. Sure, master, Madam Julia, Harry, Mrs. Kate, and the postillion, be all come.

Fag. Indeed!

Coach. Ay! master thought another fit of the gout was coming to make him a visit; so he'd a mind to gi't the slip, and whip! we were all off at an hour's warning.

Fag. Ay, ay! hasty in everything, or it would not be Sir Anthony Absolute!

Coach. But tell us, Mr. Fag, how does young master? Odd! Sir Anthony will stare to see the captain here!

Fag. I do not serve Captain Absolute now.

Coach. Why sure!

Fag. At present I am employed by Ensign Beverley.

Coach. I doubt, Mr. Fag, you ha'n't changed for the better.

Fag. I have not changed, Thomas.

Coach. No! Why, didn't you say you had left young master?

Fag. No. Well, honest Thomas, I must puzzle you no further. Briefly, then, Captain Absolute and Ensign Beverley are one and the same person.

Coach. The devil they are!

Fag. So it is indeed, Thomas; and the *ensign* half of my master being on guard at present, the *captain* has nothing to do with me.

Coach. So, so! What! this is some freak, I warrant. Do tell us, Mr. Fag, the meaning o't; you know I ha' trusted you.

Fag. You'll be secret, Thomas?

Coach. As a coach-horse.

Fag. Why, then, the cause of all this is—Love. Love, Thomas, who (as you may get read to you) has been a masquerader ever since the days of Jupiter.

Coach. Ay, ay; I guess'd there was a lady in the case. But, pray, why does your master pass only for *ensign?* Now if he had shamm'd *general* indeed——

Fag. Ah! Thomas, there lies the mystery o' the matter. Hark'ee, Thomas, my master is in love with a lady of a very singular taste: a lady who likes him better as a *half-pay ensign* than if she knew he was son and heir to Sir Anthony Absolute, a baronet of three thousand a year.

Coach. That is an odd taste indeed! But has she got the stuff, Mr. Fag? Is she rich, hey?

Fag. Rich! why, I believe she owns half the stocks. Z—ds! Thomas, she could pay the national debt as easily as I could my washerwoman! She has a lap-dog that eats out of gold, she feeds her parrot with small pearls, and all her thread-papers are made of bank-notes!

Coach. Bravo, faith! Odd! I warrant she has a set of thousands at least. But does she draw kindly with the captain?

Fag. As fond as pigeons.

Coach. May one hear her name?

Fag. Miss Lydia Languish. But there is an old tough aunt in the way: though, by-the-bye, she has never seen my master, for we got acquainted with miss while on a visit in Gloucestershire.

Coach. Well, I wish they were once harnessed together in matrimony. But pray, Mr. Fag, what kind of a place is this Bath? I ha' heard a deal of it; here's a mort o' merrymaking, hey?

Fag. Pretty well, Thomas, pretty well; 'tis a good lounge. In the morning we go to the Pump-room, though neither my master nor I drink the waters: after breakfast we saunter on the parades, or play a game at billiards; at night we dance; but d—n the place, I'm tired of it: their regular hours stupefy me; not a fiddle nor a card after eleven! However, Mr. Faulkland's gentleman and I keep it up a little in private parties. I'll introduce you there, Thomas; you'll like him much.

Coach. Sure I know Mr. Du-Peigne; you know his master is to marry Madam Julia.

Fag. I had forgot. But, Thomas, you must polish a little; indeed you must. Here now, this wig! What the devil do you do with a wig, Thomas? None of the London whips of any degree of *ton* wear wigs now.

Coach. More's the pity! more's the pity, I say. Odd's life! when I heard how the lawyers and doctors had took to their own hair, I thought how 'twould go next. Odd rabbit it! when the fashion had got foot on the Bar, I guess'd 'twould mount to the Box! But 'tis all out of character, believe me, Mr. Fag; and look'ee, I'll never gi' up mine; the lawyers and doctors may do as they will.

Fag. Well, Thomas, we'll not quarrel about that.

Coach. Why, bless you, the gentlemen of they professions ben't all of a mind; for in our village now, thoff Jack Gauge the exciseman has ta'en to his carrots, there's little Dick the farrier swears he'll never forsake his bob, tho' all the college should appear with their own heads!

Fag. Indeed! well said, Dick! But hold. Mark! mark! Thomas.

Coach. Zooks! 'tis the captain. Is that the lady with him?

Fag. No! no! that is Madam Lucy, my master's mistress's maid. They lodge at that house. But I must after him to tell him the news.

Coach. Odd! he's giving her money! Well, Mr. Fag——

Fag. Good bye, Thomas. I have an appointment in Gyde's Porch this evening at eight; meet me there, and we'll make a little party.

[*Exeunt severally.*

SCENE II.

A Dressing-room in Mrs. MALAPROP'S *Lodgings.*

LYDIA *sitting on a sofa, with a book in her hand.*

LUCY, *as just returned from a message.*

Lucy. Indeed, ma'am, I traversed half the town in search of it. I don't believe there's a circulating library in Bath I ha'n't been at.

Lydia. And could you not get 'The Reward of Constancy'?

Lucy. No, indeed, ma'am.

Lydia. Nor 'The Fatal Connexion'?

Lucy. No, indeed, ma'am.

Lydia. Nor 'The Mistakes of the Heart'?

Lucy. Ma'am, as ill luck would have it, Mr. Bull said Miss Sukey Saunter had just fetched it away.

Lydia. Heigh-ho! Did you inquire for 'The Delicate Distress'?

Lucy. Or, 'The Memoirs of Lady Woodford'? Yes, indeed, ma'am. I asked everywhere for it; and I might have brought it from Mr. Frederick's, but Lady Slattern Lounger, who had just sent it home, had so soiled and dogs'-eared it, it wa'n't fit for a Christian to read.

Lydia. Heigh-ho! Yes, I always know when Lady Slattern has been before me. She has a most observing thumb; and, I believe, cherishes her nails for the convenience of making marginal notes. Well, child, what have you brought me?

Lucy. Oh! here, ma'am.

[*Taking books from under her cloak, and from her pockets.*]

This is 'The Gordian Knot,' and this 'Peregrine Pickle.' Here are 'The Tears of Sensibility,' and 'Humphrey Clinker.' This is 'The Memoirs of a Lady of Quality, written by herself,' and here the second volume of 'The Sentimental Journey.'

Lydia. Heigh-ho! What are those books by the glass?

Lucy. The great one is only 'The Whole Duty of Man,' where I press a few blonds, ma'am.

Lydia. Very well; give me the *sal volatile*.

Lucy. Is it in a blue cover, ma'am?

Lydia. My smelling-bottle, you simpleton!

Lucy. O, the drops! Here, ma'am.

Lydia. Hold! here's some one coming. Quick, see who it is. [*Exit* LUCY.
Surely I heard my cousin Julia's voice!

[*Re-enter* LUCY.

Lucy. Lud! ma'am, here is Miss Melville.

Lydia. Is it possible!—

Enter JULIA.

Lydia. My dearest Julia, how delighted am I! (*Embrace.*) How unexpected was this happiness!

Julia. True, Lydia, and our pleasure is the greater. But what has been the matter? You were denied to me at first.

Lydia. Ah, Julia, I have a thousand things to tell you. But first inform me what has conjured you to Bath? Is Sir Anthony here?

Julia. He is; we are arrived within this hour, and I suppose he will be here to wait on Mrs. Malaprop as soon as he is dress'd.

Lydia. Then before we are interrupted, let me impart to you some of my distress! I know your gentle nature will sympathize with me, though your prudence may condemn me! My letters have informed you of my whole connexion with Beverley; but I have lost him, Julia! My aunt has discovered our intercourse by a note she intercepted, and has confined me ever since! Yet, would you believe it? she has fallen absolutely in love with a tall Irish baronet she met one night since we have been here at Lady Macshuffle's rout.

Julia. You jest, Lydia!

Lydia. No, upon my word. She really carries on a kind of correspondence with him, under a feigned name though, till she chooses to be known to him; but it is a Delia or a Celia, I assure you.

Julia. Then, surely, she is now more indulgent to her niece.

Lydia. Quite the contrary. Since she has discovered her own frailty, she is become more suspicious of mine. Then I must inform you of another plague! That odious Acres is to be in Bath to-day; so that I protest I shall be teased out of all spirits!

Julia. Come, come, Lydia, hope for the best. Sir Anthony shall use his interest with Mrs. Malaprop.

Lydia. But you have not heard the worst. Unfortunately I had quarrelled with my poor Beverley, just before my aunt made the discovery, and I have not seen him since, to make it up.

Julia. What was his offence?

Lydia. Nothing at all! But, I don't know how it was, as often as we had been together, we had never had a quarrel! And, somehow, I was afraid he would never give me an opportunity. So, last Thursday, I wrote a letter to myself, to inform myself that Beverley was at that time paying his addresses to another woman. I signed it 'your friend unknown,' showed it to Beverley, charged him with his falsehood, put myself in a violent passion, and vowed I'd never see him more.

Julia. And you let him depart so, and have not seen him since?

Lydia. 'Twas the next day my aunt found the matter out. I intended only to have teased him three days and a half, and now I've lost him for ever.

Julia. If he is as deserving and sincere as you have represented him to me, he will never give you up so. Yet consider, Lydia, you tell me he is but an ensign, and you have thirty thousand pounds!

Lydia. But you know I lose most of my fortune if I marry without my aunt's consent, till of age; and that is what I have determined to do, ever since I knew the penalty. Nor could I love the man, who would wish to wait a day for the alternative.

Julia. Nay, this is caprice!

Lydia. What, does Julia tax me with caprice? I thought her lover Faulkland had inured her to it.

Julia. I do not love even *his* faults.

Lydia. But apropos, you have sent to him, I suppose?

Julia. Not yet, upon my word; nor has he the least idea of my being in Bath. Sir Anthony's resolution was so sudden, I could not inform him of it.

Lydia. Well, Julia, you are your own mistress (though under the protection of Sir Anthony), yet have you, for this long year, been a slave to the caprice, the whim, the jealousy of this ungrateful Faulkland, who will ever delay assuming the right of a husband, while you suffer him to be equally imperious as a lover.

Julia. Nay, you are wrong entirely. We were contracted before my father's death. That, and some consequent embarrassments, have delayed what I know to be my Faulkland's most ardent wish. He is too generous to trifle on such a point. And for his character, you wrong him there too. No, Lydia, he is too proud, too noble to be jealous; if he is captious, 'tis without dissembling; if fretful, without rudeness. Unused to the fopperies of love, he is negligent of the little duties expected from a lover; but being unhackneyed in his passion, his affection is ardent and sincere; and as it engrosses his whole soul, he expects every thought and emotion of his mistress to move in unison with his. Yet, though his pride calls for this full return, his humility makes him undervalue those qualities in him which would entitle him to it; and not feeling why he should be loved to the degree he wishes, he still suspects that he is not loved enough. This temper, I must own, has cost me many unhappy hours; but I have learned to think myself his debtor, for those imperfections which arise from the ardour of his attachment.

Lydia. Well, I cannot blame you for defending him. But tell me candidly, Julia, had he never saved your life, do you think you should have been attached to him as you are? Believe me, the rude blast that overset your boat was a prosperous gale of love to him.

Julia. Gratitude may have strengthened my attachment to Mr. Faulkland, but I loved him before he had preserved me; yet surely that alone were an obligation sufficient——

Lydia. Obligation! Why a water-spaniel would have done as much! Well, I should never think of giving my heart to a man because he could swim!

Julia. Come, Lydia, you are too inconsiderate.

Lydia. Nay, I do but jest. What's here?

Enter LUCY *in a hurry.*

Lucy. O ma'am, here is Sir Anthony Absolute just come home with your aunt.

Lydia. They'll not come here. Lucy, do you watch.
[*Exit* LUCY.

Julia. Yet I must go. Sir Anthony does not know I am here, and if we meet he'll detain me, to show me the town. I'll take another opportunity of paying my respects to Mrs. Malaprop, when she shall treat me, as long as she chooses, with her select words so ingeniously *misapplied*, without being *mispronounced*.

Re-enter LUCY.

Lucy. O Lud! ma'am, they are both coming upstairs.

Lydia. Well, I'll not detain you, coz. Adieu, my dear Julia, I'm sure you are in haste to send to Faulkland. There, through my room, you'll find another staircase.

Julia. Adieu! (*Embrace.*) [*Exit* JULIA.

Lydia. Here, my dear Lucy, hide these books. Quick, quick. Fling 'Peregrine Pickle' under the toilet; throw 'Roderick Random' into the closet; put 'The Innocent Adultery' into 'The Whole Duty of Man'; thrust 'Lord Aimworth' under the sofa; cram 'Ovid' behind the bolster. There, put 'The Man of Feeling' into your pocket; so, so, now lay 'Mrs. Chapone' in sight, and leave 'Fordyce's Sermons' open on the table.

Lucy. O burn it, ma'am, the hairdresser has torn away as far as 'Proper Pride.'

Lydia. Never mind, open at 'Sobriety.' Fling me 'Lord Chesterfield's Letters.' Now for 'em.

Enter Mrs. MALAPROP *and* Sir ANTHONY ABSOLUTE.

Mrs. Mal. There, Sir Anthony, there sits the deliberate simpleton, who wants to disgrace her family, and lavish herself on a fellow not worth a shilling.

Lydia. Madam, I thought you once——

Mrs. Mal. You thought, miss! I don't know any business you have to think at all; thought does not become a young woman. But the point we would request of you is, that you will promise to forget this fellow—to illiterate him, I say, quite from your memory.

Lydia. Ah, madam! our memories are independent of our wills. It is not so easy to forget.

Mrs. Mal. But I say it is, miss; there is nothing on earth so easy as to *forget*, if a person chooses to set about it. I'm sure I have as much forgot your poor dear uncle as if he had never existed—and I thought it my duty so to do; and let me tell you, Lydia, these violent memories don't become a young woman.

Sir Anth. Why, sure she won't pretend to remember what she's ordered not! Ay, this comes of her reading!

Lydia. What crime, madam, have I committed, to be treated thus?

Mrs. Mal. Now, don't attempt to extirpate yourself from the matter; you know I have proof controvertible of it. But, tell me, will you promise to do as you're bid? Will you take a husband of your friends' choosing?

Lydia. Madam, I must tell you plainly, that had I no preference for any one else, the choice you have made would be my aversion.

Mrs. Mal. What business have you, miss, with *preference* and *aversion?* They don't become a young woman; and you ought to know, that as both always wear off, 'tis safest in matrimony to begin with a little *aversion.* I am sure I hated your poor dear uncle before marriage as if he'd been a black-a-moor; and yet, miss, you are sensible what a wife I made! and when it pleased Heaven to release me from him, 'tis unknown what tears I shed! But, suppose we were going to give you another choice, will you promise us to give up this Beverley?

Lydia. Could I belie my thoughts so far as to give that promise, my actions would certainly as far belie my words.

Mrs. Mal. Take yourself to your room. You are fit company for nothing but your own ill humours.

Lydia. Willingly, ma'am; I cannot change for the worse. [*Exit* LYDIA.

Mrs. Mal. There's a little intricate hussy for you!

Sir Anth. It is not to be wondered at, ma'am; all this is the natural consequence of teaching girls to read. Had I a thousand daughters, by heaven! I'd as soon have them taught the black art as their alphabet!

Mrs. Mal. Nay, nay, Sir Anthony, you are an absolute misanthropy.

Sir Anth. In my way hither, Mrs. Malaprop, I observed your niece's maid coming forth from a circulating library! She had a book in each hand; they were half-bound volumes, with marble covers! From that moment I guessed how full of duty I should see her mistress!

Mrs. Mal. Those are vile places, indeed!

Sir Anth. Madam, a circulating library in a town is as an evergreen tree of diabolical knowledge! It blossoms through the year! And depend on it, Mrs.

Malaprop, that they who are so fond of handling the leaves will long for the fruit at last.

Mrs. Mal. Fie, fie, Sir Anthony, you surely speak laconically.

Sir Anth. Why, Mrs. Malaprop, in moderation, now, what would you have a woman know?

Mrs. Mal. Observe me, Sir Anthony. I would by no means wish a daughter of mine to be a progeny of learning; I don't think so much learning becomes a young woman; for instance, I would never let her meddle with Greek, or Hebrew, or Algebra, or Simony, or Fluxions, or Paradoxes, or such inflammatory branches of learning; neither would it be necessary for her to handle any of your mathematical, astronomical, diabolical instruments. But, Sir Anthony, I would send her, at nine years old, to a boarding-school, in order to learn a little ingenuity and artifice. Then, sir, she should have a supercilious knowledge in accounts; and as she grew up, I would have her instructed in geometry, that she might know something of the contagious countries; but above all, Sir Anthony, she should be mistress of orthodoxy, that she might not misspell, and mispronounce words so shamefully as girls usually do; and likewise that she might reprehend the true meaning of what she is saying. This, Sir Anthony, is what I would have a woman know; and I don't think there is a superstitious article in it.

Sir Anth. Well, well, Mrs. Malaprop, I will dispute the point no further with you; though I must confess, that you are a truly moderate and polite arguer, for almost every third word you say is on my side of the question. But, Mrs. Malaprop, to the more important point in debate: you say, you have no objection to my proposal?

Mrs. Mal. None, I assure you. I am under no positive engagement with Mr. Acres, and as Lydia is so obstinate against him, perhaps your son may have better success.

Sir Anth. Well, madam, I will write for the boy directly. He knows not a syllable of this yet, though I have for some time had the proposal in my head. He is at present with his regiment.

Mrs. Mal. We have never seen your son, Sir Anthony; but I hope no objection on his side.

Sir Anth. Objection! Let him object if he dare! No, no, Mrs. Malaprop, Jack knows that the least demur puts me in a frenzy directly. My process was always very simple in their younger days: 'twas 'Jack, do this.' If he demurred, I knocked him down; and if he grumbled at that, I always sent him out of the room.

Mrs. Mal. Ay, and the properest way, o'my conscience! Nothing is so conciliating to young people as severity. Well, Sir Anthony, I shall give Mr. Acres his discharge, and prepare Lydia to receive your son's invocations; and I hope you will represent *her* to the captain as an object not altogether illegible.

Sir Anth. Madam, I will handle the subject prudently. Well, I must leave you; and let me beg you, Mrs. Malaprop, to enforce this matter roundly to the girl. Take my advice: keep a tight hand. If she rejects this proposal, clap her under lock and key; and if you were just to let the servants forget to bring her dinner for three or four days, you can't conceive how she'd come about. [*Exit* Sir Anth.

Mrs. Mal. Well, at any rate I shall be glad to get her from under my intuition. She has somehow discovered my partiality for Sir Lucius O'Trigger. Sure, Lucy can't have betrayed me! No; the girl is such a simpleton, I should have made her confess it. Lucy! Lucy! (*calls.*) Had she been one of your artificial ones, I should never have trusted her.

Enter LUCY.

Lucy. Did you call, ma'am?

Mrs. Mal. Yes, girl. Did you see Sir Lucius while you was out?

Lucy. No, indeed, ma'am, not a glimpse of him.

Mrs. Mal. You are sure, Lucy, that you never mentioned——

Lucy. O Gemini! I'd sooner cut my tongue out.

Mrs. Mal. Well, don't let your simplicity be imposed on.

Lucy. No, ma'am.

Mrs. Mal. So, come to me presently, and I'll give you another letter to Sir Lucius; but mind, Lucy, if ever you betray what you are intrusted with (unless it be other people's secrets to me), you forfeit my malevolence for ever; and your being a simpleton shall be no excuse for your locality. [*Exit* Mrs. MAL.

Lucy. Ha! ha! ha! So, my dear *simplicity*, let me give you a little respite (*altering her manner*). Let girls in my station be as fond as they please of appearing expert, and knowing in their trusts; commend me to a mask of *silliness*, and a pair of sharp eyes for my own interest under it! Let me see to what account have I turned my *simplicity* lately (*looks at a paper*). For *abetting Miss Lydia Languish in a design of running away with an ensign! in money, sundry times, twelve pound twelve; gowns, five; hats, ruffles, caps, &c., &c., numberless! From the said ensign, within this last month, six guineas and a half.* About a quarter's pay! Item, *from Mrs. Malaprop, for betraying the young people to her*—when I found matters were likely to be discovered—*two guineas, and a black padusoy.* Item, *from Mr. Acres, for carrying divers letters,* which I never delivered, *two guineas, and a pair of buckles.* Item, *from Sir Lucius O'Trigger, three crowns, two gold pocket pieces, and a silver snuff-box!* Well done, *simplicity!* yet I was forced to make my Hibernian believe, that he was corresponding, not with the *aunt,* but with the *niece:* for though not over rich, I found he had too much pride and delicacy to sacrifice the feelings of a gentleman to the necessities of fortune. [*Exit.*

ACT II.—SCENE I.

Captain ABSOLUTE's *Lodgings.*

Captain ABSOLUTE *and* FAG.

Fag. Sir, while I was there Sir Anthony came in: I told him, you had sent me to inquire after his health, and to know if he was at leisure to see you.

Abs. And what did he say, on hearing I was at Bath?

Fag. Sir, in my life I never saw an elderly gentleman more astonished! He started back two or three paces, rapt out a dozen interjectural oaths, and asked, what the devil had brought you here?

Abs. Well, sir, and what did you say?

Fag. O, I lied, sir. I forget the precise lie; but you may depend on't, he got no truth from me. Yet, with submission, for fear of blunders in future, I should be glad to fix what *has* brought us to Bath, in order that we may lie a little consistently. Sir Anthony's servants were curious, sir, very curious indeed.

Abs. You have said nothing to them——?

Fag. O, not a word, sir,—not a word. Mr. Thomas, indeed, the coachman (whom I take to be the discreetest of whips)——

Abs. 'Sdeath! you rascal! you have not trusted him!

Fag. O, *no*, sir; no, no, not a syllable, upon my veracity! He was, indeed, a little inquisitive; but I was sly, sir; devilish sly! My master (said I), honest Thomas (you know, sir, one says *honest* to one's inferiors), is come to Bath to *recruit*. Yes, sir, I said *to recruit;* and whether for men, money, or constitution, you know, sir, is nothing to him, nor any one else.

Abs. Well, *recruit* will do; let it be so.

Fag. O, sir, recruit will do surprisingly; indeed, to give the thing an air, I told Thomas, that your Honour had already enlisted five disbanded chairmen, seven minority waiters, and thirteen billiard-markers.

Abs. You blockhead, never say more than is necessary.

Fag. I beg pardon, sir; I beg pardon. But, with submission, a lie is nothing unless one supports it. Sir, whenever I draw on my invention for a good current lie, I always forge indorsements as well as the bill.

Abs. Well, take care you don't hurt your credit, by offering too much security. Is Mr. Faulkland returned?

Fag. He is above, sir, changing his dress.

Abs. Can you tell whether he has been informed of Sir Anthony's and Miss Melville's arrival?

Fag. I fancy not, sir; he has seen no one since he came in but his gentleman, who was with him at

Bristol. I think, sir, I hear Mr. Faulkland coming down——

Abs. Go, tell him, I am here.

Fag. Yes, sir—(*going*)—I beg pardon, sir, but should Sir Anthony call, you will do me the favour to remember, that we are *recruiting*, if you please.

Abs. Well, well.

Fag. And in tenderness to my character, if your Honour could bring in the chairmen and waiters, I should esteem it as an obligation; for though I never scruple a lie to serve my master, yet it hurts one's conscience to be found out. [*Exit.*

Abs. Now for my whimsical friend; if he does not know that his mistress is here, I'll tease him a little before I tell him.

Enter FAULKLAND.

Faulkland, you're welcome to Bath again; you are punctual in your return.

Faulk. Yes; I had nothing to detain me, when I had finished the business I went on. Well, what news since I left you? How stand matters between you and Lydia?

Abs. Faith, much as they were; I have not seen her since our quarrel; however, I expect to be recalled every hour.

Faulk. Why don't you persuade her to go off with you at once?

Abs. What, and lose two-thirds of her fortune? You forget that, my friend. No, no, I could have brought her to that long ago.

Faulk. Nay, then, you trifle too long. If you are sure of *her*, propose to the aunt *in your own character*, and write to Sir Anthony for his consent.

Abs. Softly, softly; for though I am convinced my little Lydia would elope with me as Ensign Beverley, yet am I by no means certain that she would take me with the impediment of our friends' consent, a regular humdrum wedding, and the reversion of a good fortune on my side: no, no; I must prepare her gradually for the discovery, and make myself necessary to her, before I risk it. Well, but Faulkland, you'll dine with us to-day at the hotel?

Faulk. Indeed I cannot; I am not in spirits to be of such a party.

Abs. By heavens! I shall forswear your company. You are the most teasing, captious, incorrigible lover! Do love like a man.

Faulk. I own I am unfit for company.

Abs. Am not *I* a lover; ay, and a romantic one too? Yet do I carry everywhere with me such a confounded farrago of doubts, fears, hopes, wishes, and all the flimsy furniture of a country miss's brain!

Faulk. Ah! Jack, your heart and soul are not, like mine, fixed immutably on one only object. You throw for a large stake, but losing, you could stake, and throw again. But I have set my sum of happiness on this cast, and not to succeed were to be stripped of all.

Abs. But, for Heaven's sake! what grounds for apprehension can your whimsical brain conjure up at present?

Faulk. What grounds for apprehension, did you say? Heavens! are there not a thousand! I fear for her spirits, her health, her life. My absence may fret her; her anxiety for my return, her fears for me, may oppress her gentle temper. And for her health, does not every hour bring me cause to be alarmed? If it rains, some shower may even then have chilled her delicate frame! If the wind be keen, some rude blast may have affected her. The heat of noon, the dews of the evening, may endanger the life of her, for whom only I value mine. O Jack! when delicate and feeling souls are separated, there is not a feature in the sky, not a movement of the elements, not an aspiration of the breeze, but hints some cause for a lover's apprehension!

Abs. Ay, but we may choose whether we will take the hint or not. So, then, Faulkland, if you were convinced that Julia were well and in spirits, you would be entirely content.

Faulk. I should be happy beyond measure. I am anxious only for that.

Abs. Then to cure your anxiety at once, Miss Melville is in perfect health, and is at this moment in Bath.

Faulk. Nay, Jack; don't trifle with me.

Abs. She is arrived here with my father within this hour.

Faulk. Can you be serious?

Abs. I thought you knew Sir Anthony better than to be surprised at a sudden whim of this kind. Seriously then, it is as I tell you; upon my honour.

Faulk. My dear friend! Hollo, Du Peigne! my hat. My dear Jack, now nothing on earth can give me a moment's uneasiness.

Enter FAG.

Fag. Sir, Mr. Acres, just arrived, is below.

Abs. Stay, Faulkland, this Acres lives within a mile of Sir Anthony, and he shall tell you how your mistress has been ever since you left her. Fag, show the gentleman up.   [*Exit* FAG.

Faulk. What, is he much acquainted in the family?

Abs. O, very intimate. I insist on your not going; besides, his character will divert you.

Faulk. Well, I should like to ask him a few questions.

Abs. He is likewise a rival of mine—that is, of my *other self's*, for he does not think his friend Captain Absolute ever saw the lady in question; and it is ridiculous enough to hear him complain to me of *one Beverley*, a concealed skulking rival, who——

Faulk. Hush! He's here.

Enter ACRES.

Acres. Hah! my dear friend, noble captain, and honest Jack, how do'st thou? just arrived, faith, as you see. Sir, your humble servant. Warm work on the roads, Jack. Odds whips and wheels! I've travelled like a comet, with a tail of dust all the way as long as the Mall.

Abs. Ah! Bob, you are indeed an eccentric planet, but we know your attraction hither. Give me leave to introduce Mr. Faulkland to you. Mr. Faulkland, Mr. Acres.

Acres. Sir, I am most heartily glad to see you. Sir, I solicit your connexions. Hey, Jack—what, this is Mr. Faulkland, who——

Abs. Ay, Bob; Miss Melville's Mr. Faulkland.

Acres. Od'so! she and your father can be but just arrived before me. I suppose you have seen them. Ah! Mr. Faulkland, you are indeed a happy man.

Faulk. I have not seen Miss Melville yet, sir. I hope she enjoyed full health and spirits in Devonshire?

Acres. Never knew her better in my life, sir—never better. Odds blushes and blooms! she has been as healthy as the German Spa.

Faulk. Indeed! I did hear that she had been a little indisposed.

Acres. False, false, sir—only said to vex you: quite the reverse, I assure you.

Faulk. There, Jack, you see she has the advantage of me; I had almost fretted myself ill.

Abs. Now are you angry with your mistress for not having been sick.

Faulk. No, no, you misunderstand me; yet surely a little trifling indisposition is not an unnatural consequence of absence from those we love. Now confess—isn't there something unkind in this violent, robust, unfeeling health?

Abs. O, it was very unkind of her to be well in your absence to be sure!

Acres. Good apartments, Jack.

Faulk. Well, sir, but you was saying that Miss Melville has been so *exceedingly* well—what then she has been merry and gay, I suppose? Always in spirits—hey?

Acres. Merry, odds crickets! she has been the belle and spirit of the company wherever she has been—so lively and entertaining! so full of wit and humour!

Faulk. There, Jack, there. O, by my soul! there is an innate levity in woman, that nothing can overcome. What! happy, and I away!

Abs. Have done. How foolish this is! Just now you were only apprehensive for your mistress's *spirits.*

Faulk. Why, Jack, have I been the joy and spirit of the company?

Abs. No, indeed, you have not.

Faulk. Have I been lively and entertaining?

Abs. O, upon my word, I acquit you.

Faulk. Have I been full of wit and humour?

Abs. No, faith; to do you justice, you have been confoundedly stupid indeed.

Acres. What's the matter with the gentleman?

Abs. He is only expressing his great satisfaction at hearing that Julia has been so well and happy—that's all—hey, Faulkland?

Faulk. Oh! I am rejoiced to hear it—yes, yes, she has a *happy* disposition!

Acres. That she has indeed. Then she is so accomplished—so sweet a voice—so expert at her harpsichord—such a mistress of flat and sharp, squallante, rumblante, and quiverante! There was this time month—Odds minnums and crotchets! how she did chirup at Mrs. Piano's concert!

Faulk. There again, what say you to this? You see she has been all mirth and song—not a thought of me!

Abs. Pho! man, is not music the food of love?

Faulk. Well, well, it may be so. Pray, Mr. —, what's his d—d name! Do you remember what songs Miss Melville sung?

Acres. Not I indeed.

Abs. Stay now, they were some pretty melancholy purling-stream airs, I warrant; perhaps you may recollect; did she sing, 'When absent from my soul's delight?'

Acres. No, that wa'n't it.

Abs. Or, 'Go, gentle gales!' 'Go, gentle gales!' (*sings*).

Acres. O no! nothing like it. Odds! now I recollect one of them—'My heart's my own, my will is free' (*sings*).

Faulk. Fool! fool that I am! to fix all my happiness on such a trifler. 'Sdeath! to make herself the pipe and ballad-monger of a circle! to soothe her light heart with catches and glees! What can you say to this, sir?

Abs. Why, that I should be glad to hear my mistress had been so merry, *sir*.

Faulk. Nay, nay, nay—I'm not sorry that she has been happy—no, no, I am glad of that. I would not have had her sad or sick—yet surely a sympathetic heart would have shown itself even in the choice of a song—she might have been temperately healthy, and somehow, plaintively gay; but she has been dancing too, I doubt not!

Acres. What does the gentleman say about dancing?

Abs. He says the lady we speak of dances as well as she sings.

Acres. Ay truly, does she. There was at our last race ball——

Faulk. Hell and the devil! There! there, I told you so! I told you so! Oh! she thrives in my absence! Dancing! but her whole feelings have been in opposition with mine; I have been anxious, silent, pensive, sedentary; my days have been hours of care, my nights of watchfulness. She has been all health! spirit! laugh! song! dance! Oh! d—n'd, d—n'd levity!

Abs. For Heaven's sake, Faulkland, don't expose yourself so. Suppose she has danced, what then? Does not the ceremony of society often oblige——

Faulk. Well, well, I'll contain myself; perhaps, as you say, for form sake. What, Mr. Acres, you were praising Miss Melville's manner of dancing a *minuet*, hey?

Acres. O, I dare insure her for that; but what I was going to speak of was her *country-dancing*. Odds swimmings! she has such an air with her!

Faulk. Now, disappointment on her! Defend this, Absolute; why don't you defend this? Country-dances! jigs and reels! am I to blame now? A minuet I could have forgiven; I should not have minded that. I say I should not have regarded a minuet; but *country-dances*, Z—ds! had she made one in a *cotillion*, I believe I could have forgiven even that; but to be monkey-led for a night; to run the gauntlet through a string of amorous palming puppies; to show paces like a managed filly! O Jack, there never can be but *one* man in the world, whom a truly modest and delicate woman ought to pair with in a *country-dance;* and even then, the rest of the couples should be her great uncles and aunts!

Abs. Ay, to be sure; grandfathers and grandmothers!

Faulk. If there be but one vicious mind in the set, 'twill spread like a contagion; the action of their pulse beats to the lascivious movement of the jig; their quivering, warm-breathed sighs impregnate the very air; the atmosphere becomes electrical to love, and each amorous spark darts through every link of the chain! I must leave you; I own I am somewhat flurried, and that confounded looby has perceived it.

[*Going.*

Abs. Nay, but stay, Faulkland, and thank Mr. Acres for his good news.

Faulk. D—n his news! [*Exit* FAULKLAND.

Abs. Ha! ha! ha! Poor Faulkland, five minutes since, ' nothing on earth could give him a moment's uneasiness!'

Acres. The gentleman wa'n't angry at my praising his mistress, was he?

Abs. A little jealous, I believe, Bob.

Acres. You don't say so? Ha! ha! jealous of me! That's a good joke.

Abs. There's nothing strange in that, Bob; let me

tell you, that sprightly grace and insinuating manner of yours will do some mischief among the girls here.

Acres. Ah! you joke. Ha! ha! mischief—ha! ha! But you know I am not my own property; my dear Lydia has forestalled me. She could never abide me in the country, because I used to dress so badly; but odds frogs and tambours! I sha'n't take matters so here, now ancient madam has no voice in it. I'll make my old clothes know who's master. I shall straight-way cashier the hunting-frock, and render my leather breeches incapable. My hair has been in training some time.

Abs. Indeed!

Acres. Ay; and tho'ff the side curls are a little restive, my hind-part takes it very kindly.

Abs. O, you'll polish, I doubt not.

Acres. Absolutely I propose so; then, if I can find out this Ensign Beverley, odds triggers and flints! I'll make him know the difference o't.

Abs. Spoke like a man. But pray, Bob, I observe you have got an odd kind of a new method of swearing——

Acres. Ha! ha! you've taken notice of it. 'Tis genteel, isn't *it?* I didn't invent it myself, though; but a commander in our militia—a great scholar, I assure you—says that there is no meaning in the common oaths, and that nothing but their antiquity makes them respectable; because, he says, the ancients would never stick to an oath or two, but would say, by Jove! or by Bacchus! or by Mars! or by Venus! or by Pallas! according to the sentiment: so that to swear with propriety, says my little major, the ' oath should be an echo to the sense;' and this we call the *oath referential,* or *sentimental swearing.* Ha! ha! ha! 'Tis genteel, isn't it?

Abs. Very genteel, and very new indeed; and I dare say will supplant all other figures of imprecation.

Acres. Ay, ay, the best terms will grow obsolete. Damns have had their day.

Enter FAG.

Fag. Sir, there is a gentleman below desires to see you. Shall I show him into the parlour?

Abs. Ay, you may.

Acres. Well, I must be gone——

Abs. Stay; who is it, Fag?

Fag. Your father, sir.

Abs. You puppy, why didn't you show him up directly? [*Exit* FAG.

Acres. You have business with Sir Anthony. I expect a message from Mrs. Malaprop at my lodgings. I have sent also to my dear friend, Sir Lucius O'Trigger. Adieu, Jack; we must meet at night, when you shall give me a dozen bumpers to little Lydia.

Abs. That I will, with all my heart. [*Exit* ACRES. Now for a parental lecture. I hope he has heard nothing of the business that has brought me here. I wish the gout had held him fast in Devonshire, with all my soul!

Enter Sir ANTHONY.

Sir, I am delighted to see you here, and looking so well. Your sudden arrival at Bath made me apprehensive for your health.

Sir Anth. Very apprehensive, I dare say, Jack. What! you are recruiting here, hey!

Abs. Yes, sir, I am on duty.

Sir Anth. Well, Jack, I am glad to see you, though I did not expect it, for I was going to write to you on a little matter of business. Jack, I have been considering that I grow old and infirm, and shall probably not trouble you long.

Abs. Pardon me, sir, I never saw you look more strong and hearty; and I pray frequently that you may continue so.

Sir Anth. I hope your prayers may be heard, with all my heart. Well then, Jack, I have been considering that I am so strong and hearty, I may continue to plague you a long time. Now, Jack, I am sensible that the income of your commission, and what I have hitherto allowed you, is but a small pittance for a lad of your spirit.

Abs. Sir, you are very good.

Sir Anth. And it is my wish, while yet I live, to have my boy make some figure in the world. I have resolved, therefore, to fix you at once in a noble independence.

Abs. Sir, your kindness overpowers me; such generosity makes the gratitude of reason more lively than the sensations even of filial affection.

Sir Anth. I am glad you are so sensible of my attention, and you shall be master of a large estate in a few weeks.

Abs. Let my future life, sir, speak my gratitude; I cannot express the sense I have of your munificence. Yet, sir, I presume you would not wish me to quit the army.

Sir Anth. O, that shall be as your wife chooses.

Abs. My wife, sir!

Sir Anth. Ay, ay, settle that between you—settle that between you.

Abs. A *wife*, sir, did you say?

Sir Anth. Ay, a wife. Why, did not I mention her before?

Abs. Not a word of her, sir.

Sir Anth. Odd so! I mustn't forget *her* though. Yes, Jack, the independence I was talking of is by a marriage—the fortune is saddled with a wife; but I suppose that makes no difference.

Abs. Sir! Sir! you amaze me!

Sir Anth. Why, what the devil's the matter with the fool? Just now you were all gratitude and duty.

Abs. I was, sir; you talked to me of independence and a fortune, but not a word of a wife.

Sir Anth. Why, what difference does that make? Odds life, sir! if you have the estate, you must take it with the live stock on it, as it stands.

Abs. If my happiness is to be the price, I must beg leave to decline the purchase. Pray, sir, who is the lady?

Sir Anth. What's that to you, sir? Come, give me your promise to love, and to marry her directly.

Abs. Sure, sir, this is not very reasonable, to summon my affection for a lady I know nothing of!

Sir Anth. I am sure, sir, 'tis more unreasonable in you to *object* to a lady you know nothing of.

Abs. Then, sir, I must tell you plainly, that my inclinations are fixed on another—my heart is engaged to an angel.

Sir Anth. Then pray let it send an excuse. It is very sorry, but *business* prevents its waiting on her.

Abs. But my vows are pledged to her.

Sir Anth. Let her foreclose, Jack; let her foreclose; they are not worth redeeming; besides, you have the angel's vows in exchange, I suppose; so there can be no loss there.

Abs. You must excuse me, sir, if I tell you, once for all, that in this point I cannot obey you.

Sir Anth. Hark'ee, Jack; I have heard you for some time with patience. I have been cool—quite cool; but take care. You know I am complaisance itself, when I am not thwarted; no one more easily led when I have my own way, but don't put me in a frenzy.

Abs. Sir, I must repeat it—in this I cannot obey you.

Sir Anth. Now, d—n me! if ever I call you *Jack* again while I live!

Abs. Nay, sir, but hear me.

Sir Anth. Sir, I won't hear a word—not a word! not one word! so give me your promise by a nod; and I'll tell you what, Jack—I mean, you dog—if you don't by——

Abs. What, sir, promise to link myself to some mass of ugliness! to——

Sir Anth. Z—ds! sirrah! the lady shall be as ugly as I choose. She shall have a hump on each shoulder; she shall be as crooked as the Crescent; her one eye shall roll like the bull's in Cox's Museum; she shall have a skin like a mummy, and the beard of a Jew; she shall be all this, sirrah! yet I will make you ogle her all day, and sit up all night to write sonnets on her beauty.

Abs. This is reason and moderation indeed!

Sir Anth. None of your sneering, puppy! no grinning, jackanapes!

Abs. Indeed, sir, I never was in a worse humour for mirth in my life.

Sir Anth. 'Tis false, sir; I know you are laughing in your sleeve; I know you'll grin when I am gone, sirrah!

Abs. Sir, I hope I know my duty better.

Sir Anth. None of your passion, sir! none of your

violence; if you please. It won't do with me, I promise you.

Abs. Indeed, sir, I never was cooler in my life.

Sir Anth. 'Tis a confounded lie! I know you are in a passion in your heart; I know you are, you hypocritical young dog! but it won't do.

Abs. Nay, sir, upon my word.

Sir Anth. So you will fly out! Can't you be cool like me? What the devil good can *passion* do? *Passion* is of no service, you impudent, insolent, overbearing reprobate! There you sneer again! don't provoke me! but you rely upon the mildness of my temper—you do, you dog! you play upon the meekness of my disposition! Yet take care, the patience of a saint may be overcome at last! but mark! I give you six hours and a half to consider of this; if you then agree, without any condition, to do everything on earth that I choose, why, confound you! I may in time forgive you. If not, z—ds! don't enter the same hemisphere with me! don't dare to breathe the same air, or use the same light with me; but get an atmosphere and a sun of your own! I'll strip you of your commission; I'll lodge a five-and-threepence in the hands of trustees, and you shall live on the interest. I'll disown you, I'll disinherit you, I'll unget you! and d—n me! if ever I call you Jack again!

[*Exit* Sir ANTHONY.

ABSOLUTE *solus.*

Abs. Mild, gentle, considerate father, I kiss your hands. What a tender method of giving his opinion in these matters Sir Anthony has! I dare not trust him with the truth. I wonder what old wealthy hag it is that he wants to bestow on me! yet he married himself for love! and was in his youth a bold intriguer, and a gay companion!

Enter FAG.

Fag. Assuredly, sir, your father is wrath to a degree; he comes downstairs eight or ten steps at a time—muttering, growling, and thumping the banisters all the way; I and the cook's dog stand bowing at the door—rap! he gives me a stroke on the head with his cane; bids me carry that to my master; then kicking the poor turnspit into the area, d—ns us all, for a puppy triumvirate! Upon my credit, sir, were I in your place, and found my father such very bad company, I should certainly drop his acquaintance.

Abs. Cease your impertinence, sir, at present. Did you come in for nothing more? Stand out of the way! [*Pushes him aside, and exit.*

FAG *solus.*

Fag. Soh! Sir Anthony trims my master; he is afraid to reply to his father—then vents his spleen on poor Fag! When one is vexed by one person, to revenge one's self on another, who happens to come in the way, is the vilest injustice! Ah! it shows the worst temper—the basest——

Enter ERRAND BOY.

Boy. Mr. Fag! Mr. Fag! your master calls you.
Fag. Well! you little dirty puppy, you need not bawl so!—The meanest disposition! the——
Boy. Quick, quick, Mr. Fag.
Fag. Quick! quick! you impudent jackanapes! am I to be commanded by you too? you little, impertinent, insolent, kitchen-bred—— [*Exit kicking and beating him.*

SCENE II.

The NORTH PARADE.

Enter LUCY.

Lucy. So, I shall have another rival to add to my mistress's list, Captain Absolute. However, I shall not enter his name till my purse has received notice in form. Poor Acres is dismissed! Well, I have done him a last friendly office, in letting him know that Beverley was here before him. Sir Lucius is generally more punctual, when he expects to hear from his *dear Delia*, as he calls her. I wonder he's not here! I have a little scruple of conscience from this deceit; though I should not be paid so well, if my hero knew that *Delia* was near fifty, and her own mistress.

Enter Sir LUCIUS O'TRIGGER.

Sir Luc. Hah! my little ambassadress, upon my conscience, I have been looking for you; I have been on the South Parade this half hour.

Lucy. (*Speaking simply*). O gemini! and I have been waiting for your worship here on the North.

Sir Luc. Faith! may be, that was the reason we did not meet; and it is very comical too, how you could go out and I not see you, for I was only taking a nap at the Parade Coffee-house, and I chose the *window* on purpose that I might not miss you.

Lucy. My stars! Now I'd wager a sixpence I went by while you were asleep.

Sir Luc. Sure enough it must have been so, and I never dreamt it was so late, till I waked. Well, but my little girl, have you got nothing for me?

Lucy. Yes, but I have. I've got a letter for you in my pocket.

Sir Luc. O faith! I guessed you weren't come empty-handed. Well, let me see what the dear creature says.

Lucy. There, Sir Lucius. (*Gives him a letter.*)

Sir Luc. (Reads) ' *Sir, there is often a sudden incentive impulse in love, that has a greater induction than years of domestic combination: such was the commotion I felt at the first superfluous view of Sir Lucius O'Trigger.*' Very pretty, upon my word. ' *Female punctuation forbids me to say more; yet let me add, that it will give me joy infallible to find Sir Lucius worthy the last criterion of my affections.* DELIA.'
Upon my conscience! Lucy, your lady is a great mistress of language. Faith, she's quite the queen of the dictionary! for the devil a word dare refuse coming at her call, though one would think it was quite out of hearing.

Lucy. Ay, sir, a lady of her experience.

Sir Luc. Experience? what, at seventeen?

Lucy. O true, sir; but then she reads so. My stars! how she will read off hand!

Sir Luc. Faith, she must be very deep read to write this way; though she is rather an arbitrary writer too, for here are a great many poor words pressed into the service of this note, that would get their *habeas corpus* from any court in Christendom.

Lucy. Ah! Sir Lucius, if you were to hear how she talks of you!

Sir Luc. O tell her I'll make her the best husband in the world, and Lady O'Trigger into the bargain!

But we must get the old gentlewoman's consent, and do everything fairly.

Lucy. Nay, Sir Lucius, I thought you wa'n't rich enough to be so nice!

Sir Luc. Upon my word, young woman, you have hit it: I am so poor, that I can't afford to do a dirty action. If I did not want money, I'd steal your mistress and her fortune with a great deal of pleasure. However, my pretty girl (*gives her money*), here's a little something to buy you a riband; and meet me in the evening, and I'll give you an answer to this. So, hussy, take a kiss beforehand, to put you in mind. (*Kisses her.*)

Lucy. O lud! Sir Lucius, I never seed such a gemman! My lady won't like you if you're so impudent.

Sir Luc. Faith she will, Lucy—that same—pho! what's the name of it? *Modesty!*—is a quality in a lover more praised by the women than liked; so, if your mistress asks you whether Sir Lucius ever gave you a kiss, tell her fifty, my dear.

Lucy. What, would you have me tell her a lie?

Sir Luc. Ah then, you baggage! I'll make it a truth presently.

Lucy. For shame now; here is some one coming.

Sir Luc. O faith, I'll quiet your conscience!

[*Sees* FAG. *Exit, humming a tune.*

Enter FAG.

Fag. So, so, ma'am. I humbly beg pardon.

Lucy. O lud! now, Mr. Fag, you flurry me so.

Fag. Come, come, Lucy, here's no one by, so a little less simplicity, with a grain or two more sincerity, if you please. You play false with us, madam. I saw you give the baronet a letter. My master shall know this, and if he don't call him out, I will.

Lucy. Ha! ha! ha! you gentlemen's gentlemen are so hasty. That letter was from Mrs. Malaprop, simpleton. She is taken with Sir Lucius's address.

Fag. How! what tastes some people have! Why, I suppose I have walked by her window a hundred times. But what says our young lady? Any message to my master?

Lucy. Sad news! Mr. Fag. A worse rival than Acres! Sir Anthony Absolute has proposed his son.

Fag. What, Captain Absolute?

Lucy. Even so. I overheard it all.

Fag. Ha! ha! ah! very good, faith. Good-bye, Lucy, I must away with this news.

Lucy. Well, you may laugh; but it is true, I assure you. (*Going.*) But—Mr. Fag—tell your master not to be cast down by this.

Fag. O, he'll be so disconsolate!

Lucy. And charge him not to think of quarrelling with young Absolute.

Fag. Never fear! never fear!

Lucy. Be sure, bid him keep up his spirits.

Fag. We will, we will. [*Exeunt severally.*

ACT III.—SCENE I.

The NORTH PARADE.

Enter ABSOLUTE.

Abs. 'Tis just as Fag told me, indeed. Whimsical enough, faith! My father wants to *force* me to marry the very girl I am plotting to run away with! He must not know of my connexion with her yet awhile. He has too summary a method of proceeding in these matters. However, I'll read my incantation instantly. My conversion is something sudden, indeed—but I can assure him it is very *sincere*. So, so, here he comes. He looks plaguy gruff. [*Steps aside.*

Enter Sir ANTHONY.

Sir Anth. No, I'll die sooner than forgive him. *Die,* did I say? I'll live these fifty years to plague him. At our last meeting, his impudence had almost put me out of temper. An obstinate, passionate, self-willed boy! Who can he take after? This is my return for getting him before all his brothers and sisters! for putting him, at twelve years old, into a marching regiment, and allowing him fifty pounds a year, besides his pay, ever since! But I have done with him; he's anybody's son for me. I never will see him more—never—never—never—never.

Abs. Now for a penitential face.

Sir Anth. Fellow, get out of my way.

Abs. Sir, you see a penitent before you.

Sir Anth. I see an impudent scoundrel before me.

Abs. A sincere penitent. I am come, sir, to acknowledge my error, and to submit entirely to your will.

Sir Anth. What's that?

Abs. I have been revolving, and reflecting, and considering on your past goodness, and kindness, and condescension to me.

Sir Anth. Well, sir?

Abs. I have been likewise weighing and balancing what you were pleased to mention concerning duty, and obedience, and authority.

Sir Anth. Well, puppy?

Abs. Why then, sir, the result of my reflections is—a resolution to sacrifice every inclination of my own to your satisfaction.

Sir Anth. Why now you talk sense—absolute sense. I never heard anything more sensible in my life. Confound you! you shall be Jack again.

Abs. I am happy in the appellation.

Sir Anth. Why then, Jack, my dear Jack, I will now inform you who the lady really is. Nothing but your passion and violence, you silly fellow, prevented my telling you at first. Prepare, Jack, for wonder and rapture—prepare. What think you of Miss Lydia Languish?

Abs. Languish? What the Languishes of Worcestershire?

Sir Anth. Worcestershire! No. Did you never meet Mrs. Malaprop and her niece, Miss Languish, who came into our country just before you were last ordered to your regiment?

Abs. Malaprop! Languish! I don't remember ever to have heard the names before. Yet, stay—I think I do recollect something. *Languish! Languish!* She squints, don't she? A little red-haired girl?

Sir Anth. Squints! A red-haired girl! Z—ds! no.

Abs. Then I must have forgot; it can't be the same person.

Sir Anth. Jack! Jack! what think you of blooming, love-breathing seventeen?

Abs. As to that, sir, I am quite indifferent. If I can please you in the matter, 'tis all I desire.

Sir Anth. Nay, but Jack, such eyes! such eyes! so innocently wild! so bashfully irresolute! Not a glance but speaks and kindles some thought of love! Then,

Jack, her cheeks! her cheeks, Jack! so deeply blushing at the insinuations of her tell-tale eyes! Then, Jack, her lips! O Jack, lips smiling at their own discretion; and if not smiling, more sweetly pouting; more lovely in sullenness!

Abs. That's she indeed. Well done, old gentleman!

Sir Anth. Then Jack, her neck! O Jack! Jack!

Abs. And which is to be mine, sir; the niece or the aunt?

Sir Anth. Why, you unfeeling, insensible puppy, I despise you. When I was of your age, such a description would have made me fly like a rocket! The *aunt*, indeed! Odds life! when I ran away with your mother, I would not have touched anything old or ugly to gain an empire.

Abs. Not to please your father, sir?

Sir Anth. To please my father! Z—ds! not to please——Oh, my father—Odd so!—yes, yes; if my father indeed had desired—that's quite another matter. Though he wa'n't the indulgent father that I am, Jack.

Abs. I dare say not, sir.

Sir Anth. But, Jack, you are not sorry to find your mistress so beautiful?

Abs. Sir, I repeat it—if I please you in this affair, 'tis all I desire. Not that I think a woman the worse for being handsome; but, sir, if you please to recollect, you before hinted something about a hump or two, one eye, and a few more graces of that kind. Now, without being very nice, I own I should rather choose a wife of mine to have the usual number of limbs, and a limited quantity of back; and though *one* eye may be very agreable, yet as the prejudice has always run in favour of *two*, I would not wish to affect a singularity in that article.

Sir Anth. What a phlegmatic sot it is! Why, sirrah, you're an anchorite! a vile, insensible stock. You a soldier! You're a walking block, fit only to dust the company's regimentals on! Odds life! I've a great mind to marry the girl myself!

Abs. I am entirely at your disposal, sir. If you should think of addressing Miss Languish yourself, I suppose you would have me marry the *aunt;* or if you should change your mind, and take the old lady— 'tis the same to me—I'll marry the *niece.*

Sir Anth. Upon my word, Jack, thou'rt either a very great hypocrite, or——but, come, I know your indifference on such a subject must be all a lie. I'm sure it must. Come, now—d—— your demure face! Come, confess, Jack—you have been lying—ha'n't you? You have been playing the hypocrite, hey? I'll never forgive you, if you ha'n't been lying and playing the hypocrite.

Abs. I'm sorry, sir, that the respect and duty which I bear to you should be so mistaken.

Sir Anth. Hang your respect and duty! But come along with me, I'll write a note to Mrs. Malaprop, and you shall visit the lady directly. Her eyes shall be the Promethean torch to you. Come along! I'll never forgive you, if you don't come back stark mad with rapture and impatience—if you don't, egad, I'll marry the girl myself! [*Exeunt.*

SCENE II.

Julia's *Dressing-room.*

Faulkland *solus.*

Faulk. They told me Julia would return directly; I wonder she is not yet come! How mean does this captious, unsatisfied temper of mine appear to my cooler judgment! Yet I know not that I indulge it in any other point: but on this one subject, and to this one subject, whom I think I love beyond my life, I am ever ungenerously fretful and madly capricious! I am conscious of it, yet I cannot correct myself! What tender honest joy sparkled in her eyes when we met! How delicate was the warmth of her expressions! I was ashamed to appear less happy, though I had come resolved to wear a face of coolness and upbraiding. Sir Anthony's presence prevented my proposed expostulations: yet I must be satisfied that she has not been so *very* happy in my absence. She is coming! Yes! I know the nimbleness of her tread, when she thinks her impatient Faulkland counts the moments of her stay.

Enter JULIA.

Julia. I had not hoped to see you again so soon.

Faulk. Could I, Julia, be contented with my first welcome, restrained as we were by the presence of a third person?

Julia. O Faulkland, when your kindness can make me thus happy, let me not think that I discovered something of coldness in your first salutation.

Faulk. 'Twas but your fancy, Julia. I *was* rejoiced to see you—to see you in such health. Sure I had no cause for coldness?

Julia. Nay, then, I see you have taken something ill. You must not conceal from me what it is.

Faulk. Well, then, shall I own to you that my joy at hearing of your health and arrival here, by your neighbour Acres, was somewhat damped by his dwelling much on the high spirits you had enjoyed in Devonshire

—on your mirth, your singing, dancing, and I know not what! For such is my temper, Julia, that I should regard every mirthful moment in your absence as a treason to constancy. The mutual tear that steals down the cheeks of parting lovers is a compact, that no smile shall live there till they meet again.

Julia. Must I never cease to tax my Faulkland with this teasing minute caprice? Can the idle reports of a silly boor weigh in your breast against my tried affection?

Faulk. They have no weight with me, Julia. No, no; I am happy if you have been so; yet only say that you did not sing with *mirth;* say that you *thought* of Faulkland in the dance.

Julia. I never can be happy in your absence. If I wear a countenance of content, it is to show that my mind holds no doubt of my Faulkland's truth. If I seemed sad, it were to make malice triumph; and say, that I had fixed my heart on one, who left me to lament his roving and my own credulity. Believe me, Faulkland, I mean not to upbraid you, when I say, that I have often dressed sorrow in smiles, lest my friends should guess whose unkindness had caused my tears.

Faulk. You were ever all goodness to me. O, I am a brute, when I admit a doubt of your true constancy!

Julia. If ever without such cause from you, as I will not suppose possible, you find my affections veering but a point, may I become a proverbial scoff for levity and base ingratitude.

Faulk. Ah! Julia, that last word is grating to me. I would I had no title to your *gratitude!* Search your heart, Julia; perhaps what you have mistaken for love, is but the warm effusion of a too thankful heart!

Julia. For what quality must I love you?

Faulk. For no quality! To regard me for any

quality of mind or understanding, were only to *esteem* me. And for person, I have often wished myself deformed, to be convinced that I owed no obligation *there* for any part of your affection.

Julia. Where nature has bestowed a show of nice attention in the features of a man, he should laugh at it as misplaced. I have seen men, who in *this* vain article, perhaps, might rank above you; but my heart has never asked my eyes if it were so or not.

Faulk. Now this is not well from *you*, Julia; I despise person in a man; yet, if you loved me as I wish, though I were an Æthiop, you'd think none so fair.

Julia. I see you are determined to be unkind. The *contract* which my poor father bound us in gives you more than a lover's privilege.

Faulk. Again, Julia, you raise ideas that feed and justify my doubts. I would not have been more free; no, I am proud of my restraint. Yet—yet, perhaps your high respect alone for this solemn compact has fettered your inclinations, which else had made a worthier choice. How shall I be sure, had you remained unbound in thought and promise, that I should still have been the object of your persevering love?

Julia. Then try me now. Let us be free as strangers as to what has past; *my* heart will not feel more liberty!

Faulk. There now! so hasty, Julia! so anxious to be free! If your love for me were fixed and ardent, you would not lose your hold, even though I wished it!

Julia. O! you torture me to the heart! I cannot bear it.

Faulk. I do not mean to distress you. If I loved you less, I should never give you an uneasy moment. But hear me. All my fretful doubts arise from this. Women are not used to weigh, and separate the motives of their affections: the cold dictates of prudence, gratitude, or filial duty, may sometimes be mistaken for the pleadings of the heart. I would not boast, yet let me say, that I have neither age, person, nor character to found dislike on; my fortune such as few ladies could be charged with *indiscretion* in the match. O, Julia! when *Love* receives such countenance from *Prudence*, nice minds will be suspicious of its birth.

Julia. I know not whither your insinuations would tend; but as they seem pressing to insult me, I will spare you the regret of having done so. I have given you no cause for this! [*Exit in tears.*

Faulk. In tears! Stay, Julia; stay but for a moment. The door is fastened! Julia! my soul, but for one moment. I hear her sobbing! 'Sdeath! what a brute am I to use her thus! Yet stay. Ay, she is coming now; how little resolution there is in woman! How a few soft words can turn them! No, faith! she is *not* coming either. Why, Julia, my love, say but that you forgive me—come but to tell me that; now this is being *too* resentful. Stay! she is coming too. I thought she would; no *steadiness* in anything! Her going away must have been a mere trick then; she sha'n't see that I was hurt by it. I'll affect indifference (*hums a tune: then listens*). No, Z—nds! she's *not* coming! nor don't intend it, I suppose. This is not *steadiness* but *obstinacy!* Yet I deserve it. What, after so long an absence to quarrel with her tenderness! 'Twas barbarous and unmanly! I should be ashamed to see her now. I'll wait till her just resentment is abated, and when I distress her so again, may I lose her for ever! and be linked instead to some antique virago, whose gnawing passions, and long-hoarded spleen, shall make me curse my folly half the day and all the night. [*Exit.*

SCENE III.

Mrs. Malaprop's *Lodgings.*

Mrs. Malaprop, *with a letter in her hand, and* Captain Absolute.

Mrs. Mal. Your being Sir Anthony's son, captain, would itself be a sufficient accommodation; but from the ingenuity of your appearance, I am convinced you deserve the character here given of you.

Abs. Permit me to say, madam, that as I never yet have had the pleasure of seeing Miss Languish, my principal inducement in this affair at present is the honour of being allied to Mrs. Malaprop; of whose intellectual accomplishments, elegant manners, and unaffected learning, no tongue is silent.

Mrs. Mal. Sir, you do me infinite honour! I beg, captain, you'll be seated. (*Sit.*) Ah! few gentlemen, now-a-days, know how to value the ineffectual qualities in a woman! few think how a little knowledge becomes a gentlewoman! Men have no sense now but for the worthless flower of beauty!

Abs. It is but too true indeed, ma'am; yet I fear our ladies should share the blame; they think our admiration of *beauty* so great, that *knowledge* in *them* would be superfluous. Thus, like garden-trees, they seldom show fruit, till time has robbed them of the more specious blossom. Few, like Mrs. Malaprop and the orange-tree, are rich in both at once!

Mrs. Mal. Sir, you overpower me with good-breeding.—He is the very pine-apple of politeness! You are not ignorant, captain, that this giddy girl has somehow contrived to fix her affections on a beggarly, strolling, eaves-dropping ensign, whom none of us have seen, and nobody knows anything of.

Abs. O, I have heard the silly affair before. I'm not at all prejudiced against her on *that* account.

Mrs. Mal. You are very good and very considerate, captain. I am sure I have done everything in my power since I exploded the affair; long ago I laid my positive conjunctions on her, never to think on the fellow again; I have since laid Sir Anthony's preposition before her; but, I am sorry to say, she seems resolved to decline every particle that I enjoin her.

Abs. It must be very distressing, indeed, ma'am.

Mrs. Mal. Oh! it gives me the hydrostatics to such a degree; I thought she had persisted from corresponding with him; but, behold, this very day, I have interceded another letter from the fellow. I believe I have it in my pocket.

Abs. O the devil! my last note. [*Aside.*

Mrs. Mal. Ay, here it is.

Abs. Ay, my note indeed! O the little traitress Lucy. [*Aside.*

Mrs. Mal. There, perhaps you may know the writing. [*Gives him the letter.*

Abs. I think I have seen the hand before; yes, I certainly must have seen this hand before——

Mrs. Mal. Nay, but read it, captain.

Abs. (*Reads*) ' *My soul's idol, my adored Lydia!* ' Very tender indeed.

Mrs. Mal. Tender! ay, and profane too, o'my conscience!

Abs. ' *I am excessively alarmed at the intelligence you send me, the more so as my new rival* '——

Mrs. Mal. That's *you*, sir.

Abs. ' *Has universally the character of being an ac-*

complished gentleman, and a man of honour.' Well, that's handsome enough.

Mrs. Mal. O, the fellow has some design in writing so.

Abs. That he had, I'll answer for him, ma'am.

Mrs. Mal. But go on, sir; you'll see presently.

Abs. '*As for the old weather-beaten she-dragon who guards you.*' Who can he mean by that?

Mrs. Mal. Me, sir; *me:* he means *me* there. What do you think now? But go on a little further.

Abs. Impudent scoundrel!—'*it shall go hard but I will elude her vigilance, as I am told that the same ridiculous vanity, which makes her dress up her coarse features, and deck her dull chat with hard words which she don't understand*'——

Mrs. Mal. There, sir, an attack upon my language! what do you think of that?—an aspersion upon my parts of speech! was ever such a brute! Sure if I reprehend anything in this world, it is the use of my oracular tongue, and a nice derangement of epitaphs!

Abs. He deserves to be hanged and quartered! let me see—'*same ridiculous vanity*'——

Mrs. Mal. You need not read it again, sir.

Abs. I beg pardon, ma'am—'*does also lay her open to the grossest deceptions from flattery and pretended admiration*'—an impudent coxcomb! '*so that I have a scheme to see you shortly with the old harridan's consent, and even to make her a go-between in our interview.*' Was ever such assurance!

Mrs. Mal. Did you ever hear anything like it? He'll elude my vigilance, will he—yes, yes! ha! ha! he's very likely to enter these doors! We'll try who can plot best!

Abs. So we will, ma'am—so we will. Ha! ha! ha! a conceited puppy, ha! ha! ha! Well, but Mrs.

Malaprop, as the girl seems so infatuated by this fellow, suppose you were to wink at her corresponding with him for a little time—let her even plot an elopement with him—then do you connive at her escape— while I, just in the nick, will have the fellow laid by the heels, and fairly contrive to carry her off in his stead.

Mrs. Mal. I am delighted with the scheme; never was anything better perpetrated!

Abs. But, pray, could not I see the lady for a few minutes now? I should like to try her temper a little.

Mrs. Mal. Why, I don't know—I doubt she is not prepared for a visit of this kind. There is a decorum in these matters.

Abs. O Lord, she won't mind *me*—only tell her Beverley——

Mrs. Mal. Sir!

Abs. Gently, good tongue. [*Aside.*

Mrs. Mal. What did you say of Beverley?

Abs. O, I was going to propose that you should tell her, by way of jest, that it was Beverley who was below; she'd come down fast enough then. Ha! ha! ha!

Mrs. Mal. 'Twould be a trick she well deserves— besides, you know the fellow tells her he'll get my consent to see her—ha! ha! Let him if he can, I say again. Lydia, come down here! (*Calling.*) He'll make me a *go-between in their interviews*—ha! ha! ha! Come down, I say, Lydia! I don't wonder at your laughing. Ha! ha! ha! His impudence is truly ridiculous.

Abs. 'Tis very ridiculous, upon my soul, ma'am; ha! ha! ha!

Mrs. Mal. The little hussy won't hear. Well, I'll go and tell her at once who it is; she shall know that

Captain Absolute is come to wait on her. And I'll make her behave as becomes a young woman.

Abs. As you please, ma'am.

Mrs. Mal. For the present, captain, your servant. Ah! you've not done laughing yet, I see—*clude my vigilance!* yes, yes; ha! ha! ha! [*Exit.*

Abs. Ha! ha! ha! one would think now that I might throw off all disguise at once, and seize my prize with security; but such is Lydia's caprice, that to undeceive were probably to lose her. I'll see whether she knows me.

[*Walks aside, and seems engaged in looking at the pictures.*

Enter LYDIA.

Lydia. What a scene am I now to go through! surely nothing can be more dreadful than to be obliged to listen to the loathsome addresses of a stranger to one's heart. I have heard of girls persecuted as I am, who have appealed in behalf of their favoured lover to the generosity of his rival; suppose I were to try it. There stands the hated rival—an officer too! but O how unlike my Beverley! I wonder he don't begin. Truly he seems a very negligent wooer! quite at his ease, upon my word! I'll speak first. Mr. Absolute.

Abs. Ma'am. [*Turns round.*

Lydia. O heavens! Beverley!

Abs. Hush! hush, my life! softly! Be not surprised!

Lydia. I am so astonished! and so terrified! and so overjoyed! For heaven's sake, how came you here?

Abs. Briefly, I have deceived your aunt. I was informed that my new rival was to visit here this evening, and contriving to have him kept away, have passed myself on *her* for Captain Absolute.

Lydia. O charming! And she really takes you for young Absolute?

Abs. O, she's convinced of it.

Lydia. Ha! ha! ha! I can't forbear laughing to think how her sagacity is overreached.

Abs. But we trifle with our precious moments—such another opportunity may not occur—then let me now conjure my kind, my condescending angel, to fix the time when I may rescue her from undeserving persecution, and with a licensed warmth plead for my reward.

Lydia. Will you then, Beverley, consent to forfeit that portion of my paltry wealth? that burden on the wings of love?

Abs. O, come to me, rich only thus, in loveliness. Bring no portion to me but thy love; 'twill be generous in you, Lydia; for well you know, it is the only dower your poor Beverley can repay.

Lydia. How persuasive are his words! how charming will poverty be with him!

Abs. Ah! my soul, what a life will we then live! Love shall be our idol and support! we will worship him with a monastic strictness; abjuring all worldly toys, to centre every thought and action there. Proud of calamity, we will enjoy the wreck of wealth; while the surrounding gloom of adversity shall make the flame of our pure love show doubly bright. By heavens! I would fling all goods of fortune from me with a prodigal hand, to enjoy the scene where I might clasp my Lydia to my bosom, and say, the world affords no smile to me but here—— [*Embracing her.* If she holds out now, the devil is in it! [*Aside.*

Lydia. Now could I fly with him to the Antipodes! but my persecution is not yet come to a crisis.

Enter Mrs. Malaprop, *listening.*

Mrs. Mal. I am impatient to know how the little hussy deports herself. [*Aside.*

Abs. So pensive, Lydia! is then your warmth abated?

Mrs. Mal. Warmth abated! so! she has been in a passion, I suppose.

Lydia. No, nor ever can while I have life.

Mrs. Mal. An ill-tempered little devil! She'll be in a passion all her life, will she?

Lydia. Think not the idle threats of my ridiculous aunt can ever have any weight with me.

Mrs. Mal. Very dutiful, upon my word!

Lydia. Let her choice be Captain Absolute, but Beverley is mine.

Mrs. Mal. I am astonished at her assurance! to his face—this is to his face!

Abs. Thus then let me enforce my suit. [*Kneeling.*

Mrs. Mal. Ay, poor young man! down on his knees entreating for pity! I can contain no longer. Why, thou vixen! I have overheard you.

Abs. O, confound her vigilance? [*Aside.*

Mrs. Mal. Captain Absolute, I know not how to apologize for her shocking rudeness.

Abs. So, all's safe, I find. [*Aside.* I have hopes, madam, that time will bring the young lady——

Mrs. Mal. O, there's nothing to be hoped for from her! she's as headstrong as an allegory on the banks of Nile.

Lydia. Nay, madam, what do you charge me with now?

Mrs. Mal. Why, thou unblushing rebel, didn't you

tell this gentleman to his face that you loved another better? Didn't you say you never would be his?

Lydia. No, madam, I did not.

Mrs. Mal. Good heavens! what assurance! Lydia, Lydia, you ought to know that lying don't become a young woman! Didn't you boast that Beverley, that stroller Beverley, possessed your heart? Tell me that, I say.

Lydia. 'Tis true, ma'am, and none but Beverley.

Mrs. Mal. Hold! hold, Assurance! you shall not be so rude.

Abs. Nay, pray, Mrs. Malaprop, don't stop the young lady's speech: she's very welcome to talk thus; it does not hurt *me* in the least, I assure you.

Mrs. Mal. You are *too* good, captain; *too* amiably patient; but come with me, miss. Let us see you again soon, captain. Remember what we have fixed.

Abs. I shall, ma'am.

Mrs. Mal. Come, take a graceful leave of the gentleman.

Lydia. May every blessing wait on my Beverley, my loved Bev——

Mrs. Mal. Hussy! I'll choke the word in your throat! Come along, come along. [*Exeunt severally.*
          [ABSOLUTE *kissing his hand to* LYDIA, Mrs.
              MALAPROP *stopping her from speaking.*

SCENE IV.

Acres's *Lodgings.*

Acres *and* David.

Acres *as just dressed.*

Acres. Indeed, David, do you think I become it so?

David. You are quite another creature, believe me, master, by the mass! an' we've any luck we shall see the Devon monkerony in all the print shops in Bath!

Acres. Dress *does* make a difference, David.

David. 'Tis all in all, I think—difference! why, an' you were to go now to Clod-Hall, I am certain the old lady wouldn't know you: Master Butler wouldn't believe his own eyes, and Mrs. Pickle would cry, 'Lard presarve me!' our dairymaid would come giggling to the door, and I warrant Dolly Tester, your honour's favourite, would blush like my waistcoat. Oons! I'll a gallon, there an't a dog in the house but would bark, and I question whether Phillis would wag a hair of her tail!

Acres. Ay, David, there's nothing like polishing.

David. So I says of your honour's boots; but the boy never heeds me!

Acres. But, David, has Mr. De-la-grace been here? I must rub up my balancing, and chasing, and boring.

David. I'll call again, sir.

Acres. Do, and see if there are any letters for me at the post-office.

David. I will. By the mass, I can't help looking at

your head! if I hadn't been by at the cooking, I wish I may die if I should have known the dish again myself!
[*Exit.*

[ACRES *comes forward, practising a dancing step.*

Acres. Sink, slide, *coupée.* Confound the first inventors of cotillons! say I, they are as bad as algebra to us country gentlemen; I can walk a minuet easy enough when I am forced! and I have been accounted a good stick in a country-dance. Odds jigs and tabors! I never valued your cross-over to couple—figure in— right and left; and I'd foot it with e'er a captain in the county! but these outlandish heathen allemandes and cotillons are quite beyond me! I shall never prosper at 'em, that's sure; mine are true-born English legs, they don't understand their curst French lingo! their *pas* this, and *pas* that, and *pas* t'other! Damn me! my feet don't like to be called paws! no, 'tis certain I have most anti-Gallican toes!

Enter SERVANT.

Serv. Here is Sir Lucius O'Trigger to wait on you, sir.

Acres. Show him in.

Enter Sir LUCIUS.

Sir Luc. Mr. Acres, I am delighted to embrace you.
Acres. My dear Sir Lucius, I kiss your hands.
Sir Luc. Pray, my friend, what has brought you so suddenly to Bath?
Acres. Faith! I have followed Cupid's Jack-a-lantern, and find myself in a quagmire at last. In short, I have been very ill used, Sir Lucius. I don't choose to mention names, but look on me as on a very ill-used gentleman.

Sir Luc. Pray, what is the case? I ask no names.

Acres. Mark me, Sir Lucius, I fall as deep as need be in love with a young lady—her friends take my part—I follow her to Bath—send word of my arrival; and receive answer, that the lady is to be otherwise disposed of. This, Sir Lucius, I call being ill used.

Sir Luc. Very ill, upon my conscience. Pray, can you divine the cause of it?

Acres. Why, there's the matter: she has another lover, one Beverley, who, I am told, is now in Bath. Odds slanders and lies! he must be at the bottom of it.

Sir Luc. A rival in the case, is there? and you think he has supplanted you unfairly?

Acres. Unfairly! to be sure he has. He never could have done it fairly.

Sir Luc. Then sure you know what is to be done!

Acres. Not I, upon my soul!

Sir Luc. We wear no swords here, but you understand me.

Acres. What! fight him!

Sir Luc. Ay, to be sure: what can I mean else?

Acres. But he has given me no provocation.

Sir Luc. Now, I think he has given you the greatest provocation in the world. Can a man commit a more heinous offence against another than to fall in love with the same woman? O, by my soul! it is the most unpardonable breach of friendship.

Acres. Breach of friendship! Ay, ay; but I have no acquaintance with this man. I never saw him in my life.

Sir Luc. That's no argument at all: he has the less right then to take such a liberty.

Acres. Gad, that's true. I grow full of anger, Sir Lucius! I fire apace! Odds hilts and blades! I find a man may have a deal of valour in him, and not know it! But couldn't I contrive to have a little right of my side?

Sir Luc. What the devil signified *right*, when your *honour* is concerned? Do you think Achilles, or my little Alexander the Great, ever inquired where the right lay? No, by my soul, they drew their broadswords, and left the lazy sons of peace to settle the justice of it.

Acres. Your words are a Grenadier's march to my heart! I believe courage must be catching! I certainly do feel a kind of valour rising as it were—a kind of courage, as I may say. Odds flints, pans, and triggers! I'll challenge him directly.

Sir Luc. Ah, my little friend! if I had *Blunderbuss-Hall* here, I could show you a range of ancestry, in the O'Trigger line, that would furnish the new room; every one of whom had killed his man! For though the mansion-house and dirty acres have slipt through my fingers, I thank heaven our honour and the family-pictures are as fresh as ever.

Acres. O, Sir Lucius! I have had ancestors too! every man of 'em colonel or captain in the militia! Odds balls and barrels! say no more; I'm braced for it. The thunder of your words has soured the milk of human kindness in my breast! Z—ds! as the man in the play says, 'I could do such deeds——'

Sir Luc. Come, come, there must be no passion at all in the case; these things should always be done civilly.

Acres. I must be in a passion, Sir Lucius—I must be in a rage. Dear, Sir Lucius, let me be in a rage, if you love me. Come, here's pen and paper. (*Sits down to write.*) I would the ink were red! Indite, I say indite! How shall I begin? Odds bullets and blades! I'll write a good bold hand, however.

Sir Luc. Pray compose yourself.

Acres. Come, now, shall I begin with an oath? Do, Sir Lucius, let me begin with a damme.

Sir Luc. Pho! pho! do the thing decently, and like a Christian. Begin now, ' *Sir,*'——

Acres. That's too civil by half.

Sir Luc. ' *To prevent the confusion that might arise* '——

Acres. Well——

Sir Luc. ' *From our both addressing the same lady* '——

Acres. Ay—there's the reason—' same lady '—Well——

Sir Luc. ' *I shall expect the honour of your company* '——

Acres. Z—ds! I'm not asking him to dinner.

Sir Luc. Pray be easy.

Acres. Well then, ' honour of your company '—

Sir Luc. ' *To settle our pretensions* '——

Acres. Well.

Sir Luc. Let me see, ay, King's Mead-field will do—' *in King's Mead-fields.*'

Acres. So that's done. Well, I'll fold it up presently; my own crest, a hand and dagger, shall be the seal.

Sir Luc. You see now this little explanation will put a stop at once to all confusion or misunderstanding that might arise between you.

Acres. Ay, we fight to prevent any misunderstanding.

Sir Luc. Now, I'll leave you to fix your own time. Take my advice, and you'll decide it this evening if you can; then let the worst come of it, 'twill be off your mind to-morrow.

Acres. Very true.

Sir Luc. So I shall see nothing more of you, unless it be by letter, till the evening. I would do myself the honour to carry your message; but, to tell you a secret, I believe I shall have just such another affair on my own hands. There is a gay captain here, who put a jest on me lately, at the expense of my country, and I only want to fall in with the gentleman, to call him out.

Acres. By my valour, I should like to see you fight first! Odds life! I should like to see you kill him, if it was only to get a little lesson.

Sir Luc. I shall be very proud of instructing you. Well for the present—but remember now, when you meet your antagonist, do everything in a mild and agreeable manner. Let your courage be as keen, but at the same time as polished, as your sword.

[*Exeunt severally.*

ACT IV.—SCENE I.

Acres's *Lodgings.*

Acres *and* David.

David. Then, by the mass, sir! I would do no such thing—ne'er a Sir Lucius O'Trigger in the kingdom should make me fight, when I wa'n't so minded. Oons! what will the old lady say, when she hears o't?

Acres. Ah! David, if you had heard Sir Lucius! Odds sparks and flames! he would have roused your valour.

David. Not he, indeed. I hates such blood-thirsty cormorants. Look'ee, master, if you'd wanted a bout at boxing, quarter-staff, or short-staff, I should never be the man to bid you cry off: but for your curst sharps and snaps, I never knew any good come of 'em.

Acres. But my honour, David, my honour! I must be very careful of my honour.

David. Ay, by the mass! and I would be very careful of it; and I think in return my *honour* couldn't do less than to be very careful of *me.*

Acres. Odds blades! David, no gentleman will ever risk the loss of his honour!

David. I say then, it would be but civil in *honour* never to risk the loss of a *gentleman.* Look'ee, master, this *honour* seems to me to be a marvellous false friend: ay, truly, a very courtier-like servant. Put the case, I was a gentleman (which, thank God, no one can say of me); well, my honour makes me quarrel with another gentleman of my acquaintance. So, we fight. (Pleasant enough that.) Boh! I kill him (the more's my luck). Now, pray who gets the profit of it? Why, my *honour.* But put the case that he kills me! by the mass! I go to the worms, and my honour whips over to my enemy.

Acres. No, David, in that case! Odds crowns and laurels! your honour follows you to the grave.

David. Now, that's just the place where I could make a shift to do without it.

Acres. Z—ds! David, you are a coward! It doesn't become my valour to listen to you. What, shall I disgrace my ancestors? Think of that, David—think what it would be to disgrace my ancestors!

David. Under favour, the surest way of not disgracing them, is to keep as long as you can out of their company. Look'ee now, master, to go to them in such haste, with an ounce of lead in your brains, I should think might as well be let alone. Our ancestors are very good kind of folks; but they are the last people I should choose to have a visiting acquaintance with.

Acres. But, David, now, you don't think there is such very, very, *very* great danger, hey? Odds life! people often fight without any mischief done!

David. By the mass, I think 'tis ten to one against you! Oons! here to meet some lion-headed fellow, I warrant, with his d—n'd double-barrelled swords, and cut-and-thrust pistols! Lord bless us! it makes me tremble to think o't! Those be such desperate bloody-minded weapons! Well, I never could abide 'em; from a child I never could fancy 'em! I suppose there a'n't been so merciless a beast in the world as your loaded pistol!

Acres. Z—ds! I *won't* be afraid. Odds fire and fury! you sha'n't make me afraid. Here is the challenge, and I have sent for my dear friend Jack Absolute to carry it for me.

David. Ay, i' the name of mischief, let *him* be the messenger. For my part, I wouldn't lend a hand in it for the best horse in your stable. By the mass! it don't look like another letter! It is, as I may say, a designing and malicious looking letter; and I warrant smells of gunpowder like a soldier's pouch! Oons! I wouldn't swear it mayn't go off!

Acres. Out, you poltroon! you ha'n't the valour of a grasshopper.

David. Well, I say no more; 'twill be sad news, to be sure, at Clod Hall! but I ha' done. How Phillis will howl when she hears of it! Ah, poor bitch, she little thinks what shooting her master's going after! And I warrant old Crop, who has carried your honour, field and road, these ten years, will curse the hour he was born. (*Whimpering.*)

Acres. It won't do, David; I am determined to fight, so get along, you coward, while I'm in the mind.

Enter SERVANT.

Ser. Captain Absolute, sir.

Acres. O! show him up.   [*Exit* SERVANT.

David. Well, Heaven send we be all alive this time to-morrow.

Acres. What's that? Don't provoke me, David!

David. Good-bye, master.   (*Whimpering.*)

Acres. Get along, you cowardly, dastardly, croaking raven.   [*Exit* DAVID.

Enter ABSOLUTE.

Abs. What's the matter, Bob?

Acres. A vile, sheep-hearted blockhead! If I hadn't the valour of St. George and the dragon to boot——

Abs. But what did you want with me, Bob?

Acres. O! There—(*Gives him the challenge*).

Abs. '*To Ensign Beverley.*' So, what's going on now!   [*Aside.*
Well, what's this?

Acres. A challenge!

Abs. Indeed! Why, you won't fight him; will you, Bob?

Acres. 'Egad, but I will, Jack. Sir Lucius has wrought me to it. He has left me full of rage, and I'll fight this evening, that so much good passion mayn't be wasted.

Abs. But what have I to do with this?

Acres. Why, as I think you know something of this fellow, I want you to find him out for me, and give him this mortal defiance.

Abs. Well, give it to me, and trust me he gets it.

Acres. Thank you, my dear friend, my dear Jack; but it is giving you a great deal of trouble.

Abs. Not in the least; I beg you won't mention it. No trouble in the world I assure you.

Acres. You are very kind. What it is to have a friend! You couldn't be my second—could you, Jack?

Abs. Why no, Bob—not in *this* affair—it would not be quite so proper.

Acres. Well, then, I must get my friend Sir Lucius. I shall have your good wishes, however, Jack.

Abs. Whenever he meets you, believe me.

Enter SERVANT.

Ser. Sir Anthony Absolute is below, inquiring for the captain.

Abs. I'll come instantly. Well, my little hero, success attend you. (*Going.*)

Acres. Stay—stay, Jack. If Beverley should ask you what kind of a man your friend Acres is, do tell him I am a devil of a fellow—will you, Jack?

Abs. To be sure I shall. I'll say you are a determined dog—hey, Bob!

Acres. Ay, do, do—and if that frightens him, 'egad, perhaps he mayn't come. So tell him I generally kill a man a-week; will you, Jack?

Abs. I will, I will; I'll say you are called in the country '*Fighting Bob.*'

Acres. Right—right—'tis all to prevent mischief; for I don't want to take his life if I clear my honour.

Abs. No!—that's very kind of you.

Acres. Why, you don't wish me to kill him—do you, Jack?

Abs. No, upon my soul, I do not. But a devil of a fellow, hey? (*Going.*)

Acres. True, true—but stay—stay, Jack—you may

add, that you never saw me in such a rage before—a most devouring rage!

Abs. I will, I will.

Acres. Remember, Jack—a determined dog!

Abs. Ay, ay, ' *Fighting Bob?*'   [*Exeunt severally.*

SCENE II.

Mrs. MALAPROP's *Lodgings.*

Mrs. MALAPROP *and* LYDIA.

Mrs. Mal. Why, thou perverse one!—tell me what you can object to him? Isn't he a handsome man?—tell me that. A genteel man? a pretty figure of a man?

Lydia. She little thinks whom she is praising! (*Aside.*) So is Beverley, ma'am.

Mrs. Mal. No caparisons, miss, if you please. Caparisons don't become a young woman. No! Captain Absolute is indeed a fine gentleman!

Lydia. Ay, the Captain Absolute *you* have seen.
                                                                [*Aside.*

Mrs. Mal. Then he's *so* well bred; *so* full of alacrity and adulation!—and has *so much* to say for himself:—in such good language too! His physiognomy so grammatical! Then his presence is so noble! I protest when I saw him, I thought of what Hamlet says in the play:—' Hesperian curls—the front of *Job* himself!—an eye, like *March*, to threaten at command!—a station, like Harry Mercury, new——' Something about kissing—on a hill—however, the similitude struck me directly.

Lydia. How enraged she'll be presently when she discovers her mistake!   [*Aside.*

Enter SERVANT.

Ser. Sir Anthony and Captain Absolute are below, ma'am.

Mrs. Mal. Show them up here. [*Exit* SERVANT. Now, Lydia, I insist on your behaving as becomes a young woman. Show your good breeding, at least, though you have forgot your duty.

Lydia. Madam, I have told you my resolution! I shall not only give him no encouragement, but I won't even speak to, or look at him.

[*Flings herself into a chair, with her face from the door.*

Enter Sir ANTHONY *and* ABSOLUTE.

Sir Anth. Here we are, Mrs. Malaprop; come to mitigate the frowns of unrelenting beauty, and difficulty enough I had to bring this fellow. I don't know what's the matter; but if I had not held him by force, he'd have given me the slip.

Mrs. Mal. You have infinite trouble, Sir Anthony, in the affair. I am ashamed for the cause! Lydia, Lydia, rise, I beseech you!—pay your respects!
[*Aside to her.*

Sir Anth. I hope, madam, that Miss Languish has reflected on the worth of this gentleman, and the regard due to her aunt's choice, and *my* alliance. Now, Jack, speak to her. [*Aside to him.*

Abs. What the d—l shall I do! (*Aside.*) You see, sir, she won't even look at me, whilst you are here. I knew she wouldn't! I told you so. Let me entreat you, sir, to leave us together!

[ABSOLUTE *seems to expostulate with his father.*

Lydia. (*Aside.*) I wonder I ha'n't heard my aunt exclaim yet! sure she can't have looked at him!—

perhaps their regimentals are alike, and she is something blind.

Sir Anth. I say, sir, I won't stir a foot yet.

Mrs. Mal. I am sorry to say, Sir Anthony, that my affluence over my niece is very small. Turn round, Lydia; I blush for you. [*Aside to her.*

Sir Anth. May I not flatter myself, that Miss Languish will assign what cause of dislike she can have to my son, Why don't you begin, Jack? Speak, you puppy—speak! [*Aside to him.*

Mrs. Mal. It is impossible, Sir Anthony, she can have any. She will not say she has. Answer, hussy! why don't you answer? [*Aside to her.*

Sir Anth. Then, madam, I trust that a childish and hasty predilection will be no bar to Jack's happiness. Z—ds, sirrah! why don't you speak?
[*Aside to him.*

Lydia. (*Aside.*) I think my lover seems as little inclined to conversation as myself. How strangely blind my aunt must be!

Abs. Hem! hem! madam—hem (ABSOLUTE *attempts to speak, then returns to* Sir ANTHONY)—Faith! sir, I am so confounded!—and—so—so—confused! I told you I should be so, sir—I knew it. The—the—tremor of my passion entirely takes away my presence of mind.

Sir Anth. But it don't take away your voice, fool, does it? Go up, and speak to her directly!

[ABSOLUTE *makes signs to* Mrs. MALAPROP *to leave them together.*

Mrs. Mal. Sir Anthony, shall we leave them together? Ah! you stubborn little vixen!
[*Aside to her.*

Sir Anth. Not yet, ma'am, not yet? What the d—l are you at? Unlock your jaws, sirrah, or—
[*Aside to him.*

[ABSOLUTE *draws near* LYDIA.]

Abs. Now Heaven send she may be too sullen to look round. I must disguise my voice. (*Aside.*)

[*Speaks in a low hoarse tone.*
—Will not Miss Languish lend an ear to the mild accents of true love? Will not——

Sir Anth. What the d—l ails the fellow? Why don't you speak out? not stand croaking like a frog in a quinsy!

Abs. The—the—excess of my awe, and my modesty, quite choke me!

Sir Anth. Ah! your *modesty* again! I'll tell you what, Jack, if you don't speak out directly, and glibly too, I shall be in such a rage! Mrs. Malaprop, I wish the lady would favour us with something more than a side-front. [Mrs. MALAPROP *seems to chide* LYDIA.

Abs. So all will out, I see.

[*Goes up to* LYDIA, *speaks softly.*
Be not surprised, my Lydia, suppress all surprise at present.

Lydia (*Aside*). Heavens! 'tis Beverley's voice. Sure he can't have imposed on Sir Anthony too!

[*Looks round by degrees, then starts up.*
Is this possible?—my Beverley!—how can this be?—my Beverley?

Abs. Ah! 'tis all over. [*Aside.*

Sir Anth. Beverley! the devil—Beverley! What can the girl mean? This is my son, Jack Absolute.

Mrs. Mal. For shame, hussy! for shame!—your head runs so on that fellow, that you have him always in your eyes! Beg Captain Absolute's pardon directly.

Lydia. I see no Captain Absolute, but my loved Beverley.

Sir Anth. Z—ds! the girl's mad—her brain's turned by reading.

Mrs. Mal. O' my conscience, I believe so! What do you mean by Beverley, hussy? You saw Captain Absolute before to-day; there he is—your husband that shall be.

Lydia. With all my soul, ma'am—when I refuse my Beverley——

Sir Anth. O! she's as mad as Bedlam!—or has this fellow been playing us a rogue's trick! Come here, sirrah, who the d—l are you?

Abs. Faith, sir, I am not quite clear myself; but I'll endeavour to recollect.

Sir Anth. Are you my son or not? Answer for your mother, you dog, if you won't for me.

Mrs. Mal. Ay, sir, who are you? O mercy! I begin to suspect!——

Abs. Ye powers of Impudence, befriend me! (*Aside.*) Sir Anthony, most assuredly I am your wife's son: and that I sincerely believe myself to be *yours* also, I hope my duty has always shown. Mrs. Malaprop, I am your most respectful admirer, and shall be proud to add affectionate nephew. I need not tell my Lydia that she sees her faithful Beverley, who, knowing the singular generosity of her temper, assumed that name, and a station, which has proved a test of the most disinterested love, which he now hopes to enjoy in a more elevated character.

Lydia. So! there will be no elopement after all! (*sullenly.*)

Sir Anth. Upon my soul, Jack, thou art a very impudent fellow! to do you justice, I think I never saw a piece of more consummate assurance!

Abs. O, you flatter me, sir—you compliment; 'tis my *modesty* you know, sir—my *modesty* that has stood in my way.

Sir Anth. Well, I am glad you are not the dull,

insensible varlet you pretended to be, however! I'm glad you have made a fool of your father, you dog, I am. So this was your *penitence*, your *duty*, and *obedience!* I thought it was d—n'd sudden! You *never heard their names before*, not you! What, The Languishes *of* Worcestershire, hey?—*if you could please me in the affair, 'twas all you desired!* Ah! you dissembling villain! What! (*pointing to* Lydia) *she squints, don't she?—a little red-haired girl!*—hey? Why, you hypocritical young rascal! I wonder you a'n't ashamed to hold up your head!

Abs. 'Tis with difficulty, sir; I *am* confused—very much confused, as you must perceive.

Mrs. Mal. O Lud! Sir Anthony! a new light breaks in upon me! hey! how! what! Captain, did *you* write the letters then? What, am I to thank *you* for the elegant compilation of '*an old weather-beaten she-dragon*,' hey? O mercy! was it *you* that reflected on my parts of speech?

Abs. Dear sir! my modesty will be overpowered at last, if you don't assist me. I shall certainly not be able to stand it!

Sir Anth. Come, come, Mrs. Malaprop, we must forget and forgive. Odds life! matters have taken so clever a turn all of a sudden, that I could find in my heart to be so good-humoured! and so gallant! hey! Mrs. Malaprop!

Mrs. Mal. Well, Sir Anthony, since *you* desire it, we will not anticipate the past; so mind, young people, our retrospection will be all to the future.

Sir Anth. Come, we must leave them together; Mrs. Malaprop, they long to fly into each other's arms, I warrant! Jack, isn't the cheek as I said, hey? and the eye, you rogue! and the lip, hey? Come, Mrs. Malaprop, we'll not disturb their tenderness—theirs is the time of life for happiness! 'Youth's the season made for joy' (*sings*), hey! Odds life! I'm in such spirits, I don't know what I could not do! Permit me, ma'am (*gives his hand to* Mrs. MALAPROP). (*Sings*) Tol-de-rol—'gad, I should like to have a little fooling myself—Tol-de-rol! de-rol.

[*Exit singing and handing* Mrs. MALAPROP.

(LYDIA *sits sullenly in her chair.*)

Abs. So much thought bodes me no good.   (*Aside.*) So grave, Lydia!

Lydia. Sir!

Abs. So! egad! I thought as much! that d—n'd monosyllable has froze me! (*Aside.*) What, Lydia, now that we are as happy in our friends' consent, as in our mutual vows——

Lydia. Friends' consent indeed! (*peevishly.*)

Abs. Come, come, we must lay aside some of our romance—a little *wealth* and *comfort* may be endured after all. And for your fortune, the lawyers shall make such settlements as——

Lydia. Lawyers! I hate lawyers!

Abs. Nay, then, we will not wait for their lingering forms, but instantly procure the licence, and——

Lydia. The *licence*! I hate license!

Abs. O, my love! be not so unkind! thus let me entreat—— [*Kneeling.*

Lydia. Pshaw! what signifies kneeling, when you know I *must* have you!

Abs. (*Rising.*) Nay, madam, there shall be no constraint upon your inclinations, I promise you. If I have lost your heart, I resign the rest. 'Gad, I must try what a little *spirit* will do. [*Aside.*

Lydia. (*Rising.*) Then, sir, let me tell you, the interest you had there was acquired by a mean, unmanly imposition, and deserves the punishment of fraud. What, you have been treating *me* like a child! humouring my romance! and laughing, I suppose, at your success!

Abs. You wrong me, Lydia, you wrong me—only hear——

Lydia. So, while *I* fondly imagined we were deceiving my relations, and flattered myself that I should outwit and incense them all, behold my hopes are to be crushed at once by my aunt's consent and approbation, and *I* am myself the only dupe at last! [*Walking about in a heat.*] But here, sir, here is the picture—Beverley's picture! (*taking a miniature from her bosom*) which I have worn, night and day, in spite of threats and entreaties! There, sir (*flings it to him*), and be assured I throw the original from my heart as easily.

Abs. Nay, nay, ma'am, we will not differ as to that. Here (*taking out a picture*), here is Miss Lydia Languish. What a difference! ay, *there* is the heavenly assenting smile that first gave soul and spirit to my hopes! those are the lips which sealed a vow, as yet scarce dry, in Cupid's calendar! and there the half-resentful blush, that *would* have checked the ardour of my thanks. Well, all that's past! all over indeed! There, madam, in beauty, that copy is not equal to you, but in my mind its merit over the original, in being still the same, is such—that—I cannot find in my heart to part with it.
[*Puts it up again.*

Lydia. (*Softening.*) 'Tis *your own* doing, sir—I, I, I suppose you are perfectly satisfied.

Abs. O, most certainly; sure, now, this is much better than being in love! ha! ha! ha! there's some spirit in *this*! What signifies breaking some scores of solemn promises: all that's of no consequence, you know. To be sure people will say, that miss didn't know her own mind, but never mind that! or, perhaps, they may be ill-natured enough to hint that the gentleman grew tired of the lady and forsook her; but don't let that fret you.

Lydia. There's no bearing his insolence.
[*Bursts into tears.*

Enter Mrs. MALAPROP *and* Sir ANTHONY.

Mrs. Mal. (Entering). Come, we must interrupt your billing and cooing awhile.

Lydia. This is worse than your treachery and deceit, you base ingrate. [*Sobbing.*

Sir Anth. What the devil's the matter now! Z—ds! Mrs. Malaprop, this is the *oddest billing* and *cooing* I ever heard! but what the deuce is the meaning of it? I am quite astonished!

Abs. Ask the lady, sir.

Mrs. Mal. O, mercy! I'm quite analysed, for my part! Why, Lydia, what is the reason of this?

Lydia. Ask the gentleman, ma'am.

Sir Anth. Z—ds! I shall be in a phrenzy! why, Jack, you are not come out to be any one else, are you?

Mrs. Mal. Ay, sir, there's no more trick, is there? you are not like Cerberus, *three* gentlemen at once, are you?

Abs. You'll not let me speak—I say the lady can account for this much better than I can.

Lydia. Ma'am, you once commanded me never to think of Beverley again—there is the man, I now obey you: for, from this moment, I renounce him for ever.
[*Exit* LYDIA.

Mrs. Mal. O mercy! and miracles! what a turn here is; why sure, captain, you haven't behaved disrespectfully to my niece.

Sir Anth. Ha! ha! ha!—ha! ha! ha! now I see

it. Ha! ha! ha! now I see it; you have been too lively, Jack.

Abs. Nay, sir, upon my word——

Sir Anth. Come, no lying, Jack; I'm sure '*twas* so.

Mrs. Mal. O lud! Sir Anthony! O fie, captain!

Abs. Upon my soul, ma'am——

Sir Anth. Come, no excuses, Jack; why, your father, you rogue, was so before you: the blood of the Absolutes was always impatient. Ha! ha! ha! poor little Lydia! why, you've frightened her, you dog, you have.

Abs. By all that's good, sir——

Sir Anth. Z—ds! say no more, I tell you; Mrs. Malaprop shall make your peace. You must make his peace, Mrs. Malaprop: you must tell her 'tis Jack's way; tell her 'tis all our ways; it runs in the blood of our family! Come away, Jack. Ha! ha! ha! Mrs. Malaprop, a young villain! [*Pushes him out.*

Mrs. Mal. O! Sir Anthony! O fie, captain!
[*Exeunt severally.*

SCENE III.

The NORTH PARADE.

Enter Sir LUCIUS O'TRIGGER.

Sir Luc. I wonder where this Captain Absolute hides himself. Upon my conscience! these officers are always in one's way in love affairs: I remember I might have married Lady Dorothy Carmine, if it had not been for a little rogue of a major, who ran away with her before she could get a sight of me! And I wonder too what it is the ladies can see in them to be so fond of them; unless it be a touch of the old serpent in 'em, that makes the little creatures be caught, like vipers, with a bit of red cloth. Hah! isn't this the captain coming? faith it is! There is a probability of succeeding about that fellow that is mighty provoking! Who the devil is he talking to? [*Steps aside.*

Enter Captain ABSOLUTE.

Abs. To what fine purpose I have been plotting! a noble reward for all my schemes, upon my soul! a little gypsy! I did not think her romance could have made her so d——n'd absurd either. 'Sdeath, I never was in a worse humour in my life! I could cut my own throat, or any other person's, with the greatest pleasure in the world!

Sir Luc. O, faith! I'm in the luck of it. I never could have found him in a sweeter temper for my purpose; to be sure I'm just come in the nick! Now to enter into conversation with him, and so quarrel genteelly. [Sir LUCIUS *goes up to* ABSOLUTE. With regard to that matter, captain, I must beg leave to differ in opinion with you.

Abs. Upon my word, then, you must be a very subtle disputant: because, sir, I happened just then to be giving no opinion at all.

Sir Luc. That's no reason. For give me leave to tell you, a man may *think* an untruth as well as speak one.

Abs. Very true, sir; but if a man never utters his thoughts, I should think they might stand a chance of escaping controversy.

Sir Luc. Then, sir, you differ in opinion with me, which amounts to the same thing.

Abs. Hark'ee, Sir Lucius, if I had not before known you to be a gentleman, upon my soul I should not have discovered it at this interview: for what you can drive at, unless you mean to quarrel with me, I cannot conceive!

Sir Luc. I humbly thank you, sir, for the quickness of your apprehension (*Bowing*)—you have named the very thing I would be at.

Abs. Very well, sir; I shall certainly not balk your inclinations; but I should be glad you would please to explain your motives.

Sir Luc. Pray, sir, be easy; the quarrel is a very pretty quarrel as it stands; we should only spoil it by trying to explain it. However, your memory is very short, or you could not have forgot an affront you passed on me within this week. So, no more, but name your time and place.

Abs. Well, sir, since you are so bent on it, the sooner the better; let it be this evening—here by the Spring Gardens. We shall scarcely be interrupted.

Sir Luc. Faith! that same interruption in affairs of this nature shows very great ill-breeding. I don't know what's the reason, but in England, if a thing of this kind gets wind, people make such a pother, that a gentleman can never fight in peace and quietness. However, if it's the same to you, captain, I should take it as a particular kindness, if you'd let us meet in King's Mead Fields, as a little business will call me there about six o'clock, and I may despatch both matters at once.

Abs. 'Tis the same to me exactly. A little after six, then, we will discuss this matter more seriously.

Sir Luc. If you please, sir; there will be very pretty small-sword light, though it won't do for a long shot. So that matter's settled! and my mind's at ease. [*Exit* Sir Lucius.

Enter FAULKLAND, *meeting* ABSOLUTE.

Abs. Well met. I was going to look for you. O, Faulkland! all the demons of spite and disappointment have conspired against me! I'm so vexed, that if I had not the prospect of a resource in being knocked o'the head by-and-bye, I should scarce have spirits to tell you the cause.

Faulk. What can you mean? Has Lydia changed her mind? I should have thought her duty and inclination would now have pointed to the same object.

Abs. Ay, just as the eyes do of a person who squints: when her love-eye was fixed on me, t'other, her eye of duty, was finely obliqued; but when duty bid her point that the same way, off t'other turned on a swivel, and secured its retreat with a frown!

Faulk. But what's the resource you——

Abs. O, to wind up the whole, a good-natured Irishman here has (*mimicking* Sir Lucius) begged leave to have the pleasure of cutting my throat, and I mean to indulge him, that's all.

Faulk. Prithee, be serious.

Abs. 'Tis fact, upon my soul. Sir Lucius O'Trigger —you know him by sight—for some affront, which I am sure I never intended, has obliged me to meet him this evening at six o'clock; 'tis on that account I wished to see you: you must go with me.

Faulk. Nay, there must be some mistake, sure. Sir Lucius shall explain himself, and I dare say matters may be accommodated: but this evening, did you say? I wish it had been any other time.

Abs. Why? there will be light enough: there will (as Sir Lucius says) 'be very pretty small-sword light, though it will not do for a long shot.' Confound his long shots!

Faulk. But I am myself a good deal ruffled, by a difference I have had with Julia; my vile tormenting temper has made me treat her so cruelly, that I shall not be myself till we are reconciled.

Abs. By heaven! Faulkland, you don't deserve her.

Enter SERVANT, *gives* FAULKLAND *a letter.*

Faulk. O Jack! this is from Julia. I dread to open it. I fear it may be to take a last leave, perhaps to bid me to return her letters, and restore——O! how I suffer for my folly!

Abs. Here—let me see.

[*Takes the letter and opens it.*
Ay, a final sentence, indeed! 'Tis all over with you, faith!

Faulk. Nay, Jack, don't keep me in suspense.

Abs. Hear then. '*As I am convinced that my dear Faulkland's own reflections have already upbraided him for his last unkindness to me, I will not add a word on the subject. I wish to speak with you as soon as possible. —Yours ever and truly,* JULIA.' There's stubbornness and resentment for you! [*Gives him the letter.* Why, man, you don't seem one whit the happier at this.

Faulk. O, yes, I am—but—but——

Abs. Confound your *buts*! You never hear anything that would make another man bless himself, but you immediately d—n it with a *but.*

Faulk. Now, Jack, as you are my friend, own honestly, don't you think there is something forward—something indelicate in this haste to forgive? Women should never sue for reconciliation; that should always come from us. They should retain their coldness till woo'd to kindness; and their *pardon*, like their *love*, should 'not unsought be won.'

Abs. I have no patience to listen to you; thou'rt incorrigible! so say no more on the subject. I must go to settle a few matters; let me see you before six, remember, at my lodgings. A poor industrious devil like me, who have toiled, and drudged, and plotted to gain my ends, and am at last disappointed by other people's folly, may in pity be allowed to swear and grumble a little; but a captious sceptic in love, a slave to fretfulness and whim, who has no difficulties but of his own creating, is a subject more fit for ridicule than compassion! [*Exit* ABSOLUTE.

Faulk. I feel his reproaches; yet I would not change this too exquisite nicety, for the gross content with which *he* tramples on the thorns of love. His engaging me in this duel has started an idea in my head, which I will instantly pursue. I'll use it as the touchstone of Julia's sincerity and disinterestedness; if her love prove pure and sterling ore, my name will rest on it with honour! And once I've stamped it there, I lay aside my doubts for ever; but if the dross of selfishness, the allay of pride predominate, 'twill be best to leave her as a toy for some less cautious fool to sigh for.

[*Exit* FAULKLAND.

ACT V.—SCENE I.

JULIA'S *Dressing-room.*

JULIA *sola.*

How this message has alarmed me! what dreadful accident can he mean? why such charge to be alone?

O Faulkland! how many unhappy moments, how many tears have you cost me!

Enter FAULKLAND.

Julia. What means this? why this caution, Faulkland?

Faulk. Alas! Julia, I am come to take a long farewell.

Julia. Heavens! what do you mean?

Faulk. You see before you a wretch, whose life is forfeited. Nay, start not! the infirmity of my temper has drawn all this misery on me. I left you fretful and passionate—an untoward accident drew me into a quarrel—the event is, that I must fly this kingdom instantly. O Julia, had I been so fortunate as to have called you mine entirely, before this mischance had fallen on me, I should not so deeply dread my banishment!

Julia. My soul is oppressed with sorrow at the nature of your misfortune: had these adverse circumstances arisen from a less fatal cause, I should have felt strong comfort in the thought that I could now chase from your bosom every doubt of the warm sincerity of my love. My heart has long known no other guardian. I now intrust my person to your honour— we will fly together. When safe from pursuit, my father's will may be fulfilled, and I receive a legal claim to be the partner of your sorrows, and tenderest comforter. Then on the bosom of your wedded Julia, you may lull your keen regret to slumbering; while virtuous love, with a cherub's hand, shall smooth the brow of upbraiding thought, and pluck the thorn from compunction.

Faulk. O Julia! I am bankrupt in gratitude! but the time is so pressing, it calls on you for so hasty a resolution. Would you not wish some hours to weigh the advantages you forego, and what little compensation poor Faulkland can make you beside his solitary love?

Julia. I ask not a moment. No, Faulkland, I have loved you for yourself: and if I now, more than ever, prize the solemn engagement which so long has pledged us to each other, it is because it leaves no room for hard aspersions on my fame, and puts the seal of duty to an act of love. But let us not linger. Perhaps this delay——

Faulk. 'Twill be better I should not venture out again till dark. Yet am I grieved to think what numberless distresses will press heavy on your gentle disposition!

Julia. Perhaps your fortune may be forfeited by this unhappy act. I know not whether 'tis so, but sure that alone can never make us unhappy. The little I have will be sufficient to support us; and exile never should be splendid.

Faulk. Ay, but in such an abject state of life, my wounded pride perhaps may increase the natural fretfulness of my temper, till I become a rude, morose companion, beyond your patience to endure. Perhaps the recollection of a deed my conscience cannot justify may haunt me in such gloomy and unsocial fits, that I shall hate the tenderness that would relieve me, break from your arms, and quarrel with your fondness!

Julia. If your thoughts should assume so unhappy a bent, you will the more want some mild and affectionate spirit to watch over and console you: one who, by bearing *your* infirmities with gentleness and resignation, may teach you *so* to bear the evils of your fortune.

Faulk. Julia, I have proved you to the quick! and

with this useless device I throw away all my doubts. How shall I plead to be forgiven this last unworthy effect of my restless, unsatisfied disposition?

Julia. Has no such disaster happened as you related?

Faulk. I am ashamed to own that it was pretended; yet in pity, Julia, do not kill me with resenting a fault which never can be repeated: but sealing, this once, my pardon, let me to-morrow, in the face of Heaven, receive my future guide and monitress, and expiate my past folly, by years of tender adoration.

Julia. Hold, Faulkland! that you are free from a crime, which I before feared to name, Heaven knows how sincerely I rejoice! These are tears of thankfulness for that! But that your cruel doubts should have urged you to an imposition that has wrung my heart, gives me now a pang, more keen than I can express!

Faulk. By heavens! Julia——

Julia. Yet hear me. My father loved you, Faulkland! and you preserved the life that tender parent gave me; in his presence I pledged my hand—joyfully pledged it—where before I had given my heart. When, soon after, I lost that parent, it seemed to me that Providence had, in Faulkland, shown me whither to transfer, without a pause, my grateful duty, as well as my affection: hence I have been content to bear from you what pride and delicacy would have forbid me from another. I will not upbraid you, by repeating how you have trifled with my sincerity.

Faulk. I confess it all! yet hear——

Julia. After such a year of trial, I might have flattered myself that I should not have been insulted with a new probation of my sincerity, as cruel as unnecessary! I now see it is not in your nature to be content, or confident in love. With this conviction

I never will be yours. While I had hopes that my persevering attention, and unreproaching kindness, might in time reform your temper, I should have been happy to have gained a dearer influence over you; but I will not furnish you with a licensed power to keep alive an incorrigible fault, at the expense of one who never would contend with you.

Faulk. Nay, but, Julia, by my soul and honour, if after this——

Julia. But one word more. As my faith has once been given to you, I never will barter it with another. I shall pray for your happiness with the truest sincerity; and the dearest blessing I can ask of Heaven to send you will be to charm you from that unhappy temper, which alone has prevented the performance of our solemn engagement. All I request of *you* is, that you will yourself reflect upon this infirmity, and when you number up the many true delights it has deprived you of, let it not be your *least* regret, that it lost you the love of one—who would have followed you in beggary through the world! [*Exit.*

Faulk. She's gone!—for ever! There was an awful resolution in her manner, that riveted me to my place. O fool! dolt! barbarian! Curst as I am with more imperfections than my fellow-wretches, kind Fortune sent a heaven-gifted cherub to my aid, and, like a ruffian, I have driven her from my side! I must now haste to my appointment. Well, my mind is tuned for such a scene. I shall wish only to become a principal in it, and reverse the tale my cursed folly put me upon forging here. O Love! tormentor! fiend! whose influence, like the moon's, acting on men of dull souls, makes idiots of them, but meeting subtler spirits, betrays their course, and urges sensibility to madness!

[*Exit.*

Enter MAID *and* LYDIA.

Maid. My mistress, ma'am, I know, was here just now—perhaps she is only in the next room.
[*Exit* MAID.

Lydia. Heigh-ho! Though he has used me so, this fellow runs strangely in my head. I believe one lecture from my grave cousin will make me recall him.

Enter JULIA.

Lydia. O, Julia, I am come to you with such an appetite for consolation. Lud! child, what's the matter with you? You have been crying! I'll be hanged, if that Faulkland has not been tormenting you!

Julia. You mistake the cause of my uneasiness! Something *has* flurried me a little. Nothing that you can guess at. I would not accuse Faulkland to a sister! [*Aside.*

Lydia. Ah! whatever vexations you may have, I can assure you mine surpass them. You know who Beverley proves to be?

Julia. I will now own to you, Lydia, that Mr. Faulkland had before informed me of the whole affair. Had young Absolute been the person you took him for, I should not have accepted your confidence on the subject, without a serious endeavour to counteract your caprice.

Lydia. So, then, I see I have been deceived by every one! but I don't care—I'll never have him.

Julia. Nay, Lydia——

Lydia. Why, is it not provoking? when I thought we were coming to the prettiest distress imaginable, to find myself made a mere Smithfield bargain of at last. There had I projected one of the most sentimental elopements! so becoming a disguise! so amiable a ladder of ropes! Conscious moon—four horses—Scotch parson—with such surprise to Mrs. Malaprop—and such paragraphs in the newspapers! O, I shall die with disappointment!

Julia. I don't wonder at it!

Lydia. Now, sad reverse! What have I to expect, but, after a deal of flimsy preparation with a bishop's licence, and my aunt's blessing, to go simpering up to the altar; or perhaps be cried three times in a country church, and have an unmannerly fat clerk ask the consent of every butcher in the parish to join John Absolute and Lydia Languish, spinster! O, that I should live to hear myself called Spinster!

Julia. Melancholy, indeed!

Lydia. How mortifying, to remember the dear delicious shifts I used to be put to, to gain half a minute's conversation with this fellow! How often have I stole forth, in the coldest night in January, and found him in the garden, stuck like a dripping statue! There would he kneel to me in the snow, and sneeze and cough so pathetically! he shivering with cold and I with apprehension! and while the freezing blast numbed our joints, how warmly would he press me to pity his flame, and glow with mutual ardour! Ah, Julia, that was something like being in love.

Julia. If I were in spirits, Lydia, I should chide you only by laughing heartily at you; but it suits more the situation of my mind, at present, earnestly to entreat you not to let a man, who loves you with sincerity, suffer that unhappiness from your caprice, which I know too well caprice can inflict.

Lydia. Oh lud! what has brought my aunt here?

Enter Mrs. MALAPROP, FAG, *and* DAVID.

Mrs. Mal. So! so! here's fine work! here's fine

suicide, paracide, and simulation going on in the fields! and Sir Anthony not to be found to prevent the antistrophe!

Julia. For Heaven's sake, madam, what's the meaning of this?

Mrs. Mal. That gentleman can tell you; 'twas he enveloped the affair to me.

Lydia. Do, sir, will you inform us? (*To* Fag.)

Fag. Ma'am, I should hold myself very deficient in every requisite that forms the man of breeding, if I delayed a moment to give all the information in my power to a lady so deeply interested in the affair as you are.

Lydia. But quick! quick, sir!

Fag. True, ma'am, as you say, one should be quick in divulging matters of this nature; for should we be tedious, perhaps while we are flourishing on the subject, two or three lives may be lost!

Lydia. O patience! Do, ma'am, for Heaven's sake! tell us what is the matter?

Mrs. Mal. Why! murder's the matter! slaughter's the matter! killing's the matter! But he can tell you the perpendiculars.

Lydia. Then, prithee, sir, be brief.

Fag. Why then, ma'am, as to murder, I cannot take upon me to say; and as to slaughter, or manslaughter, that will be as the jury finds it

Lydia. But who, sir—who are engaged in this?

Fag. Faith, ma'am, one is a young gentleman whom I should be very sorry anything was to happen to, a very pretty behaved gentleman! We have lived much together, and always on terms.

Lydia. But who is this? who? who? who?

Fag. My master, ma'am—my master. I speak of my master.

Lydia. Heavens! What, Captain Absolute?

Mrs. Mal. O, to be sure, you are frightened now!

Julia. But who are with him, sir?

Fag. As to the rest, ma'am, this gentleman can inform you better than I.

Julia. Do speak, friend. (*To* David.)

David. Look'ee, my lady. By the mass! there's mischief going on. Folks don't use to meet for amusement with fire-arms, firelocks, fire-engines, fire-screens, fire-office, and the devil knows what other crackers beside! This, my lady, I say, has an angry savour.

Julia. But, who is there beside Captain Absolute, friend!

David. My poor master; under favour for mentioning him first. You know me, my lady; I am David, and my master of course is, or *was*, 'Squire Acres. Then comes 'Squire Faulkland.

Julia. Do, ma'am, let us instantly endeavour to prevent mischief.

Mrs. Mal. O fie, it would be very inelegant in us: we should only participate things.

David. Ah! do, Mrs. Aunt, save a few lives; they are desperately given, believe me. Above all, there is that blood-thirsty Philistine, Sir Lucius O'Trigger.

Mrs. Mal. Sir Lucius O'Trigger! O mercy! have they drawn poor little dear Sir Lucius into the scrape? Why, how you stand, girl! you have no more feeling than one of the Derbyshire petrefactions!

Lydia. What are we to do, madam?

Mrs. Mal. Why, fly with the utmost felicity, to be sure, to prevent mischief! Here, friend, you can show us the place.

Fag. If you please, ma'am, I will conduct you. David, do you look for Sir Anthony. [*Exit* David.

Mrs. Mal. Come, girls! this gentleman will exhort

us. Come, sir, you're our envoy; lead the way, and we'll precede.

Fag. Not a step before the ladies for the world!

Mrs. Mal. You're sure you know the spot?

Fag. I think I can find it, ma'am; and one good thing is, we shall hear the report of the pistols as we draw near, so we can't well miss them; never fear, ma'am, never fear. [*Exeunt, he talking.*

SCENE II.

SOUTH PARADE.

Enter ABSOLUTE, *putting his sword under his great coat.*

Abs. A sword seen in the streets of Bath would raise as great an alarm as a mad dog. How provoking this is in Faulkland! never punctual! I shall be obliged to go without him at last. O, the devil! here's Sir Anthony! How shall I escape him?
       [*Muffles up his face, and takes a circle to go off.*

Enter Sir ANTHONY.

Sir Anth. How one may be deceived at a little distance! only that I see he don't know me, I could have sworn that was Jack! Hey! Gad's life! it is. Why, Jack, what are you afraid of? hey!—sure I'm right. Why, Jack—Jack Absolute! [*Goes up to him.*

Abs. Really, sir, you have the advantage of me. I don't remember ever to have had the honour——my name is Saunderson, at your service.

Sir Anth. Sir, I beg your pardon. I took you—hey?—why, z—ds! it is——Stay——
          [*Looks up to his face.*

So, so; your humble servant, Mr. Saunderson! Why, you scoundrel, what tricks are you after now?

Abs. O! a joke, sir, a joke! I came here on purpose to look for you, sir.

Sir Anth. You did! Well, I am glad you were so lucky; but what are you muffled up so for? What's this for? hey?

Abs. 'Tis cool, sir; isn't it? Rather chilly, somehow. But I shall be late. I have a particular engagement.

Sir Anth. Stay. Why, I thought you were looking for me? Pray, Jack, where is't you are going?

Abs. Going, sir?

Sir Anth. Ay, where are you going?

Abs. Where am I going?

Sir Anth. You unmannerly puppy!

Abs. I was going, sir, to—to—to—to Lydia, sir; to Lydia; to make matters up if I could; and I was looking for you, sir, to—to——

Sir Anth. To go with you, I suppose. Well, come along.

Abs. O! z—ds! no, sir, not for the world! I wished to meet with you, sir, to—to—to——You find it cool, I'm sure, sir; you'd better not stay out.

Sir Anth. Cool! not at all. Well, Jack, and what will you say to Lydia?

Abs. O, sir, beg her pardon, humour her; promise and vow: but I detain you, sir; consider the cold air on your gout.

Sir Anth. O, not at all! not at all! I'm in no hurry. Ah! Jack, you youngsters, when once you are wounded here——

[*Putting his hand to* ABSOLUTE'S *breast.* Hey! what the deuce have you got here?

Abs. Nothing, sir; nothing.

Sir Anth. What's this? Here's something d—n'd hard.

Abs. O, trinkets, sir! trinkets—a bauble for Lydia!

Sir Anth. Nay, let me see your taste.

[*Pulls his coat open, the sword falls.*

Trinkets!—a bauble for Lydia! Z—ds! sirrah, you are not going to cut her throat, are you?

Abs. Ha! ha! ha! I thought it would divert you, sir, though I didn't mean to tell you till afterwards.

Sir Anth. You didn't? Yes, this is a very diverting trinket, truly.

Abs. Sir, I'll explain to you. You know, sir, Lydia is romantic—dev'lish romantic, and very absurd of course. Now, sir, I intend, if she refuses to forgive me—to unsheath this sword—and swear—I'll fall upon its point, and expire at her feet!

Sir Anth. Fall upon a fiddlestick's end! Why, I suppose it is the very thing that would please her. Get along, you fool.

Abs. Well, sir, you shall hear of my success—you shall hear. 'O, Lydia! forgive me, or this pointed steel'—says I.

Sir Anth. 'O, booby! stab away, and welcome'—says she. Get along! and d—n your trinkets!

[*Exit* ABSOLUTE.

Enter DAVID, *running.*

David. Stop him! Stop him! Murder! Thief! Fire! Stop fire! Stop fire! O! Sir Anthony—call! call! bid 'm stop! Murder! Fire!

Sir Anth. Fire! Murder! Where?

David. Oons! he's out of sight! and I'm out of breath! for my part! O, Sir Anthony, why didn't you stop him? why didn't you stop him?

Sir Anth. Z—ds! the fellow's mad! Stop whom! stop Jack?

David. Ay, the captain, sir! There's murder and slaughter——

Sir Anth. Murder!

David. Ay, please you, Sir Anthony, there's all kinds of murder, all sorts of slaughter to be seen in the fields: there's fighting going on, sir—bloody sword-and-gun-fighting!

Sir Anth. Who are going to fight, dunce?

David. Everybody that I know of, Sir Anthony:— everybody is going to fight, my poor master, Sir Lucius O'Trigger, your son, the captain——

Sir Anth. O, the dog! I see his tricks; do you know the place?

David. King's Mead-fields.

Sir Anth. You know the way?

David. Not an inch; but I'll call the mayor, aldermen, constables, churchwardens, and beadles; we can't be too many to part them.

Sir Anth. Come along; give me your shoulder! we'll get assistance as we go; the lying villain! Well, I shall be in such a phrensy. So, this was the history of his trinkets! I'll bauble him! [*Exeunt.*

SCENE III.

King's Mead-fields.

Sir Lucius and Acres with pistols.

Acres. By my valour! then, Sir Lucius, forty yards is a good distance. Odds levels and aims! I say it is a good distance.

Sir Luc. Is it for muskets or small field-pieces? upon my conscience, Mr. Acres, you must leave those things to me. Stay now; I'll show you.

[*Measures paces along the stage.*

There now, that is a very pretty distance—a pretty gentleman's distance.

Acres. Z—ds! we might as well fight in a sentry-box! I tell you, Sir Lucius, the farther he is off, the cooler I shall take my aim.

Sir Luc. Faith! then I suppose you would aim at him best of all if he was out of sight!

Acres. No, Sir Lucius, but I should think forty or eight-and-thirty yards——

Sir Luc. Pho! pho! nonsense! three or four feet between the mouths of your pistols is as good as a mile.

Acres. Odds bullets, no!—by my valour! there is no merit in killing him so near: do, my dear Sir Lucius, let me bring him down at a long shot:—a long shot, Sir Lucius, if you love me!

Sir Luc. Well, the gentleman's friend and I must settle that. But tell me now, Mr. Acres, in case of an accident, is there any little will or commission I could execute for you?

Acres. I am much obliged to you, Sir Lucius; but I don't understand——

Sir Luc. Why, you may think there's no being shot at without a little risk—and if an unlucky bullet should carry a quietus with it—I say it will be no time then to be bothering you about family matters.

Acres. A quietus!

Sir Luc. For instance, now, if that should be the case, would you choose to be pickled and sent home? or would it be the same to you to lie here in the Abbey? I'm told there is very snug lying in the Abbey.

Acres. Pickled! Snug lying in the Abbey! Odds tremors! Sir Lucius, don't talk so!

Sir Luc. I suppose, Mr. Acres, you never were engaged in an affair of this kind before?

Acres. No, Sir Lucius, never before.

Sir Luc. Ah! that's a pity! there's nothing like being used to a thing. Pray now, how would you receive the gentleman's shot?

Acres. Odds files! I've practised that—there, Sir Lucius—there.   [*Puts himself in an attitude.*—a side-front, hey? Odd! I'll make myself small enough. I'll stand edgeways.

Sir Luc. Now, you're quite out, for if you stand so when I take my aim——   [*Levelling at him.*

Acres. Z—ds! Sir Lucius—are you sure it is not cock'd?

Sir Luc. Never fear.

Acres. But—but—you don't know—it may go off of its own head!

Sir Luc. Pho! be easy. Well, now if I hit you in the body, my bullet has a double chance, for if it misses a vital part of your right side, 'twill be very hard if it don't succeed on the left!

Acres. A vital part!

Sir Luc. But, there—fix yourself so— [*Placing him.* let him see the broad-side of your full front—there—now a ball or two may pass clean through your body, and never do any harm at all.

Acres. Clean through me!—a ball or two clean through me!

Sir Luc. Ay — may they — and it is much the genteelest attitude into the bargain.

Acres. Look'ee! Sir Lucius—I'd just as lieve be shot in an awkward posture as a genteel one—so, by my valour! I will stand edgeways.

Sir Luc. (*Looking at his watch.*) Sure they don't mean to disappoint us. Hah! no faith—I think I see them coming.

Acres. Hey!—what!—coming!——

Sir Luc. Ay. Who are those yonder getting over the stile?

Acres. There are two of them indeed!—well—let them come; hey, Sir Lucius!—we—we—we—we—won't run.

Sir Luc. Run!

Acres. No—I say—we *won't* run, by my valour!

Sir Luc. What the devil's the matter with you?

Acres. Nothing—nothing—my dear friend—my dear Sir Lucius; but I—I—I don't feel quite so bold, somehow, as I did.

Sir Luc. O fie!—consider your honour.

Acres. Ay—true—my honour. Do, Sir Lucius, edge in a word or two every now and then about my honour.

Sir Luc. Well, here they're coming. [*Looking.*

Acres. Sir Lucius; if I wa'n't with you, I should almost think I was afraid; if my valour should leave me! Valour will come and go.

Sir Luc. Then pray keep it fast, while you have it.

Acres. Sir Lucius; I doubt it is going—yes—my valour is certainly going! it is sneaking off! I feel it oozing out as it were at the palms of my hands!

Sir Luc. Your honour—your honour. Here they are.

Acres. O mercy! now—that I was safe at Clod Hall! or could be shot before I was aware!

Enter FAULKLAND *and* ABSOLUTE.

Sir Luc. Gentlemen, your most obedient. Hah! what, Captain Absolute! So, I suppose, sir, you are come here, just like myself—to do a kind office, first for your friend—then to proceed to business on your own account.

Acres. What, Jack! my dear Jack! my dear friend!

Abs. Heark'ee, Bob, Beverley's at hand.

Sir Luc. Well, Mr. Acres; I don't blame your saluting the gentleman civilly. So, Mr. Beverley, (*to* FAULKLAND) if you'll choose your weapons, the captain and I will measure the ground.

Faulk. My weapons, sir.

Acres. Odds life! Sir Lucius, I'm not going to fight Mr. Faulkland; these are my particular friends.

Sir Luc. What, sir, did not you come here to fight Mr. Acres?

Faulk. Not I, upon my word, sir.

Sir Luc. Well, now, that's mighty provoking! But I hope, Mr. Faulkland, as there are three of us come on purpose for the game, you won't be so cantanckerous as to spoil the party by sitting out.

Abs. O pray, Faulkland, fight to oblige Sir Lucius.

Faulk. Nay, if Mr. Acres is so bent on the matter——

Acres. No, no, Mr. Faulkland, I'll bear my disappointment like a Christian. Look'ee, Sir Lucius, there's no occasion at all for me to fight; and if it is the same to you, I'd as lieve let it alone.

Sir Luc. Observe me, Mr. Acres; I must not be trifled with. You have certainly challenged somebody, and you came here to fight him. Now, if that gentleman is willing to represent him, I can't see, for my soul, why it isn't just the same thing.

Acres. Why no, Sir Lucius, I tell you, 'tis one Beverley I've challenged; a fellow, you see, that dare not show his face! If *he* were here, I'd make him give up his pretensions directly!

Abs. Hold, Bob; let me set you right; there is no

such man as Beverley in the case. The person who assumed that name is before you; and as his pretensions are the same in both characters, he is ready to support them in whatever way you please.

Sir Luc. Well, this is lucky. Now you have an opportunity——

Acres. What, quarrel with my dear friend Jack Absolute; not if he were fifty Beverleys! Z—ds! Sir Lucius, you would not have me so unnatural.

Sir Luc. Upon my conscience, Mr. Acres, your valour has *oozed* away with a vengeance!

Acres. Not in the least! Odds backs and abettors! I'll be your second with all my heart; and if you should get a *quietus*, you may command me entirely. I'll get you *snug lying* in the *Abbey here;* or *pickle* you, and send you over to Blunderbuss Hall, or anything of the kind, with the greatest pleasure.

Sir Luc. Pho! pho! you are little better than a coward.

Acres. Mind, gentlemen, he calls me a *coward;* coward was the word, by my valour!

Sir Luc. Well, sir?

Acres. Look'ee, Sir Lucius, 'tisn't that I mind the word coward; *coward* may be said in joke. But if you had called me a *poltroon*, odds daggers and balls——

Sir Luc. Well, sir?

Acres. —— I should have thought you a very ill-bred man.

Sir Luc. Pho! you are beneath my notice.

Abs. Nay, Sir Lucius, you can't have a better second than my friend Acres. He is a most *determined dog*, called in the country, *Fighting Bob.* He generally *kills a man a week*—don't you, Bob?

Acres. Ay, at home!

Sir Luc. Well then, captain, 'tis we must begin—so

come out, my little counsellor (*draws his sword*)—and ask the gentleman, whether he will resign the lady, without forcing you to proceed against him?

Abs. Come on then, sir (*draws*); since you won't let it be an amicable suit, here's my reply.

Enter Sir ANTHONY, DAVID, *and the* WOMEN.

David. Knock 'em all down, sweet Sir Anthony; knock down my master in particular, and bind his hands over to their good behaviour!

Sir Anth. Put up, Jack, put up, or I shall be in a phrensy. How came you in a duel, sir?

Abs. Faith, sir, that gentleman can tell you better than I; 'twas he called on me, and you know, sir, I serve his majesty.

Sir Anth. Here's a pretty fellow! I catch him going to cut a man's throat, and he tells me, he serves his majesty! Z—ds! sirrah, then how durst you draw the king's sword against one of his subjects?

Abs. Sir, I tell you! that gentleman called me out, without explaining his reasons.

Sir Anth. Gad! sir, how came you to call my son out, without explaining your reasons?

Sir Luc. Your son, sir, insulted me in a manner which my honour could not brook.

Sir Anth. Z—ds! Jack, how durst you insult the gentleman in a manner which his honour could not brook?

Mrs. Mal. Come, come, let's have no honour before ladies. Captain Absolute, come here. How could you intimidate us so? Here's Lydia has been terrified to death for you.

Abs. For fear I should be killed, or escape, ma'am?

Mrs. Mal. Nay, no delusions to the past. Lydia is convinced; speak, child.

Sir Luc. With your leave, ma'am, I must put in a word here. I believe I could interpret the young lady's silence. Now mark——

Lydia. What is it you mean, sir?

Sir Luc. Come, come, Delia, we must be serious now; this is no time for trifling.

Lydia. 'Tis true, sir; and your reproof bids me offer this gentleman my hand, and solicit the return of his affections.

Abs. O! my little angel, say you so? Sir Lucius, I perceive there must be some mistake here, with regard to the affront which you affirm I have given you. I can only say, that it could not have been intentional. And as you must be convinced, that I should not fear to support a real injury, you shall now see that I am not ashamed to atone for an inadvertency. I ask your pardon. But for this lady, while honoured with her approbation, I will support my claim against any man whatever.

Sir Anth. Well said, Jack, and I'll stand by you, my boy.

Acres. Mind, I give up all my claim. I make no pretensions to anything in the world; and if I can't get a wife, without fighting for her, by my valour! I'll live a bachelor.

Sir Luc. Captain, give me your hand; an affront handsomely acknowledged becomes an obligation; and as for the lady, if she chooses to deny her own handwriting, here—— [*Takes out letters.*

Mrs. Mal. O, he will dissolve my mystery! Sir Lucius, perhaps there's some mistake, perhaps I can illuminate——

Sir Luc. Pray, old gentlewoman, don't interfere where you have no business. Miss Languish, are you my Delia, or not?

Lydia. Indeed, Sir Lucius, I am not.

[LYDIA *and* ABSOLUTE *walk aside.*

Mrs. Mal. Sir Lucius O'Trigger, ungrateful as you are, I own the soft impeachment; pardon my blushes, I am Delia.

Sir Luc. You Delia—pho! pho! be easy.

Mrs. Mal. Why, thou barbarous Vandyke, those letters are mine. When you are more sensible of my benignity, perhaps I may be brought to encourage your addresses.

Sir Luc. Mrs. Malaprop, I am extremely sensible of your condescension; and whether you or Lucy have put this trick upon me, I am equally beholden to you. And, to show you I am not ungrateful, Captain Absolute, since you have taken that lady from me, I'll give you my Delia into the bargain.

Abs. I am much obliged to you, Sir Lucius; but here's my friend, fighting Bob, unprovided for.

Sir Luc. Hah! little Valour—here, will you make your fortune?

Acres. Odds wrinkles! No. But give me your hand, Sir Lucius; forget and forgive; but if ever I give you a chance of *pickling* me again, say Bob Acres is a dunce, that's all.

Sir Anth. Come, Mrs. Malaprop, don't be cast down; you are in your bloom yet.

Mrs. Mal. O Sir Anthony! men are all barbarians.

[*All retire but* JULIA *and* FAULKLAND.

Julia. He seems dejected and unhappy—not sullen; there was some foundation, however, for the tale he told me. O woman! how true should be your judgment, when your resolution is so weak!

Faulk. Julia! how can I sue for what I so little deserve? I dare not presume, yet Hope is the child of Penitence.

Julia. Oh! Faulkland, you have not been more faulty in your unkind treatment of me, than I am now in wanting inclination to resent it. As my heart honestly bids me place my weakness to the account of love, I should be ungenerous not to admit the same plea for yours.

Faulk. Now I shall be blest indeed!

[Sir ANTHONY *comes forward.*

Sir Anth. What's going on here? So you have been quarrelling too, I warrant. Come, Julia, I never interfered before; but let me have a hand in the matter at last. All the faults I have ever seen in my friend Faulkland seemed to proceed from what he calls the *delicacy* and *warmth* of his affection for you. There, marry him directly, Julia; you'll find he'll mend surprisingly! [*The rest come forward.*

Sir Luc. Come, now, I hope there is no dissatisfied person but what is content; for as I have been disappointed myself, it will be very hard if I have not the satisfaction of seeing other people succeed better——

Acres. You are right, Sir Lucius. So, Jack, I wish you joy. Mr. Faulkland the same. Ladies,—come now, to show you I'm neither vexed nor angry, odds tabors and pipes! I'll order the fiddles in half an hour to the New Rooms, and I insist on your all meeting me there.

Sir Anth. 'Gad! sir, I like your spirit; and at night we single lads will drink a health to the young couples, and a husband to Mrs. Malaprop.

Faulk. Our partners are stolen from us, Jack. I hope to be congratulated by each other; *yours* for having checked in time the errors of an ill-directed imagination, which might have betrayed an innocent heart; and *mine*, for having, by her gentleness and candour, reformed the unhappy temper of one, who by it made wretched whom he loved most, and tortured the heart he ought to have adored.

Abs. Well, Jack, we have both tasted the bitters, as well as the sweets, of love; with this difference only, that *you* always prepared the bitter cup for yourself, while *I*——

Lydia. Was always obliged to *me* for it, hey! Mr. Modesty? But come, no more of that; our happiness is now as unalloyed as general.

Julia. Then let us study to preserve it so; and while Hope pictures to us a flattering scene of future bliss, let us deny its pencil those colours which are too bright to be lasting. When hearts deserving happiness would unite their fortunes, Virtue would crown them with an unfading garland of modest, hurtless flowers; but ill-judging Passion will force the gaudier rose into the wreath, whose thorn offends them, when its leaves are dropt!

ST. PATRICK'S DAY:

or,

THE SCHEMING LIEUTENANT.

A FARCE.

DRAMATIS PERSONÆ,

AS ORIGINALLY ACTED AT COVENT GARDEN THEATRE IN NOVEMBER, 1775.

Lieutenant O'Connor . .	Mr. CLINCH.
Doctor Rosy	Mr. QUICK.
Justice Credulous . . .	Mr. LEE LEWIS.
Serjeant Trounce	Mr. BOOTH.
Corporal Flint	
Lauretta	Mrs. CARGILL.
Mrs. Bridget Credulous .	Mrs. PITT.

ST. PATRICK'S DAY.

ACT I.—SCENE I.

Enter TROUNCE, FLINT, *and four* SOLDIERS.

1st Sol. I say you are wrong; we should all speak together, each for himself, and all at once, that we may be heard the better.

2nd Sol. Right, Jack, we'll argue in platoons.

3rd Sol. Ay, ay, let him have our grievances in a volley, and if we be to have a spokesman, there's the corporal is the lieutenant's countryman, and knows his humour.

Cor. Let me alone for that. I served three years, within a bit, under his honour, in the Royal Inniskillions, and I never will see a sweeter tempered gentleman, nor one more free with his purse. I put a great shamrock in his hat this morning, and I'll be bound for him he'll wear it, was it as big as Steven's Green.

4th Sol. I say again then you talk like youngsters, like militia striplings: there's discipline, look'ee, in all things, whereof the sergeant must be our guide; he's a gentleman of words; he understands your foreign lingo, your figures, and such like auxiliaries in scoring. Confess now for a reckoning, whether in chalk or writing, ben't he your only man?

Cor. Why the sergeant is a scholar to be sure, and has the gift of reading.

Serg. Good soldiers, and fellow-gentlemen, if you make me your spokesman, you will show the more judgment; and let me alone for the argument. I'll be as loud as a drum, and point blank from the purpose.

All. Agreed, agreed.

Cor. O fait! here comes the lieutenant; now, sergeant.

Serg. So then, to order. Put on your mutiny looks; every man grumble a little to himself, and some of you hum the deserter's march.

Enter LIEUTENANT.

Lieut. Well, honest lads, what is it you have to complain of?

Sol. Ahem! hem!

Serg. So please your honour, the very grievance of the matter is this: ever since your honour differed with Justice Credulous, our innkeepers use us most scurvily. By my halbert, their treatment is such, that if your spirit was willing to put up with it, flesh and blood could by no means agree; so we humbly petition that your honour would make an end of the matter at once, by running away with the justice's daughter, or else get us fresh quarters; hem! hem!

Lieut. Indeed! Pray which of the houses use you ill?

1st Sol. There's the Red Lion an't half the civility of the old Red Lion.

2nd Sol. There's the White Horse, if he wasn't case-hardened, ought to be ashamed to show his face.

Lieut. Very well; the Horse and the Lion shall answer for it at the quarter sessions.

Serg. The two Magpies are civil enough: but the Angel uses us like devils, and the Rising Sun refuses us light to go to bed by.

Lieut. Then, upon my word, I'll have the Rising Sun put down, and the Angel shall give security for his good behaviour; but are you sure you do nothing to quit scores with them?

Cor. Nothing at all, your honour, unless now and then we happen to fling a cartridge into the kitchen fire or put a spatterdash or so into the soup; and sometimes Ned drums up and down stairs a little of a night.

Lieut. Oh, all that's fair; but hark'ee, lads, I must have no grumbling on St. Patrick's day; so here, take this, and divide it amongst you. But observe me now, show yourselves men of spirit, and don't spend sixpence of it in drink.

Serg. Nay, hang it, your honour, soldiers should never bear malice; we must drink St. Patrick's and your honour's health.

All. Oh, d—n malice! St. Patrick's and his honour by all means.

Cor. Come away, then, lads, and first we'll parade round the Market Cross, for the honour of King George.

1st Sol. Thank your honour. Come along; St. Patrick, his honour, and strong beer for ever!

[*Exit* SOLDIERS.

Lieut. Get along, you thoughtless vagabonds! yet, upon my conscience, 'tis very hard these poor fellows should scarcely have bread from the soil they would die to defend.

Enter Doctor Rosy.

Ah, my little Doctor Rosy, my Galen a-bridge, what's the news?

Doct. All things are as they were, my Alexander; the justice is as violent as ever: I felt his pulse on the matter again, and thinking his rage began to intermit, I wanted to throw in the bark of good advice, but it would not do. He says you and your cut-throats have a plot upon his life, and swears he had rather see his daughter in a scarlet fever than in the arms of a soldier.

Lieut. Upon my word the army is very much obliged to him. Well, then, I must marry the girl first, and ask his consent afterwards.

Doct. So, then, the case of her fortune is desperate, hey?

Lieut. Oh, hang fortune; let that take its chance; there is a beauty in Lauretta's simplicity, so pure a bloom upon her charms.

Doct. So there is, so there is. You are for beauty as nature made her, hey! No artificial graces, no cosmetic varnish, no beauty in grain, hey!

Lieut. Upon my word, doctor, you are right; the London ladies were always too handsome for me; then they are so defended, such a circumvallation of hoop, with a breast-work of whalebone, that would turn a pistol-bullet, much less Cupid's arrows; then turret on turret on top, with stores of concealed weapons, under pretence of black pins; and above all, a standard of feathers that would do honour to a knight of the Bath. Upon my conscience, I could as soon embrace an Amazon, armed at all points.

Doct. Right, right, my Alexander; my taste to a tittle.

Lieut. Then, doctor, though I admire modesty in women, I like to see their faces. I am for the changeable rose; but with one of these quality Amazons, if their midnight dissipations had left them blood enough to raise a blush, they have not room enough in their cheeks to show it. To be sure, bashfulness is a very pretty thing; but, in my mind, there is nothing on earth so impudent as an everlasting blush.

Doct. My taste, my taste. Well, Lauretta is none of these. Ah! I never see her but she puts me in mind of my poor dear wife.

Lieut. Ay, faith; in my opinion she can't do a worse thing. Now he is going to bother me about an old hag that has been dead these six years. [*Aside.*

Doct. Oh, poor Dolly! I never shall see her like again; such an arm for a bandage; veins that seemed to invite the lancet. Then her skin, smooth and white as a gallipot; her mouth as round and not larger than the mouth of a penny phial; her lips conserve of roses; and then her teeth—none of your sturdy fixtures—ache as they would, it was but a small pull, and out they came. I believe I have drawn half a score of her poor dear pearls (*weeps*)—but what avails her beauty? Death has no consideration; one must die as well as another.

Lieut. Oh, if he begins to moralize [*Takes out his snuff-box*].

Doct. Fair and ugly, crooked or straight, rich or poor—flesh is grass—flowers fade!

Lieut. Here, doctor, take a pinch, and keep up your spirits.

Doct. True, true, my friend; grief can't mend the matter—all's for the best; but such a woman was a great loss, lieutenant.

Lieut. To be sure, for doubtless she had mental accomplishments equal to her beauty.

Doct. Mental accomplishments! she would have stuffed an alligator, or pickled a lizard, with any apothecary's wife in the kingdom. Why, she could decipher a prescription, and invent the ingredients, almost as well as myself; then she was such a hand at making foreign waters! for Seltzer, Pyrmont, Islington, or Chalybeate, she never had her equal; and her Bath and Bristol springs exceeded the originals. Ah, poor Dolly! she fell a martyr to her own discoveries.

Lieut. How so, pray?

Doct. Poor soul! her illness was occasioned by her zeal in trying an improvement on the Spa-water, by an infusion of rum and acid.

Lieut. Ay, ay, spirits never agree with water-drinkers.

Doct. No, no, you mistake. Rum agreed with her well enough; it was not the rum that killed the poor dear creature, for she died of a dropsy. Well, she is gone never to return, and has left no pledge of our loves behind. No little babe, to hang like a label round papa's neck. Well, well, we are all mortal—sooner or later—flesh is grass—flowers fade.

Lieut. O, the devil! again!

Doct. Life's a shadow; the world a stage; we strut an hour.

Lieut. Here, doctor. [*Offers snuff.*

Doct. True, true, my friend; well, high grief can't cure it. All's for the best, hey! my little Alexander.

Lieut. Right, right; an apothecary should never be out of spirits. But come, faith, 'tis time honest Humphrey should wait on the justice; that must be our first scheme.

Doct. True, true; you should be ready; the clothes

are at my house, and I have given you such a character that he is impatient to have you; he swears you shall be his body-guard. Well, I honour the army, or I should never do so much to serve you.

Lieut. Indeed I am bound to you for ever, doctor; and when once I'm possessed of my dear Lauretta, I will endeavour to make work for you as fast as possible.

Doct. Now you put me in mind of my poor wife again.

Lieut. Ah, pray forget her a little: we shall be too late.

Doct. Poor Dolly!
Lieut. 'Tis past twelve.
Doct. Inhuman dropsy!
Lieut. The justice will wait.
Doct. Cropt in her prime!
Lieut. For heaven's sake, come!
Doct. Well, flesh is grass.
Lieut. O, the devil!
Doct. We must all die——
Lieut. Doctor!
Doct. Kings, lords, and common whores——
[*Forces him off.*

SCENE II.

Enter Lauretta *and* Bridget.

Lau. I repeat it again, mamma, officers are the prettiest men in the world, and Lieutenant O'Connor is the prettiest officer I ever saw.

Bri. For shame, Laura! how can you talk so? or if you must have a military man, there's Lieutenant Plow, or Captain Haycock, or Major Dray, the brewer, are all your admirers; and though they are peaceable, good kind of men, they have as large cockades, and become scarlet as well as the fighting folks.

Lau. Psha! you know, mamma, I hate militia officers; a set of ~~dunghill~~ cocks with spurs on—heroes scratch'd off a church door—clowns in military masquerade, wearing the dress without supporting the character. No, give me the bold upright youth, who makes love to-day, and his head shot off to-morrow. Dear! to think how the sweet fellows sleep on the ground, and fight in silk stockings and lace ruffles.

Bri. Oh, barbarous! to want a husband that may wed you to-day, and be sent the Lord knows where before night; then in a twelvemonth perhaps to have him come like a Colossus, with one leg at New York and the other at Chelsea Hospital.

Lau. Then I'll be his crutch, mamma.

Bri. No, give me a husband that knows where his limbs are, though he want the use of them: and if he should take you with him, to sleep in a baggage-cart, and stroll about the camp like a gypsy, with a knapsack and two children at your back; then, by way of entertainment in the evening, to make a party with the sergeant's wife to drink Bohea tea, and play at all-fours on a drum-head! 'Tis a precious life, to be sure.

Lau. Nay, mamma, you shouldn't be against my lieutenant, for I heard him say you were the best natured and best looking woman in the world.

Bri. Why, child, I never said but that Lieutenant O'Connor was a very well-bred and discerning young man; 'tis your papa is so violent against him.

Lau. Why, cousin Sophy married an officer.
Bri. Ay, Laury, an officer in the militia.
Lau. No, indeed, mamma, a marching regiment.
Bri. No, child, I tell you he was a major of militia.
Lau. Indeed, mamma, it wasn't.

Enter JUSTICE.

Just. Bridget, my love, I have had a message.
Lau. It was cousin Sophy told me so.
Just. I have had a message, love——
Bri. No, child, she would say no such thing.
Just. A message, I say.
Lau. How could he be in the militia, when he was ordered abroad?
Bri. Ay, girl, hold your tongue. Well, my dear.
Just. I have had a message from Doctor Rosy.
Bri. He ordered abroad! He went abroad for his health.
Just. Why, Bridget——
Bri. Well, deary. Now hold your tongue, Miss.
Just. A message from Doctor Rosy, and Doctor Rosy says——
Lau. I'm sure, mamma, his regimentals——
Just. D—n his regimentals! Why don't you listen?
Bri. Ay, girl, how durst you interrupt your papa?
Lau. Well, papa.
Just. Doctor Rosy says he'll bring——
Lau. Were blue turn'd up with red, mamma.
Just. Laury!—says he will bring the young man——
Bri. Red! yellow, if you please, Miss.
Just. Bridget; the young man that is to be hired——
Bri. Besides, Miss, it is very unbecoming in you to want to have the last word with your mamma; you should know——

Just. Why z—ds! will you hear me or no?

Bri. I am listening, my love; I am listening. But what signifies my silence, what good is my not speaking a word, if this girl will interrupt and let nobody speak but herself? Ay, I don't wonder, my life, at your impatience; your poor dear lips quiver to speak; but I suppose she'll run on, and not let you put in a word. You may very well be angry; there is nothing sure so provoking as a chattering, talking——

Lau. Nay, I'm sure, mamma, it is you will not let papa speak now.

Bri. Why, you little provoking minx——

Just. Get out of the room directly, both of you; get out!

Bri. Ay, go, girl.

Just. Go, Bridget; you are worse than she, you old hag. I wish you were both up to the neck in the canal, to argue there till I took you out.

Enter SERVANT.

Ser. Doctor Rosy, sir.

Just. Show him up. [*Exit* SERVANT.

Lau. Then you own, mamma, it was a marching regiment?

Bri. You're an obstinate fool, I tell you; for if that had been the case——

Just. You won't go?

Bri. We are going, Mr. Surly. If that had been the case, I say, how could——

Lau. Nay, mamma, one proof.

Bri. How could major——

Lau. And a full proof——

[JUSTICE *drives them off.*

Just. There they go, ding dong in for the day. Good lack! a fluent tongue is the only thing a mother don't like her daughter to resemble her in.

Enter Doctor Rosy.

Well, Doctor, where's the lad—where's trusty?

Doct. At hand; he'll be here in a minute, I'll answer for't. He's such a one as you an't met with: strong as a black draught, gentle as a saline draught.

Just. Ah, he comes in the place of a rogue, a dog that was corrupted by the lieutenant. But this is a sturdy fellow, is he, doctor?

Doct. As Hercules; and the best back-sword in the country. Egad, he'll make the red-coats keep their distance.

Just. O the villains! this is St. Patrick's Day, and the rascals have been parading my house all the morning. I know they have a design upon me; but I have taken all precautions: I have magazines of arms, and if this fellow does but prove faithful, I shall be more at ease.

Doct. Doubtless he'll be a comfort to you.

Enter SERVANT.

Ser. There is a man below, sir, inquires for Doctor Rosy.

Doct. Show him up.

Just. Hold! a little caution: how does he look?

Ser. A country-looking fellow, your worship.

Just. O, well, well, for Doctor Rosy; these rascals try all ways to get in here.

Ser. Yes, please your worship; there was one here this morning wanted to speak to you: he said his name was Corporal Breakbones.

Just. Corporal Breakbones!

Ser. And Drummer Crackskull came again.

Just. Ay! did you ever hear of such a d—d confounded crew? Well, show the lad in here!

[*Exit* SERVANT.

Doct. Ay, he'll be your porter; he'll give the rogues an answer.

Enter LIEUTENANT, *disguised as* HUMPHREY.

Just. So, a tall——Efacks! what! has lost an eye?

Doct. Only a bruise he got in taking seven or eight highwaymen.

Just. He has a d—d wicked leer somehow with the other.

Doct. O, no, he's bashful—a sheepish look——

Just. Well, my lad, what's your name?

Lieut. Humphrey Hum.

Just. Hum. I don't like Hum!

Lieut. But I be mostly call'd honest Humphrey——

Doct. There, I told you so, of noted honesty.

Just. Well, honest Humphrey, the doctor has told you my terms, and you are willing to serve, hey?

Lieut. And please your worship, I shall be well content.

Just. Well, then, hark'ee, honest Humphrey, you are sure now you will never be a rogue—never take a bribe, hey, honest Humphrey?

Lieut. A bribe! what's that?

Just. A very ignorant fellow indeed.

Doct. His worship hopes you will never part with your honesty for money.

Lieut. Noa, noa.

Just. Well said, Humphrey; my chief business with you is to watch the motions of a rake-helly fellow here, one Lieutenant O'Connor.

Doct. Ay, you don't value the soldiers, do you, Humphrey?

Lieut. Not I; they are but zwaggerers, and you'll see they'll be as much afraid of me as they would of their captain.

Just. And i'faith, Humphrey, you have a pretty cudgel there!

Lieut. Ay, the zwitch is better than nothing, but I should be glad of a stouter. Ha' you got such a thing in the house as an old coach-pole, or a spare bed-post?

Just. Oons! what a dragon it is! Well, Humphrey, come with me. I'll just show him to Bridget, doctor, and we'll agree. Come along, honest Humphrey. [*Exit.*

Lieut. My dear doctor, now remember to bring the justice presently to the walk; I have a scheme to get into his confidence at once.

Doct. I will, I will.

[*Shakes hands;* JUSTICE *enters, and sees them.*

Just. Why, honest Humphrey, hey! what the devil are you at?

Doct. I was just giving him a little advice. Well, I must go for the present. Good morning to your worship; you need not fear the lieutenant while he is in your house.

Just. Well, get in, Humphrey. Good morning to you, doctor. (*Exit* DOCTOR.) Come along, Humphrey. Now I think I am a match for the lieutenant and all his gang. [*Exeunt.*

ACT II.—SCENE I.

Enter TROUNCE, DRUMMER, *and* SOLDIERS.

Serg. Come, silence your drum; there is no valour stirring to-day. I thought St. Patrick would have given us a recruit or two to-day.

Sol. Mark, sergeant.

Enter two COUNTRYMEN.

Serg. Oh! these are the lads I was looking for; they have the looks of gentlemen. A'n't you single, my lads?

1st Coun. Yes, an please you, I be quite single; my relations be all dead, thank heavens, more or less. I have but one poor mother left in the world, and she's an helpless woman.

Serg. Indeed! a very extraordinary case; quite your own master then? the fitter to serve his majesty. Can you read?

1st Coun. Noa, I was always too lively to take to learning; but John here is main clever at it.

Serg. So, what you're a scholar, friend?

2nd Coun. I was born so, measter. Feyther kept grammar-school.

Serg. Lucky man; in a campaign or two put yourself down chaplain to the regiment. And I warrant you have read of warriors and heroes?

2nd Coun. Yes, that I have. I have read of Jack the Giantkiller, and the Dragon of Wantly, and the——Noa, I believe that's all in the hero way, except once about a comet.

Serg. Wonderful knowledge! Well, my heroes, I'll write word to the king of your good intentions, and meet me half an hour hence at the Two Magpies.

Coun. We will, your honour, we will.

Serg. But stay; for fear I shou'dn't see you again in the crowd, clap these little bits of ribbon into your hats.

1st Coun. Our hats are none of the best.

Serg. Well, meet me at the Magpies, and I'll give you money to buy new ones.

Coun. Bless your honour, thank your honour.
[*Exit.*

Serg. (*Winking at* SOL.) Jack. [*Exeunt* SOLDIERS.

Enter LIEUTENANT.

So, here comes one who would make a grenadier. Stop, friend, will you list?

Lieut. Who shall I serve under?

Serg. Under me, to be sure.

Lieut. Isn't Lieutenant O'Connor your officer?

Serg. He is, and I am commander over him.

Lieut. What! be your sergeants greater than your captains?

Serg. To be sure we are; 'tis our business to keep them in order. For instance now, the general writes to me, dear Sergeant, or dear Trounce, or dear Sergeant Trounce, according to his hurry, if your lieutenant does not demean himself accordingly, let me know. Yours, General Deluge.

Lieut. And do you complain of him often?

Serg. No, hang him, the lad is good-natured at bottom, so I pass over small things. But hark'ee, between ourselves, he is most confoundedly given to wenching.

Enter CORPORAL.

Cor. Please your honour, the doctor is coming this way with his worship. We are all ready, and have our cues.

Lieut. Then, my dear Trounce, or my dear Sergeant Trounce, take yourself away.

Serg. Z—ds! the lieutenant. I smell of the black-hole already. [*Exit.*

Enter JUSTICE *and* DOCTOR.

Just. I thought I saw some of the cut-throats.

Doct. I fancy not; there's no one but honest Humphrey. Ha! Odds life, here comes some of them; we'll stay by these trees, and let them pass.

Just. Oh, the bloody-looking dogs! [*Walks aside.*

Enter CORPORAL *and two* SOLDIERS.

Cor. Halloa, friend! do you serve Justice Credulous?

Lieut. I do.

Cor. Are you rich?

Lieut. Noa.

Cor. Nor ever will with that old stingy booby. Look here, take it. [*Gives him a purse.*

Lieut. What must I do for this?

Cor. Mark me, our lieutenant is in love with the old rogue's daughter: help us to break his worship's bones and carry off the girl, and you are a made man.

Lieut. I'll see you hanged first, you pack of skurry villains! [*Throws away the purse.*

Cor. What, sirrah, do you mutiny? Lay hold of him.

Lieut. Nay then, I'll try your armour for you.
[*Beats them.*

All. Oh! oh! Quarter! quarter! [*Exeunt.*

Just. Trim them, trounce them, break their bones, honest Humphrey. What a spirit he has!

Doct. Aquafortis.

Lieut. Betray your master!

Doct. What a miracle of fidelity!

Just. Ay, and it shall not go unrewarded. I'll give him sixpence on the spot. Here, honest Humphrey, there's for yourself: as for this bribe (*takes up the purse*), such trash is best in the hands of justice. Now then, doctor, I think I may trust him to guard the women: while he is with them I may go out with safety.

Doct. Doubtless you may. I'll answer for the lieutenant's behaviour whilst honest Humphrey is with your daughter.

Just. Ay, ay, she shall go nowhere without him. Come along, honest Humphrey. How rare it is to meet with such a servant! [*Exeunt.*

SCENE II.

A Garden. LAURETTA *discovered.*

Enter JUSTICE *and* LIEUTENANT.

Just. Why, you little truant, how durst you wander so far from the house without my leave? Do you want to invite that scoundrel lieutenant to scale the walls, and carry you off?

Lau. Lud, papa, you are so apprehensive for nothing.

Just. Why, hussy——

Lau. Well, then, I can't bear to be shut up all day so like a nun. I am sure it is enough to make one wish to be run away with, and I wish I was run away with, I do, and I wish the lieutenant knew it.

Just. You do, do you, hussy? Well, I think I'll take pretty good care of you. Here, Humphrey, I leave this lady in your care. Now you may walk about the garden, Miss Pert; but Humphrey shall go with you wherever you go. So mind, honest Humphrey, I am obliged to go abroad for a little while; let no one but yourself come near her: don't be shame-faced, you booby, but keep close to her. And now, Miss, let your lieutenant or any of his crew come near you if they can. [*Exit.*

Lau. How this booby stares after him!

[*Sits down and sings.*

Lieut. Lauretta!

Lau. Not so free, fellow! [*Sings.*

Lieut. Lauretta! look on me.

Lau. Not so free, fellow!

Lieut. No recollection!

Lau. Honest Humphrey, be quiet.

Lieut. Have you forgot your faithful soldier?

Lau. Ah! O preserve me!

Lieut. 'Tis my soul! your truest slave, passing on your father in this disguise.

Lau. Well now, I declare this is charming; you are so disguised, my dear lieutenant, and you do look so delightfully ugly. I am sure no one will find you out, ha! ha! ha! You know I am under your protection; papa charged you to keep close to me.

Lieut. True, my angel, and thus let me fulfil——

Lau. O pray now, dear Humphrey——

Lieut. Nay, 'tis but what old Mittimus commanded.
  [*Offers to kiss her—Enter* JUSTICE.

Just. Laury, my——hey! what the devil's here?

Lau. Well now, one kiss, and be quiet.

Just. Your very humble servant, honest Humphrey. Don't let me—pray don't let me interrupt you!

Lau. Lud, papa. Now that's so good-natured—indeed there's no harm. You did not mean any rudeness, did you, Humphrey?

Lieut. No, indeed, Miss; his worship knows it is not in me.

Just. I know that you are a lying, canting, hypocritical scoundrel; and if you don't take yourself out of my sight——

Lau. Indeed, papa, now I'll tell you how it was. I was sometime taken with a sudden giddiness, and Humphrey, seeing me beginning to totter, ran to my assistance, quite frightened, poor fellow! and took me in his arms.

Just. Oh! was that all; nothing but a little giddiness, hey?

Lieut. That's all, indeed, your worship; for seeing Miss change colour, I ran up instantly.

Just. O, 'twas very kind in you.

Lieut. And luckily recovered her.

Just. And who made you a doctor, you impudent rascal, hey? Get out of my sight, I say, this instant, or by all the statutes——

Lau. O now, papa, you frighten me, and I am giddy again. Oh, help!

Lieut. O, dear lady, she'll fall!
  [*Takes her into his arms.*

Just. Z—ds! what, before my face; why then, thou miracle of impudence! (*Lays hold of him, and discovers him.*) Mercy on me! who have we here? Murder! Robbery! Fire! Rape! Gunpowder! Soldiers! John! Susan! Bridget!

Lieut. Good sir, don't be alarmed; I mean you no harm.

Just. Thieves! Robbers! Soldiers!

Lieut. You know my love for your daughter——

Just. Fire! Cut-throats!

Lieut. And that alone——

Just. Treason! Gunpowder! [*Enter a Servant with a blunderbuss.*] Now, scoundrel! let her go this instant.

Lau. O papa, you'll kill me!

Just. Honest Humphrey, be advised. Ay, Miss, this way, if you please.

Lieut. Nay, sir, but hear me——

Just. I'll shoot.

Lieut. And you'll be convinced——

Just. I'll shoot.

Lieut. How injurious——

Just. I'll shoot; and so your very humble servant, honest Humphrey Hum. [*Exeunt separately.*

SCENE III.

A Walk.

Enter Doctor ROSY.

Doct. Well, I think my friend is now in a fair way of succeeding. Ah! I warrant he is full of hope and fear, doubt and anxiety; truly he has the fever of love strong upon him; faint, peevish, languishing all day, with burning, restless nights. Ah! just my case when I pined for my dear Dolly! when she used to have her daily colics, that her little doctor be sent for. Then would I interpret the language of her pulse; declare my own sufferings in my receipt for her; send her a pearl necklace in a pill-box, or a cordial draught with an acrostic on the label. Well, those days are over; no happiness lasting; all is vanity—now sunshine, now cloudy—we are, as it were, king and beggar: then what avails——

Enter LIEUTENANT.

Lieut. O doctor! ruined and undone.
Doct. The pride of beauty——
Lieut. I am discovered, and——
Doct. The gaudy palace——
Lieut. The justice is——
Doct. The pompous wig——
Lieut. Is more enraged than ever.
Doct. The gilded cane——
Lieut. Why, doctor! (*Slapping him on the shoulder.*)
Doct. Hey!
Lieut. Confound your morals! I tell you I am discovered, discomfited, disappointed.
Doct. Indeed! Good lack, good lack, to think of the instability of human affairs. Nothing certain in this world; most deceived when most confident; fools of fortune all.
Lieut. My dear doctor, I want at present a little practical wisdom; I am resolved this instant to try the scheme we were going to put into execution last week. I have the letter ready, and only want your assistance to recover my ground.

Doct. With all my heart; I'll warrant you I'll bear a part in it: but how the deuce were you discovered?

Lieut. I'll tell you as we go; there's not a moment to be lost.

Doct. Heaven send we succeed better; but there's no knowing.

Lieut. Very true.

Doct. We may, and we may not.

Lieut. Right.

Doct. Time must show.

Lieut. Certainly.

Doct. We are but blind guessers.

Lieut. Nothing more.

Doct. Thick-sighted mortals.

Lieut. Remarkably.

Doct. Wandering in error.

Lieut. Even so.

Doct. Futurity is dark.

Lieut. As a cellar.

Doct. Men are moles.

[LIEUTENANT *forcing him out.*

SCENE IV.

Justice's House.

Enter JUSTICE *and* BRIDGET.

Just. Odds life, Bridget, you are enough to make one mad! I tell you he would have deceived a chief justice: the dog seemed as ignorant as my clerk, and talked of honesty as if he had been a churchwarden.

Bri. Pho! nonsense, honesty. What had you to do, pray, with honesty? A fine business you have made of it with your Humphrey Hum; and Miss too, she must have been privy to it. Lauretta, ay, you would have her called so; but for my part, I never knew any good come of giving girls these heathen Christian names; if you had called her Deborah, or Tabitha, or Ruth, or Rebecca, or Joan, nothing of this had ever happened: but I always knew Lauretta was a runaway name.

Just. Psha, you're a fool.

Bri. No, Mr. Credulous, it is you who are a fool, and no one but such a simpleton would be so imposed on.

Just. Why, z—ds! madam, how durst you talk so? if you have no respect for your husband, I should think unus quorum might command a little deference.

Bri. Don't tell me. Unus fiddlestick! you ought to be ashamed to show your face at the sessions: you'll be a laughing-stock to the whole bench, and a by-word with all the pig-tailed lawyers and bag-wigged attorneys about town.

Just. Is this language for his majesty's representative? By the statutes, it's high treason and petty treason, both at once.

Enter SERVANT.

Serv. A letter for your worship.

Just. Who brought it?

Serv. A soldier.

Just. Take it away, and burn it.

Bri. Stay. Now you're in such a hurry; it is some canting scrawl from the lieutenant, I suppose; let me see. Ay, 'tis signed O'Connor.

Just. Well, come, read it out.

Bri. 'Revenge is sweet.'

Just. It begins so, does it? I'm glad of that; I'll let the dog know I'm of his opinion.

Bri. 'And though disappointed of my designs upon your daughter, I have still the satisfaction of knowing I'm revenged on her unnatural father; for this morning, in your chocolate, I had the pleasure to administer to you a dose of poison.' Mercy on us!

Just. No tricks, Bridget; come, you know it is not so; you know it is a lie.

Bri. Read it yourself.

Just. 'Pleasure to administer a dose of poison.' O horrible! Cut-throat villain! Bridget!

Bri. Lovee, stay; here's a postscript. 'N.B. 'Tis not in the power of medicine to save you.'

Just. Odds my life, Bridget! why don't you call for help? I've lost my voice. My brain is giddy. I shall burst, and no assistance. John! Laury! John!

Bri. You see, lovee, what you have brought on yourself.

Enter SERVANT.

Ser. Your worship.

Just. Stay, John; did you perceive anything in my chocolate cup this morning?

Ser. Nothing, your worship, unless it was a little grounds.

Just. What colour were they?

Ser. Blackish, your worship.

Just. Ay, arsenic, black arsenic. Why don't you run for Doctor Rosy, you rascal?

Ser. Now, sir?

Bri. O! lovee, you may be sure it is in vain: let him run for the lawyer to witness your will, my life.

Just. Z—ds! go for the doctor, you scoundrel. You are all confederate murderers.

Ser. O, here he is, your worship. [*Exit.*

Just. Now, Bridget, hold your tongue, and let me see if my horrid situation be apparent.

Enter DOCTOR.

Doct. I have but just called to inform——Hey! bless me, what's the matter with your worship?

Just. There, he sees it already. Poison in my face, in capitals. Yes, yes, I'm a sure job for the undertakers indeed.

Bri. Oh! oh! alas, doctor!

Just. Peace, Bridget. Why, doctor, my dear old friend, do you really see any change in me?

Doct. Change! never was man so altered. How came these black spots on your nose?

Just. Spots on my nose!

Doct. And that wild stare in your right eye?

Just. In my right eye!

Doct. Ay, and alack, alack, how you are swelled!

Just. Swelled!

Doct. Ay, don't you think he is, madam?

Bri. O, 'tis in vain to conceal it: indeed, lovee, you are as big again as you were this morning.

Just. Yes, I feel it now, I'm poisoned. Doctor, help me, for the love of justice. Give me life to see my murderer hanged.

Doct. What?

Just. I'm poisoned, I say!

Doct. Speak out!

Just. What! can't you hear me?

Doct. Your voice is so low and hollow, as it were, I can't hear a word you say.

Just. I'm gone then: hic jacet, many years one of his majesty's justices.

Bri. Read, doctor. Ah, lovee, the will. Consider, my life, how soon you will be dead.

Just. No, Bridget, I shall die by inches.

Doct. I never heard such monstrous iniquity. Oh, you are gone indeed, my friend: the mortgage of your little bit of clay is out, and the sexton has nothing to do but to close. We must all go, sooner or later, high and low. Death's a debt; his mandamus binds all alike. No bail, no demurrer.

Just. Silence, Doctor Croaker. Will you cure me, or will you not?

Doct. Alas! my dear friend, it is not in my power, but I'll certainly see justice done on your murderer.

Just. I thank you, my dear friend, but I had rather see it myself.

Doct. Ay, but if you recover, the villain will escape.

Bri. Will he? then indeed it would be a pity you should recover. I am so enraged against the villain, I can't bear the thought of his escaping the halter.

Just. That's very kind in you, my dear; but, if it's the same thing to you, my dear, I had as soon recover, notwithstanding. What, doctor, no assistance!

Doct. Efacks, I can do nothing; but there's the German quack, whom you wanted to send from town; I met him at the next door, and I know he has antidotes for all poisons.

Just. Fetch him, my dear friend, fetch him: I'll get him a diploma if he cures me.

Doct. Well, there's no time to be lost; you continue to swell immensely. [*Exit.*

Bri. What, my dear, will you submit to be cured by a quack nostrum-monger? For my part, as much as I love you, I had rather follow you to your grave than see you owe your life to any but a regular-bred physician.

Just. I'm sensible of your affection, dearest; and be assured nothing consoles me in my melancholy situation so much as the thoughts of leaving you behind.

Enter Doctor *and* Lieutenant, *disguised.*

Doct. Great luck; met him passing by the door.
Lieut. Metto dowsei pulsum.
Doct. He desires me to feel your pulse.
Just. Can't he speak English?
Doct. Not a word.
Lieut. Palio vivem mortem soonem.
Doct. He says you have not six hours to live.
Just. O mercy! does he know my distemper?
Doct. I believe not.
Just. Tell him 'tis black arsenic they have given me.
Doct. Geneable illi arsnecca.
Lieut. Pisonatus.
Just. What does he say?
Doct. He says you are poisoned.
Just. We know that; but what will be the effect?
Doct. Quid effectum?
Lieut. Diable tutellum.
Doct. He says you'll die presently.
Just. Oh horrible! What, no antidote?
Lieut. Curum benakere bono fullum.
Just. What, does he say I must row in a boat to Fulham?
Doct. He says he'll undertake to cure you for three thousand pounds.
Bri. Three thousand pounds! three thousand halters! No, lovee, you shall never submit to such

impositions: die at once, and be a customer to none of them.

Just. I won't die, Bridget; I don't like death.

Bri. Pshaw! there is nothing in it; a moment, and it is over.

Just. Ay, but it leaves a numbness behind that lasts a plaguy long time.

Bri. O my dear, pray consider the will.

Enter LAURETTA.

Lau. O, my father, what is this I hear?

Lieut. Quiddam seomriam deos tollam rosam.

Doct. The doctor is astonished at the sight of your fair daughter.

Just. How so?

Lieut. Damsellum livivum suvum rislibani.

Doct. He says that he has lost his heart to her, and that if you will give him leave to pay his addresses to the young lady, and promise your consent to the union, if he should gain her affections, he will on those conditions cure you instantly, without fee or reward.

Just. The devil! Did he say all that in so few words? What a fine language it is! Well, I agree, if he can prevail on the girl; and that I am sure he never will. [*Aside.*

Doct. Greal.

Lieut. Writhum bothum.

Doct. He says you must give this under your hand, while he writes you a miraculous receipt.

[*Both sit down to write.*

Lau. Do, mamma, tell me the meaning of this.

Bri. Don't speak to me, girl. Unnatural parent!

Just. There, doctor; there's what he requires.

Doct. And here's your receipt; read it yourself.

Just. Hey! what's here! plain English?

Doct. Read it out; a wondrous nostrum, I'll answer for it.

Just. " In reading this you are cured, by your affectionate son-in-law, O'Connor." Who, in the name of Beelzebub, sirrah, who are you?

Lieut. Your affectionate son-in-law, O'Connor, and your very humble servant, Humphrey Hum.

Just. 'Tis false, you dog, you are not my son-in-law; for I'll be poisoned again, and you shall be hanged. I'll die, sirrah, and leave Bridget my estate.

Bri. Ay, pray do, my dear, leave me your estate. I'm sure he deserves to be hanged.

Just. He does, you say; hark'ee, Bridget, you showed such a tender concern for me when you thought me poisoned, that for the future I am resolved never to take your advice again in anything. So, do you hear, sir, you are an Irishman and a soldier, an't you?

Lieut. I am, sir, and proud of both.

Just. The two things on earth I most hate; so I'll tell you what—renounce your country and sell your commission, and I'll forgive you.

Lieut. Hark'ee, Mr. Justice, if you were not the father of my Lauretta, I would pull your nose for asking the first, and break your bones for desiring the second.

Doct. Ay, ay, you're right.

Just. Is he? then I'm sure I must be wrong. Here, sir, I give my daughter to you, who are the most impudent dog I ever saw in my life.

Lieut. O, sir, say what you please; with such a gift as Lauretta, every word is a compliment.

Bri. Well, my lovee, I think this will be a good subject for us to quarrel about the rest of our lives.

Just. Why, truly, my dear, I think so, though we are seldom at a loss for that.

Doct. This is all as it should be. My Alexander, I give you joy, and you, my little god-daughter; and now my sincere wish is, that you may make just such a wife as my poor dear Dolly.

THE DUENNA:

A COMIC OPERA.

DRAMATIS PERSONÆ.

AS ORIGINALLY ACTED AT COVENT GARDEN THEATRE ON TUESDAY, NOVEMBER 21, 1775.

Don Ferdinand	Mr. MATTOCKS.
Isaac Mendoza	Mr. QUICK.
Don Jerome	Mr. WILSON.
Don Antonio	Mr. DUBELLAMY.
Father Paul	Mr. MAHON.
Lopez	Mr. WEWITZER.
Don Carlos	Mr. LEONI.
Francis	Mr. FOX.
Lay Brother	Mr. BAKER.
Donna Lousia	Mrs. MATTOCKS.
Donna Clara	Mrs. CARGILL.
The Duenna	Mrs. GREEN.

THE
DUENNA.

ACT I.—SCENE I.

A Street.

Enter LOPEZ, *with a dark lantern.*

Lop. PAST three o'clock! soh! a notable hour for one of my regular disposition, to be strolling like a bravo through the streets of Seville! Well, of all services, to serve a young lover is the hardest—not that I am an enemy to love; but my love, and my master's differ strangely. Don Ferdinand is much too gallant to eat, drink, or sleep; now, my love gives me an appetite; then I am fond of dreaming of my mistress, and I love dearly to toast her. This cannot be done without good sleep and good liquor; hence my partiality to a feather-bed and a bottle. What a pity now, that I have not further time for reflections! but my master expects thee, honest Lopez, to secure his retreat from Donna Clara's window, as I guess [*Music without*]——hey! sure, I heard music! So, so! who have we here? Oh, Don Antonio, my master's friend, come from the masquerade, to serenade my young mistress, Donna Louisa, I suppose: soh! we shall have the old gentleman up presently; lest he should miss his son, I had best lose no time in getting to my post.

[*Exit.*

Enter ANTONIO, *with Masks and Music.*

SONG.

Ant. Tell me, my lute, can thy soft strain
So gently speak thy master's pain,
So softly sing, so humbly sigh,
  That, though my sleeping love shall know
  Who sings—who sighs below,
Her rosy slumbers shall not fly?
  Thus, may some vision whisper more
  Than ever I dare speak before.

1 *Mask.* Antonio, your mistress will never wake, while you sing so dolefully: love, like a cradled infant, is lulled by a sad melody.

Ant. I do not wish to disturb her rest.

1 *Mask.* The reason is, because you know she does not regard you enough to appear, if you awaked her.

Ant. Nay, then, I'll convince you.   [*Sings.*

  The breath of morn bids hence the night,
  Unveil those beauteous eyes, my fair;
  For till the dawn of love is there,
  I feel no day, I own no light.

LOUISA—*replies from a Window.*

  Waking, I heard thy numbers chide,
    Waking, the dawn did bless my sight;
  'Tis Phœbus sure, that woos, I cried,
    Who speaks in song, who moves in light.

Don Jerome—*from a Window.*

What vagabonds are these, I hear,
Fiddling, fluting, rhyming, ranting,
Piping, scraping, whining, canting?
Fly, scurvy minstrels, fly!

TRIO.

Louisa. Nay, pr'ythee, father, why so rough?
Ant. An humble lover I.
Jerome. How durst you, daughter, lend an ear
To such deceitful stuff?
Quick, from the window fly!
Louisa. Adieu, Antonio!
Ant. Must you go?
Louisa. } We soon, perhaps, may meet again;
Ant. } For though hard fortune is our foe,
The god of love will fight for us.
Jerome. Reach me the blunderbuss.
Ant. & L. The god of love, who knows no pain——
Jerome. Hence, or these slugs are through your brain.
[*Exeunt severally.*

SCENE II.

A Piazza.

Enter Ferdinand *and* Lopez.

Lopez. Truly, sir, I think that a little sleep, once in a week or so——
Ferd. Peace, fool, don't mention sleep to me.

Lopez. No, no, sir, I don't mention your low-bred, vulgar, sound sleep; but I can't help thinking that a gentle slumber, or half an hour's dozing, if it were only for the novelty of the thing——

Ferd. Peace, booby, I say! Oh Clara, dear, cruel disturber of my rest!

Lopez. And of mine too.

Ferd. 'Sdeath! to trifle with me at such a juncture as this! now to stand on punctilios. Love me! I don't believe she ever did.

Lopez. Nor I either.

Ferd. Or is it, that her sex never know their desires for an hour together?

Lopez. Ah, they know them oftener than they'll own them.

Ferd. Is there, in the world, so inconstant a creature as Clara?

Lopez. I could name one.

Ferd. Yes; the tame fool, who submits to her caprice.

Lopez. I thought he couldn't miss it.

Ferd. Is she not capricious, teasing, tyrannical, obstinate, perverse, absurd? ay, a wilderness of faults and follies; her looks are scorn, and her very smiles ——'Sdeath! I wish I hadn't mentioned her smiles; for she does smile such beaming loveliness, such fascinating brightness. Oh, death and madness! I shall die if I lose her.

Lopez. Oh, those d—d smiles have undone all.

AIR.

Ferd.   Could I her faults remember,
       Forgetting every charm,
   Soon would impartial Reason
       The tyrant Love disarm;

> But when enraged I number
> Each failing of her mind,
> Love still suggests each beauty,
> And sees—while Reason's blind.

Lopez. Here comes Don Antonio, sir.

Ferd. Well, go you home; I shall be there presently.

Lopez. Ah, those cursed smiles! [*Exit.*

Enter ANTONIO.

Ferd. Antonio, Lopez tells me he left you chanting before our door? was my father waked?

Ant. Yes, yes; he has a singular affection for music, so I left him roaring at his barred window, like the print of Bajazet in the cage. And what brings you out so early?

Ferd. I believe I told you, that to-morrow was the day fixed by Don Pedro and Clara's unnatural stepmother, for her to enter a convent, in order that her brat might possess her fortune; made desperate by this, I procured a key to the door, and bribed Clara's maid to leave it unbolted; at two this morning I entered, unperceived, and stole to her chamber. I found her waking and weeping.

Ant. Happy Ferdinand!

Ferd. 'Sdeath! hear the conclusion. I was rated as the most confident ruffian, for daring to approach her room at that hour of night.

Ant. Ay, ay, this was at first?

Ferd. No such thing; she would not hear a word from me, but threatened to raise her mother, if I did not instantly leave her.

Ant. Well, but at last?——

Ferd. At last! why, I was forced to leave the house, as I came in.

Ant. And did you do nothing to offend her?

Ferd. Nothing, as I hope to be saved. I believe, I might snatch a dozen or two of kisses.

Ant. Was that all? well, I think, I never heard of such assurance!

Ferd. Z—ds! I tell you, I behaved with the utmost respect.

Ant. O Lord! I don't mean you, but in her——but, hark ye, Ferdinand, did you leave your key with them?

Ferd. Yes; the maid, who saw me out, took it from the door.

Ant. Then, my life for it, her mistress elopes after you.

Ferd. Ay, to bless my rival, perhaps. I am in a humour to suspect everybody. You loved her once, and thought her an angel, as I do now.

Ant. Yes, I loved her, till I found she wouldn't love me, and then I discovered that she hadn't a good feature in her face.

AIR.

I ne'er could any lustre see
In eyes that would not look on me;
I ne'er saw nectar on a lip,
But where my own did hope to sip.
Has the maid who seeks my heart
Cheeks of rose, untouch'd by art?
I will own the colour true,
When yielding blushes aid their hue.

Is her hand so soft and pure?
I must press it, to be sure;
Nor can I be certain then,
Till it, grateful, press again.

>   Must I, with attentive eye,
>   Watch her heaving bosom sigh?
>   I will do so, when I see
>   That heaving bosom sigh for me.

Besides, Ferdinand, you have full security in my love for your sister? Help me there, and I never can disturb you with Clara.

Ferd. As far as I can, consistently with the honour of our family, you know I will; but there must be no eloping.'

Ant. And yet, now, you would carry off Clara?

Ferd. Ay, that's a different case: we never mean that others should act to our sisters and wives, as we do to others'. But, to-morrow, Clara is to be forced into a convent.

Ant. Well, and am not I so unfortunately circumstanced? To-morrow, your father forces Louisa to marry Isaac, the Portuguese. But come with me, and we'll devise something, I warrant.

Ferd. I must go home.

Ant. Well, adieu!

Ferd. But, Antonio, if you did not love my sister, you have too much honour and friendship' to supplant me with Clara.

AIR.

> *Ant.* Friendship is the bond of reason;
>   But if beauty disapprove,
>   Heaven dissolves all other treason
>   In the heart that's true to love.
>
>   The faith which to my friend I swore,
>   As a civil oath I view;
>   But to the charms which I adore,
>   'Tis religion to be true.

Then if to one I false must be,
  Can I doubt which to prefer—
A breach of social faith with thee,
  Or sacrilege to love and her?   [*Exit.*

Ferd. There is always a levity in Antonio's manner of replying to me on this subject that is very alarming. 'Sdeath! if Clara should love him after all!

SONG.

Though cause for suspicion appears,
  Yet proofs of her love, too, are strong;
I'm a wretch if I'm right in my fears,
  And unworthy of bliss if I'm wrong.
What heart-breaking torments from jealousy flow,
Ah! none but the jealous—the jealous can know!

When blest with the smiles of my fair,
  I know not how much I adore:
Those smiles let another but share,
  And I wonder I prized them no more!
Then whence can I hope a relief from my woe,
When the falser she seems, still the fonder I grow!
                                        [*Exit.*

SCENE III.

A Room in DON JEROME'S *House.*

Enter LOUISA *and* DUENNA.

Louisa. But, my dear Margaret, my charming Duenna, do you think we shall succeed?

Duenna. I tell you again, I have no doubt on't; but it must be instantly put to the trial. Everything is prepared in your room, and for the rest, we must trust to fortune.

Louisa. My father's oath was, never to see me till I had consented to——

Duenna. 'Twas thus I overheard him say to his friend, Don Guzman: ' I will demand of her to-morrow, once for all, whether she will consent to marry Isaac Mendoza; if she hesitates, I will make a solemn oath never to see or speak to her, till she returns to her duty.' These were his words.

Louisa. And on his known obstinate adherence to what he has once said, you have formed this plan for my escape. But have you secured my maid in our interest?

Duenna. She is a party in the whole; but remember, if we succeed, you resign all right and title in little Isaac, the Jew, over to me.

Louisa. That I do with all my soul; get him, if you can, and I shall wish you joy, most heartily. He is twenty times as rich as my poor Antonio.

AIR.

Thou canst not boast of fortune's store,
  My love, while me they wealthy call;
But I was glad to find thee poor—
  For with my heart I'd give thee all.
    And then the grateful youth shall own
    I loved him for himself alone.

But when his worth my hand shall gain,
  No word or look of mine shall show
That I the smallest thought retain
  Of what my bounty did bestow;
    Yet still his grateful heart shall own
    I loved him for himself alone.

Duenna. I hear Don Jerome coming. Quick, give me the last letter I brought you from Antonio; you know that is to be the ground of my dismission. I must slip out to seal it up, as undelivered. [*Exit.*

Enter Don Jerome *and* Ferdinand.

Jerome. What, I suppose, you have been serenading too! Eh, disturbing some peaceable neighbourhood with villanous catgut, and lascivious piping! Out on't! you set your sister, here, a vile example; but I come to tell you, madam, that I'll suffer no more of these midnight incantations; these amorous orgies, that steal the senses in the hearing; as, they say, Egyptian embalmers serve mummies, extracting the brain through the ears; however, there's an end of your frolics. Isaac Mendoza will be here presently, and to-morrow you shall marry him.

Louisa. Never, while I have life.

Ferd. Indeed, sir, I wonder how you can think of such a man for a son-in-law.

Jerome. Sir, you are very kind, to favour me with your sentiments, and pray, what is your objection to him?

Ferd. He is a Portuguese, in the first place.

Jerome. No such thing, boy; he has forsworn his country.

Louisa. He is a Jew.

Jerome. Another mistake: he has been a Christian these six weeks.

Ferd. Ay, he left his old religion for an estate, and has not had time to get a new one.

Louisa. But stands like a dead wall between church and synagogue, or like the blank leaves between the Old and New Testament.

Jerome. Anything more?

Ferd. But the most remarkable part of his character is his passion for deceit and tricks of cunning.

Louisa. Though at the same time, the fool predominates so much over the knave, that I am told he is generally the dupe of his own art.

Ferd. True, like an unskilful gunner, he usually misses his aim, and is hurt by the recoil of his own piece.

Jerome. Anything more?

Louisa. To sum up all, he has the worst fault a husband can have; he's not my choice.

Jerome. But you are his; and choice on one side is sufficient; two lovers should never meet in marriage; be you sour as you please, he is sweet-tempered, and for your good fruit, there's nothing like engrafting on a crab.

Louisa. I detest him as a lover, and shall ten times more as a husband.

Jerome. I don't know that; marriage generally makes a great change; but, to cut the matter short, will you have him or not?

Louisa. There is nothing else I could disobey you in.

Jerome. Do you value your father's peace?

Louisa. So much, that I will not fasten on him the regret of making an only daughter wretched.

Jerome. Very well, ma'am, then mark me, never more will I see or converse with you till you return to your duty; no reply, this and your chamber shall be your apartments; I never will stir out, without leaving you under lock and key, and when I'm at home no creature can approach you but through my library; we'll try who can be most obstinate. Out of my sight; there remain till you know your duty.

[*Pushes her out.*

Ferd. Surely, sir, my sister's inclinations should be consulted in a matter of this kind, and some regard paid to Don Antonio, being my particular friend.

Jerome. That, doubtless, is a very great recommendation; I certainly have not paid sufficient respect to it.

Ferd. There is not a man living I would sooner choose for a brother-in-law.

Jerome. Very possible; and if you happen to have e'er a sister, who is not at the same time a daughter of mine, I'm sure I shall have no objection to the relationship; but at present, if you please, we'll drop the subject.

Ferd. Nay, sir, 'tis only my regard for my sister makes me speak.

Jerome. Then pray, sir, in future, let your regard for your father make you hold your tongue.

Ferd. I have done, sir; I shall only add a wish that you would reflect what at our age you would have felt, had you been crossed in your affection for the mother of her you are so severe to.

Jerome. Why, I must confess I had a great affection for your mother's ducats, but that was all, boy. I married her for her fortune, and she took me in obedience to her father, and a very happy couple we were. We never expected any love from one another, and so we were never disappointed. If we grumbled a little now and then, it was soon over, for we were never fond enough to quarrel; and when the good woman died, why, why—I had as lieve she had lived, and I wish every widower in Seville could say the same. I shall now go and get the key of this dressing-room; so, good son, if you have any lecture in support of disobedience to give your sister, it must be brief; so make the best of your time, d'ye hear? [*Exit.*

Ferd. I fear, indeed, my friend Antonio has little to hope for; however, Louisa has firmness, and my father's anger will probably only increase her affection. In our intercourse with the world it is natural for us to dislike those who are innocently the cause of our distress; but in the heart's attachment a woman never likes a man with ardour till she has suffered for his sake. [*Noise.*] Soh! what bustle is here! between my father and the Duenna too. I'll e'en get out of the way. [*Exit.*

Enter Don Jerome *with a Letter, pulling in the* Duenna.

Jerome. I'm astonished! I'm thunder-struck! here's treachery and conspiracy with a vengeance! You, Antonio's creature, and chief manager of this plot for my daughter's eloping! you, that I placed here as a scarecrow?

Duenna. What?

Jerome. A scarecrow—to prove a decoy duck. What have you to say for yourself?

Duenna. Well, sir, since you have forced that letter from me, and discovered my real sentiments, I scorn to renounce them. I am Antonio's friend, and it was my intention that your daughter should have served you as all such old tyrannical sots should be served. I delight in the tender passions, and would befriend all under their influence.

Jerome. The tender passions! yes, they would become those impenetrable features! Why, thou deceitful hag! I placed thee as a guard to the rich blossoms of my daughter's beauty. I thought that dragon's front of thine would cry aloof to the sons of gallantry—steel traps and spring guns seemed writ in every wrinkle of it—but you shall quit my house this instant. The tender passions, indeed! Go, thou wanton sybil, thou amorous woman of Endor, go!

Duenna. You base, scurrilous old — but I won't demean myself by naming what you are — yes, savage, I'll leave your den; but I suppose you don't mean to detain my apparel; I may have my things, I presume?

Jerome. I took you, mistress, with your wardrobe on. What have you pilfered, eh?

Duenna. Sir, I must take leave of my mistress; she has valuables of mine; besides, my cardinal and veil are in her room.

Jerome. Your veil, forsooth! What, do you dread being gazed at? or are you afraid of your complexion? Well, go take your leave, and get your veil and cardinal; soh! you quit the house within these five minutes — in — in — quick [*Exit* DUENNA.] Here was a precious plot of mischief! These are the comforts daughters bring us!

AIR.

If a daughter you have, she's the plague of your life,
No peace shall you know, though you've buried your wife!
At twenty she mocks at the duty you taught her—
Oh, what a plague is an obstinate daughter!
    Sighing and whining,
    Dying and pining,
Oh, what a plague is an obstinate daughter!

When scarce in their teens they have wit to perplex us,
With letters and lovers for ever they vex us;
While each still rejects the fair suitor you've brought her;
Oh, what a plague is an obstinate daughter!
    Wrangling and jangling,
    Flouting and pouting,
Oh, what a plague is an obstinate daughter!

Enter LOUISA, *dressed as the* DUENNA, *with Cardinal and Veil, seeming to cry.*

Jerome. This way, mistress, this way—what, I warrant, a tender parting; soh! tears of turpentine down those deal cheeks. Ay, you may well hide your head—yes, whine till your heart breaks; but I'll not hear one word of excuse—so you are right to be dumb. This way, this way. [*Exeunt.*

Enter DUENNA.

Duenna. So speed you well, sagacious Don Jerome! Oh, rare effects of passion and obstinacy; now shall I try whether I can't play the fine lady as well as my mistress, and if I succeed, I may be a fine lady for the rest of my life. I'll lose no time to equip myself.
[*Exit.*

SCENE IV.

The Court before DON JEROME'S *House.*

Enter DON JEROME *and* LOUISA.

Jerome. Come, mistress, there is your way. The world lies before you, so troop, thou antiquated Eve, thou original sin. Hold, yonder is some fellow skulking; perhaps it is Antonio; go to him, d'ye hear, and tell him to make you amends, and as he has got you turned away, tell him I say it is but just he should take you himself; go. [*Exit* LOUISA.] Soh! I am rid of her, thank Heaven! and now I shall be able to keep my oath, and confine my daughter with better security. [*Exit.*

SCENE V.

The Piazza.

Enter CLARA *and her* MAID.

Maid. But where, madam, is it you intend to go?

Clara. Anywhere to avoid the selfish violence of my mother-in-law, and Ferdinand's insolent importunity.

Maid. Indeed, ma'am, since we have profited by Don Ferdinand's key, in making our escape, I think we had best find him, if it were only to thank him.

Clara. No; he has offended me exceedingly.

[*Retire.*

Enter LOUISA.

Louisa. So I have succeeded in being turned out of doors; but how shall I find Antonio? I dare not inquire after him, for fear of being discovered; I would send to my friend Clara, but that I doubt her prudery would condemn me.

Maid. Then suppose, ma'am, you were to try if your friend Donna Louisa would not receive you.

Clara. No, her notions of filial duty are so severe, she would certainly betray me.

Louisa. Clara is of a cold temper, and would think this step of mine highly forward.

Clara. Louisa's respect for her father is so great, she would not credit the unkindness of mine.

[LOUISA *turns, and sees* CLARA *and* MAID.

Louisa. Ha! who are those? sure one is Clara; if it be, I'll trust her. Clara! [*Advances.*

Clara. Louisa! and in masquerade too!

Louisa. You will be more surprised when I tell you, that I have run away from my father.

Clara. Surprised indeed! and I should certainly chide you most horridly, only that I have just run away from mine.

Louisa. My dear Clara! [*Embrace.*

Clara. Dear sister truant! and whither are you going?

Louisa. To find the man I love, to be sure. And, I presume, you would have no aversion to meet with my brother?

Clara. Indeed I should; he has behaved so ill to me, I don't believe I shall ever forgive him.

AIR.

When sable night, each drooping plant restoring,
   Wept o'er the flowers her breath did cheer,
As some sad widow o'er her babe deploring,
   Wakes its beauty with a tear;
When all did sleep, whose weary hearts did borrow
   One hour from love and care to rest,
Lo! as I press'd my couch in silent sorrow,
   My lover caught me to his breast;
      He vow'd he came to save me
      From those who would enslave me!
         Then kneeling,
         Kisses stealing,
   Endless faith he swore;

> But soon I chid him thence,
> For had his fond pretence
> Obtain'd one favour then,
> And he had press'd again,
> I fear'd my treacherous heart might grant him more.

Louisa. Well, for all this, I would have sent him to plead his pardon, but that I would not yet a while have him know of my flight. And where do you hope to find protection?

Clara. The Lady Abbess of the convent of St. Catherine is a relation and kind friend of mine. I shall be secure with her, and you had best go thither with me.

Louisa. No; I am determined to find Antonio first; and, as I live, here comes the very man I will employ to seek him for me.

Clara. Who is he? he's a strange figure!

Louisa. Yes; that sweet creature is the man whom my father has fixed on for my husband.

Clara. And will you speak to him? are you mad?

Louisa. He is the fittest man in the world for my purpose; for, though I was to have married him to-morrow, he is the only man in Seville, who, I am sure, never saw me in his life.

Clara. And how do you know him?

Louisa. He arrived but yesterday, and he was shown to me from the window, as he visited my father.

Clara. Well, I'll begone.

Louisa. Hold, my dear Clara; a thought has struck me. Will you give me leave to borrow your name, as I see occasion?

Clara. It will but disgrace you; but use it as you please. I dare not stay [*Going.*]—but, Louisa, if you should see your brother, be sure you don't inform him, that I have taken refuge with the Dame Prior of the convent of St. Catherine, on the left-hand side of the Piazza, which leads to the church of St. Anthony.

Louisa. Ha! ha! ha! I'll be very particular in my directions where he may not find you. [*Exeunt* CLARA *and* MAID.] So! my swain, yonder, has done admiring himself, and draws nearer. [*Retires.*

Enter ISAAC *and* CARLOS; ISAAC *with a Pocket Glass.*

Isaac. [*Looking in the Glass.*] I tell you, friend Carlos, I will please myself in the habit of my chin.

Carlos. But, my dear friend, how can you think to please a lady with such a face?

Isaac. Why, what's the matter with the face? I think it is a very engaging face; and, I am sure, a lady must have very little taste who could dislike my beard. [*Sees* LOUISA.] See now! I'll die if here is not a little damsel struck with it already.

Louisa. Signior, are you disposed to oblige a lady, who greatly wants your assistance? [*Unveils.*

Isaac. Egad, a very pretty black-eyed girl! she has certainly taken a fancy to me, Carlos. First, ma'am, I must beg the favour of your name.

Louisa. So! it's well I am provided. [*Aside.*] My name, sir, is Donna Clara d'Almanza.

Isaac. What! Don Gusman's daughter? I'faith, I just now heard she was missing.

Louisa. But sure, sir, you have too much gallantry and honour to betray me, whose fault is love?

Isaac. So! a passion for me! poor girl! Why, ma'am, as for betraying you, I don't see how I could get anything by it; so you may rely on my honour; but as for your love, I am sorry your case is so desperate.

Louisa. Why so, signior?

Isaac. Because I am positively engaged to another—an't I, Carlos?

Louisa. Nay, but hear me.

Isaac. No, no; what should I hear for? It is impossible for me to court you in an honourable way; and, for anything else, if I were to comply now, I suppose you have some ungrateful brother, or cousin, who would want to cut my throat for my civility—so, truly, you had best go home again.

Louisa. Odious wretch! [*Aside.*] But, good signior, it is Antonio d'Ercilla, on whose account I have eloped.

Isaac. How! what! it is not with me, then, that you are in love?

Louisa. No, indeed, it is not.

Isaac. Then you are a forward, impertinent simpleton! and I shall certainly acquaint your father.

Louisa. Is this your gallantry?

Isaac. Yet hold—Antonio d'Ercilla, did you say? Egad, I may make something of this Antonio d'Ercilla?

Louisa. Yes; and, if ever you hope to prosper in love, you will bring me to him.

Isaac. By St. Iago, and I will too. Carlos, this Antonio is one who rivals me (as I have heard) with Louisa; now, if I could hamper him with this girl, I should have the field to myself; hey, Carlos! A lucky thought, isn't it?

Carlos. Yes, very good—very good—

Isaac. Ah! this little brain is never at a loss. Cunning Isaac! cunning rogue! Donna Clara, will you trust yourself a while to my friend's direction?

Louisa. May I rely on you, good signior?

Carlos. Lady, it is impossible I should deceive you.

AIR.

Had I a heart for falsehood framed,
    I ne'er could injure you;
For though your tongue no promise claim'd,
    Your charms would make me true.
To you no soul shall bear deceit,
    No stranger offer wrong;
But friends in all the aged you'll meet,
    And lovers in the young.

But when they learn that you have blest
    Another with your heart,
They'll bid aspiring passion rest,
    And act a brother's part:
Then, lady, dread not here deceit,
    Nor fear to suffer wrong;
For friends in all the aged you'll meet,
    And brothers in the young.

Isaac. I'll conduct the lady to my lodgings, Carlos; I must haste to Don Jerome. Perhaps you know Louisa, ma'am. She is divinely handsome, isn't she?

Louisa. You must excuse me not joining with you.

Isaac. Why, I have heard it on all hands.

Louisa. Her father is uncommonly partial to her; but I believe you will find she has rather a matronly air.

Isaac. Carlos, this is all envy—you pretty girls never speak well of one another—hark ye, find out Antonio, and I'll saddle him with this scrape, I warrant! Oh, 'twas the luckiest thought! Donna Clara, your very obedient. Carlos, to your post.

DUET.

Isaac.   My mistress expects me, and I must go to her,
        Or how can I hope for a smile?

Louisa. Soon may you return a prosperous wooer,
　　　　But think what I suffer the while!
　　　　Alone, and away from the man whom I love,
　　　　In strangers I'm forced to confide.
Isaac. Dear lady, my friend you may trust, and he'll prove
　　　　Your servant, protector, and guide.

AIR—CARLOS.

Gentle maid, ah! why suspect me?
Let me serve thee—then reject me.
Canst thou trust, and I deceive thee?
Art thou sad, and shall I grieve thee?
Gentle maid, ah! why suspect me?
Let me serve thee—then reject me.

TRIO.

Louisa.　Never may'st thou happy be,
　　　　　If in aught thou'rt false to me.

Isaac.　　Never may he happy be,
　　　　　If in aught he's false to thee.

Carlos.　Never may I happy be,
　　　　　If in aught I'm false to thee.

Louisa.　Never may'st thou, &c.
Isaac.　　Never may he, &c.
Carlos.　Never may I, &c.　　　　　　　[*Exeunt.*

ACT II.—SCENE I.

A Library in DON JEROME'S *House.*

Enter DON JEROME *and* ISAAC.

Jerome. Ha! ha! ha! run away from her father! has she given him the slip? Ha! ha! poor Don Gusman!

Isaac. Ay; and I am to conduct her to Antonio; by which means you see I shall hamper him so that he can give no disturbance with your daughter. This is trap, isn't it? a nice stroke of cunning, hey?

Jerome. Excellent! excellent! Yes, yes, carry her to him, hamper him by all means, ha! ha! ha! poor Don Gusman! an old fool! imposed on by a girl!

Isaac. Nay, they have the cunning of serpents, that's the truth on't.

Jerome. Psha! they are cunning only when they have fools to deal with. Why don't my girl play me such a trick; let her cunning overreach my caution, I say—hey, little Isaac!

Isaac. True, true; or let me see any of the sex make a fool of me. No, no, egad, little Solomon (as my aunt used to call me) understands tricking a little too well.

Jerome. Ay, but such a driveller as Don Gusman.

Isaac. And such a dupe as Antonio.

Jerome. True; sure never were seen such a couple of credulous simpletons; but come, 'tis time you should see my daughter—you must carry on the siege by yourself, friend Isaac.

Isaac. Sir, you'll introduce——

Jerome. No. I have sworn a solemn oath not to see or speak to her till she renounces her disobedience; win her to that, and she gains a father and a husband at once.

Isaac. Gad, I shall never be able to deal with her alone; nothing keeps me in such awe as perfect beauty. Now there is something consoling and encouraging in ugliness.

SONG.

Give Isaac the nymph who no beauty can boast,
But health and good humour to make her his toast;
If straight, I don't mind whether slender or fat,
And six feet or four—we'll ne'er quarrel for that.

Whate'er her complexion, I vow I don't care;
If brown it is lasting—more pleasing if fair:
And though in her face I no dimples should see,
Let her smile—and each dell is a dimple to me.

Let her locks be the reddest that ever were seen,
And her eyes may be e'en any colour but green;
For in eyes, though so various the lustre and hue,
I swear I've no choice—only let her have two.

'Tis true I'd dispense with a throne on her back,
And white teeth, I own, are genteeler than black;
A little round chin too's a beauty, I've heard;
But I only desire she mayn't have a beard.

Jerome. You will change your note, my friend, when you've seen Louisa.

Isaac. Oh, Don Jerome, the honour of your alliance——

Jerome. Ay, but her beauty will affect you; she is

though I say it, who am her father, a very prodigy; there you will see features with an eye like mine. Yes, i'faith, there is a kind of wicked sparkling—something of a roguish brightness, that shows her to be my own.

Isaac. Pretty rogue!

Jerome. Then, when she smiles, you'll see a little dimple in one cheek only; a beauty it is certainly, yet you shall not say which is prettiest, the cheek with the dimple, or the cheek without.

Isaac. Pretty rogue!

Jerome. Then the roses on those cheeks are shaded with a sort of velvet down, that gives a delicacy to the glow of health.

Isaac. Pretty rogue!

Jerome. Her skin pure dimity, yet more fair, being spangled here and there with a golden freckle.

Isaac. Charming pretty rogue! Pray how is the tone of her voice?

Jerome. Remarkably pleasing; but if you could prevail on her to sing, you would be enchanted: she is a nightingale—a Virginian nightingale. But come, come; her maid shall conduct you to her antechamber.

Isaac. Well, egad, I'll pluck up resolution, and meet her frowns intrepidly.

Jerome. Ay! woo her briskly—win her, and give me a proof of your address, my little Solomon.

Isaac. But hold—I expect my friend Carlos to call on me here. If he comes, will you send him to me?

Jerome. I will. Lauretta, come; she'll show you to the room. What, do you droop? Here's a mournful face to make love with! [*Exeunt.*

SCENE II.

Louisa's *Dressing-Room.*

Enter Maid *and* Isaac.

Maid. Sir, my mistress will wait on you presently.
[*Goes to the door.*
Isaac. When she's at leisure — don't hurry her. [*Exit* Maid.] I wish I had ever practised a love scene. I doubt I shall make a poor figure. I couldn't be more afraid if I was going before the Inquisition. So the door opens—yes, she's coming. The very rustling of her silk has a disdainful sound.

Enter Duenna, *dressed as* Louisa.

Now dar'n't I look round for the soul of me; her beauty will certainly strike me dumb if I do. I wish she'd speak first.
Duenna. Sir, I attend your pleasure.
Isaac. So! the ice is broke, and a pretty civil beginning too! Hem! madam—miss—I'm all attention.
Duenna. Nay, sir, 'tis I who should listen, and you propose.
Isaac. Egad, this isn't so disdainful neither. I believe I may venture to look—no—I dar'n't—one glance of those roguish sparklers would fix me again.
Duenna. You seem thoughtful, sir; let me persuade you to sit down.

Isaac. So, so; she mollifies apace—she's struck with my figure! this attitude has had its effect.

Duenna. Come, sir, here's a chair.

Isaac. Madam, the greatness of your goodness overpowers me, that a lady so lovely should deign to turn her beauteous eyes on me so.

[*She takes his hand, he turns and sees her.*

Duenna. You seem surprised at my condescension.

Isaac. Why, yes, madam, I am a little surprised at it. Z—ds! this can never be Louisa; she's as old as my mother! [*Aside.*

Duenna. But former prepossessions give way to my father's commands.

Isaac. [*Aside.*] Her father! Yes, 'tis she, then. Lord, lord, how blind some parents are!

Duenna. Signor Isaac.

Isaac. Truly, the little damsel was right: she has rather a matronly air indeed! Ah! 'tis well my affections are fixed on her fortune, and not her person.

Duenna. Signor, won't you sit? [*She sits.*

Isaac. Pardon me, madam, I have scarce recovered my astonishment at—your condescension, madam. She has the devil's own dimples to be sure! [*Aside.*

Duenna. I do not wonder, sir, that you are surprised at my affability. I own, signor, that I was vastly prepossessed against you, and being teased by my father, I did give some encouragement to Antonio; but then, sir, you were described to me as a quite different person.

Isaac. Ay, and so you were to me, upon my soul, madam.

Duenna. But when I saw you, I was never more struck in my life.

Isaac. That was just my case too, madam; I was struck all on a heap, for my part.

Duenna. Well, sir, I see our misapprehension has been mutual; you expected to find me haughty and averse, and I was taught to believe you a little, black, snub-nosed fellow, without person, manners, or address.

Isaac. Egad, I wish she had answered her picture as well.

Duenna. But, sir, your air is noble; something so liberal in your carriage, with so penetrating an eye, and so bewitching a smile!

Isaac. Egad, now I look at her again, I don't think she is so ugly.

Duenna. So little like a Jew, and so much like a gentleman!

Isaac. Well, certainly there is something pleasing in the tone of her voice.

Duenna. You will pardon this breach of decorum in praising you thus, but my joy at being so agreeably deceived has given me such a flow of spirits!

Isaac. O, dear lady, may I thank those dear lips for this goodness? [*Kisses her.*] Why, she has a pretty sort of velvet down, that's the truth on't!
[*Aside.*

Duenna. O, sir, you have the most insinuating manner, but indeed you should get rid of that odious beard; one might as well kiss a hedgehog.

Isaac. Yes, ma'am, the razor wouldn't be amiss— for either of us. [*Aside.*] Could you favour me with a song?

Duenna. Willingly, sir, though I am rather hoarse —ahem! [*Begins to sing.*

Isaac. Very like a Virginia nightingale!—ma'am, I perceive you're hoarse. I beg you will not distress——

Duenna. Oh, not in the least distressed. Now, sir.

SONG.

    When a tender maid
    Is first essay'd
By some admiring swain,
    How her blushes rise
    If she meet his eyes,
While he unfolds his pain!
If he takes her hand—she trembles quite!
Touch her lips—and she swoons outright!
    While a pit-a-pat, &c.
    Her heart avows her fright.

    But in time appear
    Fewer signs of fear!
The youth she boldly views:
    If her hand he grasp,
    Or her bosom clasp,
No mantling blush ensues!
Then to church well pleased the lovers move,
While her smiles her contentment prove;
    And a pit-a-pat, &c.
    Her heart avows her love.

Isaac. Charming, ma'am! enchanting! and, truly, your notes put me in mind of one that's very dear to me; a lady, indeed, whom you greatly resemble!

Duenna. How! is there, then, another so dear to you?

Isaac. O, no, ma'am. you mistake; it was my mother I meant.

Duenna. Come, sir, I see you are amazed and confounded at my condescension, and know not what to say.

Isaac. It is very true, indeed, ma'am; but it is a judgment, I look on it as a judgment on me, for delaying to urge the time when you'll permit me to complete my happiness, by acquainting Don Jerome with your condescension.

Duenna. Sir, I must frankly own to you, that I can never be yours with my father's consent.

Isaac. Good lack! how so?

Duenna. When my father, in his passion, swore he would never see me again till I acquiesced in his will, I also made a vow, that I never would take a husband from his hand; nothing shall make me break that oath; but if you have spirit and contrivance enough to carry me off without his knowledge, I'm yours.

Isaac. Hum!

Duenna. Nay, sir, if you hesitate——

Isaac. I'faith, no bad whim this; if I take her at her word, I shall secure her fortune, and avoid making any settlement in return; thus I shall not only cheat the lover, but the father too. Oh, cunning rogue, Isaac! Ay, ay, let this little brain alone. Egad, I'll take her in the mind.

Duenna. Well, sir, what's your determination?

Isaac. Madam, I was dumb only from rapture. I applaud your spirit, and joyfully close with your proposals; for which, thus let me, on this lily hand, express my gratitude.

Duenna. Well, sir, you must get my father's consent to walk with me in the garden. But by no means inform him of my kindness to you.

Isaac. No, to be sure, that would spoil all; but, trust me, when tricking is the word; let me alone for a piece of cunning. This very day you shall be out of his power.

Duenna. Well, I leave the management of it all to you; I perceive plain, sir, that you are not one that can be easily outwitted.

Isaac. Egad, you're right, madam; you're right, i'faith.

Enter MAID.

Maid. Here's a gentleman at the door, who begs permission to speak with Signor Isaac.

Isaac. A friend of mine, ma'am, and a trusty friend; let him come in. [*Exit* MAID.] He is one to be depended on, ma'am.

Enter CARLOS.

So, coz. [*Aside.*

Carlos. I have left Donna Clara at your lodgings; but can nowhere find Antonio.

Isaac. Well, I will search him out myself. Carlos, you rogue, I thrive, I prosper.

Carlos. Where is your mistress?

Isaac. There, you booby; there she stands.

Carlos. Why she's d—d ugly!

Isaac. Hush! [*Stops his mouth.*

Duenna. What is your friend saying, signor?

Isaac. Oh, ma'am, he is expressing his raptures at such charms as he never saw before; eh, Carlos?

Carlos. Ay, such as I never saw before, indeed!

Duenna. You are a very obliging gentleman. Well, Signor Isaac, I believe we had better part for the present. Remember our plan.

Isaac. Oh, ma'am, it is written in my heart, fixed as the image of those divine beauties! Adieu, idol of my soul! Yet once more permit me—— [*Kisses her.*

Duenna. Sweet, courteous sir, adieu!

Isaac. Your slave eternally. Come, Carlos, say something civil at taking leave.

Carlos. I'faith, Isaac, she is the hardest woman to

compliment I ever saw; however, I'll try something I had studied for the occasion.

SONG.

Ah! sure a pair was never seen
  So justly form'd to meet by nature!
The youth excelling so in mien,
  The maid in ev'ry grace of feature.
    Oh, how happy are such lovers,
      When kindred beauties each discovers!
        For surely she
        Was made for thee,
And thou to bless this lovely creature!

So mild your looks, your children thence
  Will early learn the task of duty—
The boys with all their father's sense,
  The girls with all their mother's beauty!
    Oh, how happy to inherit
      At once such graces and such spirit!
        Thus while you live
        May fortune give
Each blessing equal to your merit!
        [*Exeunt* ISAAC, CARLOS, DUENNA.

SCENE III.

A Library.

JEROME *and* FERDINAND *discovered.*

Jerome. Object to Antonio? I have said it: his poverty, can you acquit him of that?

Ferd. Sir, I own he is not over rich; but he is of as

ancient and honourable a family as any in the kingdom.

Jerome. Yes, I know the beggars are a very ancient family in most kingdoms; but never in great repute, boy.

Ferd. Antonio, sir, has many amiable qualities.

Jerome. But he is poor; can you clear him of that, I say? Is he not a gay, dissipated rake, who has squandered his patrimony?

Ferd. Sir, he inherited but little; and that his generosity, more than his profuseness, has stripped him of; but he has never sullied his honour, which, with his title, has outlived his means.

Jerome. Pshaw! you talk like a blockhead! Nobility, without an estate, is as ridiculous as gold lace on a frieze coat.

Ferd. This language, sir, would better become a Dutch or English trader than a Spaniard.

Jerome. Yes; and those Dutch and English traders, as you call them, are the wiser people. Why, booby, in England, they were formerly as nice as to birth and family as we are; but they have long discovered what a wonderful purifier gold is; and now, no one there regards pedigree in anything but a horse. Oh, here comes Isaac! I hope he has prospered in his suit.

Ferd. Doubtless, that agreeable figure of his must have helped his suit surprisingly.

Jerome. How now? [FERDINAND *walks aside.*

Enter ISAAC.

Well, my friend, have you softened her?

Isaac. Oh, yes; I have softened her.

Jerome. What, does she come to?

Isaac. Why, truly, she was kinder than I expected to find her.

Jerome. And the dear little angel was civil, hey?

Isaac. Yes, the pretty little angel was very civil.

Jerome. I'm transported to hear it. Well, and you were astonished at her beauty, hey?

Isaac. I was astonished, indeed? Pray, how old is miss?

Jerome. How old? let me see. Eight and twelve—she is twenty.

Isaac. Twenty?

Jerome. Ay, to a month.

Isaac. Then, upon my soul, she is the oldest looking girl of her age in Christendom!

Jerome. Do you think so? but, I believe, you will not see a prettier girl.

Isaac. Here and there one.

Jerome. Louisa has the family face.

Isaac. Yes, egad, I should have taken it for a family face, and one that has been in the family some time too. [*Aside.*

Jerome. She has her father's eyes.

Isaac. Truly I should have guessed them to have been so. If she had her mother's spectacles, I believe she would not see the worse. [*Aside.*

Jerome. Her aunt Ursula's nose, and her grandmother's forehead, to a hair.

Isaac. Ay, faith, and her grandfather's chin to a hair. [*Aside.*

Jerome. Well, if she was but as dutiful as she's handsome—and hark ye, friend Isaac, she is none of your made-up beauties—her charms are of the lasting kind.

Isaac. I'faith, so they should; for if she be but twenty now, she may double her age before her years will overtake her face.

Jerome. Why, z—ds, Master Isaac! you are not sneering, are you?

Isaac. Why now, seriously, Don Jerome, do you think your daughter handsome?

Jerome. By this light, she's as handsome a girl as any in Seville.

Isaac. Then, by these eyes, I think her as plain a woman as ever I beheld.

Jerome. By St. Iago! you must be blind.

Isaac. No, no; 'tis you are partial.

Jerome. How! have I neither sense nor taste? If a fair skin, fine eyes, teeth of ivory, with a lovely bloom, and a delicate shape—if these, with a heavenly voice, and a world of grace, are not charms, I know not what you call beautiful.

Isaac. Good lack, with what eyes a father sees! As I have life, she is the very reverse of all this: as for the dimity skin you told me of, I swear, 'tis a thorough nankeen as ever I saw! for her eyes, their utmost merit is not squinting; for her teeth, where there is one of ivory, its neighbour is pure ebony, black and white alternately, just like the keys of an harpsichord. Then, as to her singing, and heavenly voice, by this hand, she has a shrill, cracked pipe, that sounds, for all the world, like a child's trumpet.

Jerome. Why, you little Hebrew scoundrel, do you mean to insult me? Out of my house, I say!

Ferd. Dear sir, what's the matter?

Jerome. Why, this Israelite here has the impudence to say your sister's ugly.

Ferd. He must be either blind or insolent.

Isaac. So, I find they are all in a story. Egad, I believe I have gone too far!

Ferd. Sure, sir, there must be some mistake; it can't be my sister whom he has seen.

Jerome. 'Sdeath! you are as great a fool as he! What mistake can there be? Did not I lock up Louisa, and hav'n't I the key in my own pocket? and didn't her maid show him into the dressing-room? and yet you talk of a mistake: no, the Portuguese meant to insult me; and, but that this roof protects him, old as I am, this sword should do me justice.

Isaac. I must get off as well as I can: her fortune is not the less handsome.

DUET.

Isaac.   Believe me, good sir, I ne'er meant to offend;
My mistress I love, and I value my friend:
To win her and wed her is still my request,
For better, for worse—and I swear I don't jest.

Jerome. Z—ds! you'd best not provoke me, my rage is so high!

Isaac. Hold him fast, I beseech you, his rage is so high!
Good sir, you're too hot, and this place I must fly.

Jerome. You're a knave and a sot, and this place you'd best fly.

Isaac. Don Jerome, come now, let us lay aside all joking, and be serious.

Jerome. How?

Isaac. Ha! ha! ha! I'll be hanged if you hav'n't taken my abuse of your daughter seriously.

Jerome. You meant it so, did not you?

Isaac. O mercy, no! a joke—just to try how angry it would make you.

Jerome. Was that all, i'faith? I didn't know you had been such a wag, ha! ha! ha! By St. Iago! you made me very angry though. Well, and you do think Louisa handsome?

Isaac. Handsome! Venus de Medicis was a sybil to her.

Jerome. Give me your hand, you little jocose rogue. Egad, I thought we had been all off.

Ferd. So! I was in hope this would have been a quarrel! but I find the Jew is too cunning.

Jerome. Ay, this gust of passion has made me dry. I am seldom ruffled. Order some wine in the next room; let us drink the poor girl's health. Poor Louisa! ugly, hey! Ha! ha! ha! 'Twas a very good joke, indeed!

Isaac. And a very true one, for all that.

Jerome. And, Ferdinand, I insist upon your drinking success to my friend.

Ferd. Sir, I will drink success to my friend, with all my heart.

Jerome. Come, little Solomon, if any sparks of anger had remained, this would be the only way to quench them.

TRIO.

A bumper of good liquor
Will end a contest quicker
Than justice, judge, or vicar:
 So fill a cheerful glass,
 And let good humour pass.

But if more deep the quarrel,
Why sooner drain the barrel
Than be the hateful fellow
That's crabbed when he's mellow.
 A bumper, &c.   [*Exeunt.*

SCENE IV.

Isaac's *Lodgings.*

Enter Louisa.

Louisa. Was ever truant daughter so whimsically circumstanced as I am! I have sent my intended husband to look after my lover—the man of my father's choice is gone to bring me the man of my own—but how dispiriting is this interval of expectation!

SONG.

What bard, O Time, discover,
   With wings first made thee move?
Ah! sure it was some lover
   Who ne'er had left his love!
For who that once did prove
The pangs which absence brings,
   Though but one day
   He were away,
Could picture thee with wings?
   What bard, &c.

Enter Carlos.

So, friend, is Antonio found?

Carlos. I could not meet with him, lady: but I doubt not my friend Isaac will be here with him presently.

Louisa. Oh, shame! you have used no diligence. Is this your courtesy to a lady, who has trusted herself to your protection?

Carlos. Indeed, madam, I have not been remiss.

Louisa. Well, well; but if either of you had known how each moment of delay weighs upon the heart of her who loves, and waits the object of her love, oh, ye would not then have trifled thus!

Carlos. Alas, I know it well!

Louisa. Were you ever in love then?

Carlos. I was, lady; but while I have life, will never be again.

Louisa. Was your mistress so cruel?

Carlos. If she had always been so, I should have been happier.

SONG.

O had my love ne'er smiled on me,
   I ne'er had known such anguish;
But think how false, how cruel she,
   To bid me cease to languish;
To bid me hope her hand to gain,
   Breathe on a flame half perish'd;
And then with cold and fix'd disdain
   To kill the hope she cherish'd.

Not worse his fate, who on a wreck,
   That drove as winds did blow it,
Silent had left the shatter'd deck,
   To find a grave below it:
Then land was cried—no more resign'd,
   He glow'd with joy to hear it;
Not worse his fate, his woe to find
   The wreck must sink ere near it!

Louisa. As I live, here is your friend coming with Antonio. I'll retire for a moment to surprise him.

[*Exit.*

Enter ISAAC *and* ANTONIO.

Ant. Indeed, my good friend, you must be mistaken.

Clara D'Almanza in love with me, and employ you to bring me to meet her! It is impossible!

Isaac. That you shall see in an instant. Carlos, where is the lady? [CARLOS *points to the door.*] In the next room, is she?

Ant. Nay, if that lady is really here, she certainly wants me to conduct her to a dear friend of mine, who has long been her lover.

Isaac. Pshaw! I tell you 'tis no such thing; you are the man she wants, and nobody but you. Here's ado to persuade you to take a pretty girl that's dying for you!

Ant. But I have no affection for this lady.

Isaac. And you have for Louisa, hey? But take my word for it, Antonio, you have no chance there; so you may as well secure the good that offers itself to you.

Ant. And could you reconcile it to your conscience to supplant your friend?

Isaac. Pish! Conscience has no more to do with gallantry, than it has with politics; why, you are no honest fellow, if love can't make a rogue of you; so come, do go in, and speak to her at last.

Ant. Well, I have no objection to that.

Isaac. [*Opens the door.*] There; there she is: yonder by the window; get in, do. [*Pushes him in, and half shuts the door.*] Now, Carlos, now I shall hamper him, I warrant. Stay, I'll peep how they go on. Egad, he looks confoundedly posed. Now she's coaxing him. See, Carlos, he begins to come to—ay, ay, he'll soon forget his conscience.

Carlos. Look; now they are both laughing!

Isaac. Ay, so they are. Yes, yes, they are laughing at that dear friend he talked of. Ay, poor devil, they have outwitted him.

Carlos. Now he's kissing her hand.

Isaac. Yes, yes, 'faith, they're agreed; he's caught, he's entangled. My dear Carlos, we have brought it about. Oh, this little cunning head! I'm a Machiavel—a very Machiavel.

Carlos. I hear somebody inquiring for you. I'll see who it is. [*Exit* CARLOS.

Enter ANTONIO *and* LOUISA.

Ant. Well, my good friend, this lady has so entirely convinced me of the certainty of your success at Don Jerome's, that I now resign my pretensions there.

Isaac. You never did a wiser thing, believe me; and as for deceiving your friend, that's nothing at all; tricking is all fair in love; isn't it, ma'am?

Louisa. Certainly, sir; and I am particularly glad to find you are of that opinion.

Isaac. O lud! yes, ma'am; let any one outwit me, that can, I say. But here, let me join your hands—— there, you lucky rogue! I wish you happily married, from the bottom of my soul!

Louisa. And I am sure if you wish it, no one else should prevent it.

Isaac. Now, Antonio, we are rivals no more; so let us be friends, will you?

Ant. With all my heart, Isaac.

Isaac. It is not every man, let me tell you, that would have taken such pains, or been so generous to a rival.

Ant. No, 'faith; I don't believe there's another beside yourself in all Spain.

Isaac. Well, but you resign all pretensions to the other lady?

Ant. That I do, most sincerely.

Isaac. I doubt you have a little hankering there still.

Ant. None in the least, upon my soul.

Isaac. I mean after her fortune.

Ant. No, believe me. You are heartily welcome to everything she has.

Isaac. Well, i'faith, you have the best of the bargain, as to beauty, twenty to one. Now I'll tell you a secret. I am to carry off Louisa this very evening.

Louisa. Indeed!

Isaac. Yes; she has sworn not to take a husband from her father's hand; so I've persuaded him to trust her to walk with me in the garden, and then we shall give him the slip.

Louisa. And is Don Jerome to know nothing of this?

Isaac. O lud, no! there lies the jest. Don't you see that, by this step, I overreach him? I shall be entitled to the girl's fortune, without settling a ducat on her, ha! ha! ha! I'm a cunning dog, an't I? A sly little villain, eh?

Ant. Ha! ha! ha! you are indeed!

Isaac. Roguish, you'll say, but keen, eh?—devilish keen?

Ant. So you are indeed; keen—very keen.

Isaac. And what a laugh we shall have at Don Jerome's, when the truth comes out! hey?

Louisa. Yes, I'll answer for it, we shall have a good laugh when the truth comes out, ha! ha! ha!

Enter CARLOS.

Carlos. Here are the dancers come to practise the fandango you intended to have honoured Donna Louisa with.

Isaac. O, I sha'n't want them; but as I must pay them, I'll see a caper for my money. Will you excuse me?

Louisa. Willingly.

Isaac. Here's my friend, whom you may command for any service. Madam, your most obedient. Antonio, I wish you all happiness. Oh, the easy blockhead! what a tool I have made of him! This was a masterpiece! [*Exit.*

Louisa. Carlos, will you be my guard again, and convey me to the convent of St. Catherine?

Ant. Why, Louisa—why should you go there?

Louisa. I have my reasons, and you must not be seen to go with me. I shall write from thence to my father; perhaps, when he finds what he has driven me to, he may relent.

Ant. I have no hope from him. O Louisa! in these arms should be your sanctuary.

Louisa. Be patient but for a little while; my father cannot force me from thence. But let me see you there before evening, and I will explain myself.

Ant. I shall obey.

Louisa. Come, friend. Antonio, Carlos has been a lover himself.

Ant. Then he knows the value of his trust.

Carlos. You shall not find me unfaithful.

TRIO.

Soft pity never leaves the gentle breast
Where love has been received a welcome guest;
As wand'ring saints poor huts have sacred made,
He hallows ev'ry heart he once has sway'd;
And when his presence we no longer share,
Still leaves compassion as a relic there.

[*Exeunt.*

ACT III.—SCENE I.

A Library.

Enter JEROME *and* SERVANT.

Jerome. Why, I never was so amazed in my life! Louisa gone off with Isaac Mendoza! What! steal away with the very man whom I wanted her to marry—elope with her own husband, as it were—it is impossible!

Serv. Her maid says, sir, they had your leave to walk in the garden, while you was abroad. The door by the shrubbery was found open, and they have not been heard of since. [*Exit.*

Jerome. Well, it is the most unaccountable affair! 'Sdeath! there is certainly some infernal mystery in it, I can't comprehend!

Enter SECOND SERVANT, *with a Letter.*

Serv. Here is a letter, sir, from Signor Isaac. [*Exit.*
Jerome. So, so, this will explain. Ay, Isaac Mendoza. Let me see—— [*Reads.*

' *Dearest Sir,*
' *You must, doubtless, be much surprised at my flight with your daughter.*' Yes, 'faith, and well I may. ' *I had the happiness to gain her heart at our first interview.*' The devil you had! ' *But she having unfortunately made a vow not to receive a husband from your hands, I was obliged to comply with her whims.*' So, so! ' *We shall*

shortly throw ourselves at your feet, and I hope you will have a blessing ready for one, who will then be

'Your son-in-law,
'Isaac Mendoza.'

A whim, hey? Why, the devil's in the girl, I think! This morning, she would die sooner than have him, and before evening she runs away with him! Well, well, my will's accomplished, let the motive be what it will, and the Portuguese, sure, will never deny to fulfil the rest of the article.

Enter Servant, *with another Letter.*

Serv. Sir, here's a man below, who says he brought this from my young lady, Donna Louisa. [*Exit.*

Jerome. How! yes, it is my daughter's hand indeed! Lord, there was no occasion for them both to write. Well, let's see what she says. [*Reads.*

'*My dearest Father*,
'*How shall I entreat your pardon for the rash step I have taken—how confess the motive?*' Pish! hasn't Isaac just told me the motive? One would think they weren't together when they wrote. '*If I have a spirit too resentful of ill usage, I have also a heart as easily affected by kindness.*' So, so, here the whole matter comes out; her resentment for Antonio's ill usage has made her sensible of Isaac's kindness. Yes, yes, it is plain enough—well——'*I am not married yet, though with a man I am convinced adores me.*' Yes, yes, I dare say Isaac is very fond of her. '*But I shall anxiously expect your answer, in which, should I be so fortunate as to receive your consent, you will make completely happy,*

'*Your ever affectionate daughter,*
'Louisa.'

My consent? to be sure she shall have it! Egad, I was never better pleased. I have fulfilled my resolution. I knew I should. Oh, there's nothing like obstinacy. Lewis!

Enter SERVANT.

Let the man who brought the last letter wait, and get me a pen and ink below. I am impatient to set poor Louisa's heart at rest. Holloa! Lewis! Sancho!

Enter SERVANTS.

See that there be a noble supper provided in the saloon to-night; serve up my best wines, and let me have music; d'ye hear?

Serv. Yes, sir. [*Exeunt.*

Jerome. And order all my doors to be thrown open; admit all guests, with masks or without masks——— I'faith, we'll have a night of it. And I'll let them see how merry an old man can be.

SONG.

Oh, the days when I was young,
   When I laugh'd in fortune's spite;
Talk'd of love the whole day long,
   And with nectar crown'd the night!
Then it was, old father Care,
   Little reck'd I of thy frown;
Half thy malice youth could bear,
   And the rest a bumper drown.

Truth, they say, lies in a well,
   Why, I vow I ne'er could see:
Let the water-drinkers tell,
   There it always lay for me:

For when sparkling wine went round,
   Never saw I falsehood's mask;
But still honest truth I found
   At the bottom of each flask.

True, at length my vigour's flown,
   I have years to bring decay;
Few the locks that now I own,
   And the few I have are grey.
Yet, old Jerome, thou may'st boast,
   While thy spirits do not tire;
Still beneath thy age's frost
   Glows a spark of youthful fire.

SCENE II.

The New Piazza.

Enter FERDINAND *and* LOPEZ.

Ferd. What, could you gather no tidings of her? nor guess where she was gone? O Clara! Clara!

Lopez. In truth, sir, I could not. That she was run away from her father, was in everybody's mouth, and that Don Guzman was in pursuit of her was also a very common report; where she was gone, or what was become of her, no one could take upon them to say.

Ferd. 'Sdeath and fury, you blockhead! she can't be out of Seville.

Lopez. So I said to myself, sir. 'Sdeath and fury, you blockhead, says I, she can't be out of Seville. Then some said, she had hanged herself for love; and others have it, Don Antonio had carried her off.

Ferd. 'Tis false, scoundrel! no one said that.

Lopez. Then I misunderstood them, sir.

Ferd. Go, fool, get home, and never let me see you again, till you bring me news of her. [*Exit* LOPEZ.] Oh, how my fondness for this ungrateful girl has hurt my disposition!

Enter ISAAC.

Isaac. So, I have her safe, and have only to find a priest to marry us. Antonio now may marry Clara, or not, if he pleases.

Ferd. What? what was that you said of Clara?

Isaac. Oh, Ferdinand! my brother-in-law, that shall be, who thought of meeting you!

Ferd. But what of Clara?

Isaac. I'faith, you shall hear. This morning, as I was coming down, I met a pretty damsel, who told me her name was Clara d'Almanza, and begged my protection.

Ferd. How?

Isaac. She said she had eloped from her father, Don Guzman, but that love for a young gentleman in Seville was the cause.

Ferd. Oh, heavens! did she confess it?

Isaac. Oh, yes, she confessed at once; but then, says she, my lover is not informed of my flight, nor suspects my intention.

Ferd. Dear creature! no more I did indeed! Oh, I am the happiest fellow! [*Aside.*] Well, Isaac!

Isaac. Why, then she entreated me to find him out for her, and bring him to her.

Ferd. Good heavens, how lucky! Well, come along; let's lose no time. [*Pulling him.*

Isaac. Zooks! where are we to go?

Ferd. Why, did anything more pass?

Isaac. Anything more! yes; the end on't was, that

I was moved with her speeches, and complied with her desires.

Ferd. Well, and where is she?

Isaac. Where is she? why, don't I tell you, I complied with her request, and left her safe in the arms of her lover.

Ferd. 'Sdeath, you trifle with me! I have never seen her.

Isaac. You! O lud, no! How the devil should you? 'Twas Antonio she wanted; and with Antonio I left her.

Ferd. Hell and madness! [*Aside.*] What, Antonio d'Ercilla?

Isaac. Ay, ay, the very man; and the best part of it was, he was shy of taking her at first. He talked a good deal about honour, and conscience, and deceiving some dear friend; but, lord, we soon overruled that.

Ferd. You did!

Isaac. Oh, yes, presently. Such deceit, says he. Pish! says the lady, tricking is all fair in love. But then, my friend, says he—— Pshaw! d—n your friend, says I. So, poor wretch, he has no chance—no, no; he may hang himself as soon as he pleases.

Ferd. I must go, or I shall betray myself.

Isaac. But stay, Ferdinand, you ha'n't heard the best of the joke.

Ferd. Curse on your joke!

Isaac. Good lack! what's the matter now? I thought to have diverted you.

Ferd. Be rack'd! tortured! d—d——

Isaac. Why, sure you are not the poor devil of a lover, are you? I'faith, as sure as can be, he is. This is a better joke than t'other, ha! ha! ha!

Ferd. What, do you laugh? you vile, mischievous

varlet! [*Collars him.*] But that you're beneath my anger, I'd tear your heart out. [*Throws him from him.*

Isaac. O mercy! here's usage for a brother-in-law!

Ferd. But, hark ye, rascal! tell me directly where these false friends are gone, or, by my soul——[*Draws.*

Isaac. For Heaven's sake, now, my dear brother-in-law, don't be in a rage. I'll recollect as well as I can.

Ferd. Be quick then!

Isaac. I will, I will; but people's memories differ; some have a treacherous memory, now mine is a cowardly memory, it takes to its heels, at sight of a drawn sword, it does, i'faith; and I could as soon fight as recollect.

Ferd. Z—ds! tell me the truth, and I won't hurt you.

Isaac. No, no, I know you won't, my dear brother-in-law; but that ill-looking thing there——

Ferd. What, then, you won't tell me?

Isaac. Yes, yes, I will; I'll tell you all, upon my soul; but why need you listen sword in hand?

Ferd. Why, there. [*Puts up.*] Now.

Isaac. Why then, I believe they are gone to——that is, my friend Carlos told me, he had left Donna Clara—dear Ferdinand, keep your hands off—at the convent of St. Catharine.

Ferd. St. Catharine!

Isaac. Yes; and that Antonio was to come to her there.

Ferd. Is this the truth?

Isaac. It is indeed; and all I know, as I hope for life.

Ferd. Well, coward, take your life. 'Tis that false, dishonourable Antonio who shall feel my vengeance.

Isaac. Ay, ay, kill him; cut his throat, and welcome.

Ferd. But, for Clara, infamy on her! She is not worth my resentment.

Isaac. No more she is, my dear brother-in-law. I'faith, I would not be angry about her; she is not worth it, indeed.

Ferd. 'Tis false! she is worth the enmity of princes.

Isaac. True, true, so she is; and I pity you exceedingly for having lost her.

Ferd. 'Sdeath, you rascal! How durst you talk of pitying me?

Isaac. Oh, dear brother-in-law, I beg pardon, I don't pity you in the least, upon my soul.

Ferd. Get hence, fool, and provoke me no further; nothing but your insignificance saves you.

Isaac. I'faith, then my insignificance is the best friend I have. I'm going, dear Ferdinand. What a curst, hot-headed bully it is! [*Exeunt.*

SCENE III.

The Garden of the Convent.

Enter LOUISA *and* CLARA.

Louisa. And you really wish my brother may not find you out?

Clara. Why else have I concealed myself under this disguise?

Louisa. Why, perhaps, because the dress becomes you; for you certainly don't intend to be a nun for life.

Clara. If, indeed, Ferdinand had not offended me so last night——

Louisa. Come, come, it was his fear of losing you made him so rash.

Clara. Well, you may think me cruel; but I swear,

if he were here this instant, I believe I should forgive him.

SONG.

By him we love offended,
  How soon our anger flies!
One day apart, 'tis ended;
  Behold him, and it dies.

Last night, your roving brother,
  Enrag'd, I bade depart;
And sure his rude presumption
  Deserved to lose my heart.

Yet, were he now before me,
  In spite of injured pride,
I fear my eyes would pardon
  Before my tongue could chide.

Louisa. I protest, Clara, I shall begin to think you are seriously resolved to enter on your probation.

Clara. And, seriously, I very much doubt whether the character of a nun would not become me best.

Louisa. Why, to be sure, the character of a nun is a very becoming one at a masquerade; but no pretty woman, in her senses, ever thought of taking the veil for above a night.

Clara. Yonder I see your Antonio is returned. I shall only interrupt you. Ah, Louisa, with what happy eagerness you turn to look for him! [*Exit.*

Enter ANTONIO.

Ant. Well, my Louisa, any news since I left you?

Louisa. None. The messenger is not returned from my father.

Ant. Well, I confess, I do not perceive what we are to expect from him.

Louisa. I shall be easier, however, in having made the trial. I do not doubt your sincerity, Antonio, but there is a chilling air around poverty, that often kills affection, that was not nursed in it. If we would make love our household god, we had best secure him a comfortable roof.

SONG—ANTONIO.

How oft, Louisa, hast thou told
   (Nor wilt thou the fond boast disown),
Thou wouldst not lose Antonio's love
   To reign the partner of a throne.
And by those lips, that spoke so kind,
   And by that hand, I've press'd to mine,
To be the lord of wealth and power,
   By Heav'ns, I would not part with thine!

Then how, my soul, can we be poor,
   Who own what kingdoms could not buy?
Of this true heart thou shalt be queen,
   And, serving thee, a monarch I.
Thus uncontroll'd, in mutual bliss,
   And rich in love's exhaustless mine,
Do thou snatch treasures from my lips,
   And I'll take kingdoms back from thine!

Enter MAID, *with a Letter.*

Louisa. My father's answer, I suppose.

Ant. My dearest Louisa, you may be assured that it contains nothing but threats and reproaches.

Louisa. Let us see, however. [*Reads.*] '*Dearest daughter, make your lover happy; you have my full* consent to marry as your whim has chosen, but be sure come home and sup with your affectionate father.'

Ant. You jest, Louisa!

Louisa. [*Gives him the letter.*] Read—read.

Ant. 'Tis so, by Heavens! Sure there must be some mistake; but that's none of our business. Now, Louisa, you have no excuse for delay.

Louisa. Shall we not then return and thank my father?

Ant. But first let the priest put it out of his power to recall his word. I'll fly to procure one.

Louisa. Nay, if you part with me again, perhaps you may lose me.

Ant. Come, then, there is a friar of a neighbouring convent is my friend. You have already been diverted by the manners of a nunnery, let us see whether there is less hypocrisy among the holy fathers.

Louisa. I'm afraid not, Antonio; for in religion, as in friendship, they who profess most are ever the least sincere. [*Exeunt.*

Enter CLARA.

Clara. So, yonder they go, as happy as a mutual and confessed affection can make them, while I am left in solitude. Heigho! love may perhaps excuse the rashness of an elopement from one's friend, but I am sure, nothing but the presence of the man we love can support it. Ha! what do I see? Ferdinand, as I live! How could he gain admission? By potent gold, I suppose, as Antonio did. How eager and disturbed he seems! he shall not know me as yet.

[*Lets down her veil.*

Enter FERDINAND.

Ferd. Yes, those were certainly they; my information was right. [*Going.*

Clara. [*Stops him.*] Pray, signor, what is your business here?

Ferd. No matter—no matter. Oh, they stop [*Looks out.*] Yes, that is the perfidious Clara, indeed!

Clara. So, a jealous error. I'm glad to see him so moved. [*Aside.*

Ferd. Her disguise can't conceal her. No, no, I know her too well.

Clara. Wonderful discernment! but, signor——

Ferd. Be quiet, good nun; don't tease me. By Heavens, she leans upon his arm, hangs fondly on it! O woman! woman!

Clara. But, signor, who is it you want?

Ferd. Not you, not you, so pr'ythee don't tease me. Yet pray stay; gentle nun, was it not Donna Clara d'Almanza just parted from you?

Clara. Clara d'Almanza, signor, is not yet out of the garden.

Ferd. Ay, ay, I knew I was right. And pray is not that gentleman, now at the porch with her, Antonio d'Ercilla?

Clara. It is indeed, signor.

Ferd. So, so; now but one question more. Can you inform me for what purpose they have gone away?

Clara. They are gone to be married, I believe.

Ferd. Very well—enough; now if I don't mar their wedding! [*Exit.*

Clara [*Unveils.*] I thought jealousy had made lovers quick-sighted, but it has made mine blind. Louisa's story accounts to me for this error, and I am glad to find I have power enough over him to make him so unhappy. But why should not I be present at his surprise when undeceived? When he's through the porch, I'll follow him; and, perhaps, Louisa shall not singly be a bride.

SONG.

Adieu, thou dreary pile, where never dies
The sullen echo of repentant sighs!
Ye sister mourners of each lonely cell,
Inured to hymns and sorrow, fare ye well!
For happier scenes I fly this darksome grove,
To saints a prison, but a tomb to love!

[*Exit.*

SCENE IV.

A Court before the Priory.

Enter ISAAC, *crossing the Stage.*

Enter ANTONIO.

Ant. What, my friend Isaac!

Isaac. What, Antonio! wish me joy! I have Louisa safe.

Ant. Have you? I wish you joy with all my soul.

Isaac. Yes, I am come here to procure a priest to marry us.

Ant. So, then we are both on the same errand; I am come to look for Father Paul.

Isaac. Ha! I am glad on't; but, i'faith, he must tack me first; my love is waiting.

Ant. So is mine. I left her in the porch.

Isaac. Ay, but I am in haste to get back to Don Jerome.

Ant. And so am I too.

Isaac. Well, perhaps he'll save time, and marry us both together; or I'll be your father, and you shall be mine. Come along; but you're obliged to me for all this

Ant. Yes, yes. [*Exeunt.*

SCENE V.

A Room in the Priory—FRIARS *at the Table, drinking.*

GLEE AND CHORUS.

This bottle's the sun of our table,
   His beams are rosy wine;
We, planets, that are not able
   Without his help to shine.
Let mirth and glee abound!
   You'll soon grow bright
   With borrow'd light,
And shine as he goes round.

Paul. Brother Francis, toss the bottle about, and give me your toast.

Francis. Have we drank the abbess of St. Ursuline?

Paul. Yes, yes; she was the last.

Francis. Then I'll give you the blue-eyed nun of St. Catharine's.

Paul. With all my heart. [*Drinks.*] Pray, brother Augustine, were there any benefactions left in my absence?

Aug. Don Juan Corduba has left a hundred ducats, to remember him in our masses.

Paul. Has he? Let them be paid to our wine merchant, and we'll remember him in our cups, which will do just as well. Anything more?

Aug. Yes; Baptista, the rich miser, who died last

week, has bequeathed us a thousand pistoles, and the silver lamp he used in his own chamber, to burn before the image of St. Anthony.

Paul. 'Twas well meant; but we'll employ his money better. Baptista's bounty shall light the living, not the dead. St. Anthony is not afraid to be left in the dark, though he was——See who's there.

[*A knocking,* FRANCIS *goes to the door, and opens it.*]

Enter PORTER.

Porter. Here's one without in pressing haste to speak with Father Paul.

Francis. Brother Paul!

[PAUL *comes from behind a curtain, with a glass of wine, and in his hand a piece of cake.*

Paul. Here! how durst you, fellow, thus abruptly break in upon our devotions?

Porter. I thought they were finished.

Paul. No, they were not; were they, Brother Francis?

Francis. Not by a bottle each.

Paul. But neither you nor your fellows mark how the hours go; no, you mind nothing but the gratifying of your appetites; ye eat and swill, and sleep, and gormandize, and thrive, while we are wasting in mortification.

Porter. We ask no more than nature craves.

Paul. 'Tis false, ye have more appetites than hairs! and your flushed, sleek, and pampered appearance is the disgrace of our order; out on't. If you are hungry, can't you be content with the wholesome roots of the earth; and if you are dry, isn't there the crystal spring? [*Drinks.*] Put this away [*Gives a glass*] and show me where I'm wanted. [PORTER *drains the glass.* PAUL, *going, turns.*] So, you would have drank it, if there had been any left. Ah, glutton! glutton!

[*Exeunt.*

SCENE VI.

The Court before the Priory.

Enter ISAAC *and* ANTONIO.

Isaac. A plaguy while coming, this same Father Paul. He's detained at vespers, I suppose, poor fellow.

Ant. No, here he comes.

Enter PAUL.

Good Father Paul, I crave your blessing.

Isaac. Yes, good Father Paul, we are come to beg a favour.

Paul. What is it, pray?

Isaac. To marry us, good Father Paul; and in truth thou dost look the very priest of Hymen.

Paul. In short, I may be called so; for I deal in repentance and mortification.

Isaac. No, no, thou seemest an officer of Hymen, because thy presence speaks content and good humour.

Paul. Alas! my appearance is deceitful. Bloated I am, indeed! for fasting is a windy recreation, and it hath swol'n me like a bladder.

Ant. But thou hast a good fresh colour in thy face, father; rosy, i'faith.

Paul. Yes, I have blushed for mankind, till the hue of my shame is as fixed as their vices.

Isaac. Good man!

Paul. And I have laboured too, but to what purpose? they continue to sin under my very nose.

Isaac. Efecks, father, I should have guessed as much, for your nose seems to be put to the blush more than any other part of your face.

Paul. Go, you're a wag.

Ant. But, to the purpose, father; will you officiate for us?

Paul. To join young people thus clandestinely is not safe; and, indeed, I have in my heart many weighty reasons against it.

Ant. And I have in my hand many weighty reasons for it. Isaac, hav'n't you an argument or two in our favour about you?

Isaac. Yes, yes; here is a most unanswerable purse.

Paul. For shame! you make me angry; you forget who I am, and when importunate people have forced their trash—ay, into this pocket, here; or into this—why, then the sin was theirs. [*They put money into his pockets.*] Fie, now how you distress me! I would return it, but that I must touch it that way, and so wrong my oath.

Ant. Now then, come with us.

Isaac. Ay, now give us your title to joy and rapture.

Paul. Well, when your hour of repentance comes, don't blame me.

Ant. No bad caution to my friend Isaac. [*Aside.*] Well, well, father, do you do your part, and I'll abide the consequence.

Isaac. Ay, and so will I. [*They are going.*

Enter Louisa, *running.*

Louisa. O, Antonio, Ferdinand is at the porch, and inquiring for us.

Isaac. Who? Don Ferdinand! he's not inquiring for me, I hope.

Ant. Fear not, my love; I'll soon pacify him.

Isaac. Egad, you won't. Antonio, take my advice, and run away; this Ferdinand is the most unmerciful dog! and has the cursedest long sword! and, upon my soul, he comes on purpose to cut your throat.

Ant. Never fear, never fear.

Isaac. Well, you may stay if you will; but I'll get some one to marry me; for, by St. Iago, he shall never marry me again, while I am master of a pair of heels.

[*Runs out.*

Enter FERDINAND.

Ferd. So, sir, I have met with you at last.

Ant. Well, sir.

Ferd. Base, treacherous man! Whence can a false, deceitful soul, like yours, borrow confidence to look so steadily on the man you've injured?

Ant. Ferdinand, you are too warm. 'Tis true you find me on the point of wedding one I love beyond my life; but no argument of mine prevailed on her to elope. I scorn deceit as much as you. By Heaven, I knew not she had left her father's, till I saw her.

Ferd. What a mean excuse! You have wronged your friend, then, for one, whose wanton forwardness anticipated your treachery; of this, indeed, your Jew pander informed me; but let your conduct be consistent, and since you have dared to do a wrong, follow me, and show you have a spirit to avow it.

Louisa. Antonio, I perceive his mistake; leave him to me.

Paul. Friend, you are rude, to interrupt the union of two willing hearts.

Ferd. No, meddling priest; the hand he seeks is mine!

Paul. If so, I'll proceed no farther. Lady, did you ever promise this youth your hand?

[*To* LOUISA, *who shakes her head.*

Ferd. Clara, I thank you for your silence. I would not have heard your tongue avow such falsity; be't your punishment to remember I have not reproached you.

Enter CLARA.

Clara. What mockery is this?

Ferd. Antonio, you are protected now, but we shall meet.

[*Going,* CLARA *holds one arm, and* LOUISA *the other.*

DUET.

Louisa.	Turn thee round, I pray thee,
	Calm awhile thy rage.
Clara.	I must help to stay thee,
	And thy wrath assuage.
Louisa.	Couldst thou not discover
	One so dear to thee?
Clara.	Canst thou be a lover,
	And thus fly from me?

[*Both unveil.*

Ferd. How's this! my sister! Clara too. I'm confounded.

Louisa. 'Tis even so, good brother.

Paul. How! what impiety! Did the man want to marry his own sister?

Louisa. And ar'n't you ashamed of yourself, not to know your own sister?

Clara. To drive away your own mistress——

Louisa. Don't you see how jealousy blinds people?

Clara. Ay, and will you ever be jealous again?

Ferd. Never, never. You, sister, I know will forgive me. But how, Clara, shall I presume——

Clara. No, no, just now you told me not to tease you. 'Who do you want, good signor?' 'Not you, not you.' Oh, you blind wretch! But swear never to be jealous again, and I'll forgive you.

Ferd. By all——

Clara. There, that will do; you'll keep the oath just as well. [*Gives her hand.*

Louisa. But, brother, here is one to whom some apology is due.

Ferd. Antonio, I am ashamed to think——

Ant. Not a word of excuse, Ferdinand. I have not been in love myself without learning that a lover's anger should never be resented. But come, let us retire with this good father, and we'll explain to you the cause of this error.

GLEE AND CHORUS.

Oft does Hymen smile to hear
    Wordy vows of feigned regard;
Well he knows when they're sincere;
    Never slow to give reward:
For his glory is to prove
Kind to those who wed for love.

[*Exeunt.*

SCENE VII.

A Grand Saloon.

Enter DON JEROME, SERVANTS, *and* LOPEZ.

Jerome. Be sure now let everything be in the best order. Let all my servants have on their merriest faces, but tell them to get as little drunk as possible, till after supper. So, Lopez, where's your master? Sha'n't we have him at supper?

Lopez. Indeed, I believe not, sir. He's mad, I doubt; I'm sure he has frighted me from him.

Jerome. Ay, ay, he's after some wench, I suppose? A young rake! Well, well, we'll be merry without him.

Enter SERVANT.

Serv. Sir, here is Signor Isaac.

Enter ISAAC.

Jerome. So, my dear son-in-law — there, take my blessing and forgiveness. But where's my daughter? Where's Louisa?

Isaac. She's without, impatient for a blessing, but almost afraid to enter.

Jerome. Oh, fly and bring her in. [*Exit* ISAAC.] Poor girl, I long to see her pretty face.

Isaac. [*Without.*] Come, my charmer! my trembling angel!

Enter ISAAC *and* DUENNA; DON JEROME *runs to meet them; she kneels.*

Jerome. Come to my arms, my—— [*Starts back.*] Why, who the devil have we here?

Isaac. Nay, Don Jerome, you promised her forgiveness; see how the dear creature droops!

Jerome. Droops, indeed! Why, gad take me, this is old Margaret. But where's my daughter, where's Louisa?

Isaac. Why, here, before your eyes. Nay, don't be abashed, my sweet wife!

Jerome. Wife with a vengeance! Why, z—ds, you have not married the Duenna!

Duenna. [*Kneeling.*] O, dear papa! you'll not disown me, sure!

Jerome. Papa! papa! Why, z—ds, your impudence is as great as your ugliness!

Isaac. Rise, my charmer; go throw your snowy arms about his neck, and convince him you are——

Duenna. Oh, sir, forgive me!   [*Embraces him.*
Jerome. Help! murder!

Servants. What's the matter, sir?

Jerome. Why, here, this d—d Jew has brought an old harridan to strangle me.

Isaac. Lord, it is his own daughter, and he is so hard-hearted, he won't forgive her.

Enter ANTONIO *and* LOUISA; *they kneel.*

Jerome. Z—ds and fury! what's here now? Who sent for you, sir, and who the devil are you?

Ant. This lady's husband, sir.

Isaac. Ay, that he is, I'll be sworn; for I left them with the priest, and was to have given her away.

Jerome. You were?

Isaac. Ay; that's my honest friend, Antonio; and that's the little girl I told you I had hampered him with.

Jerome. Why, you are either drunk or mad; this is my daughter.

Isaac. No, no; 'tis you are both drunk and mad, I think. Here's your daughter.

Jerome. Hark ye, old iniquity, will you explain all this, or not?

Duenna. Come then, Don Jerome, I will; though our habits might inform you all. Look on your daughter, there, and on me.

Isaac. What's this I hear?

Duenna. The truth is, that in your passion this morning you made a small mistake; for you turned your daughter out of doors, and locked up your humble servant.

Isaac. O lud! O lud! here's a pretty fellow, to turn his daughter out of doors, instead of an old Duenna.

Jerome. And, O lud! O lud! here's a pretty fellow, to marry an old Duenna instead of my daughter. But how came the rest about?

Duenna. I have only to add, that I remained in your daughter's place, and had the good fortune to engage the affections of my sweet husband here.

Isaac. Her husband! why, you old witch, do you think I'll be your husband now? This is a trick, a cheat, and you ought all to be ashamed of yourselves.

Ant. Hark ye, Isaac, do you dare to complain of tricking? Don Jerome, I give you my word, this cunning Portuguese has brought all this upon himself, by endeavouring to overreach you, by getting your daughter's fortune, without making any settlement in return.

Jerome. Overreach me!

Louisa. 'Tis so, indeed, sir, and we can prove it to you.

Jerome. Why, gad take me, it must be so, or he could never have put up with such a face as Margaret's. So, little Solomon, I wish you joy of your wife with all my soul.

Louisa. Isaac, tricking is all fair in love; let you alone for the plot.

Ant. A cunning dog, ar'n't you? A sly little villain, heh?

Louisa. Roguish, perhaps; but keen, devilish keen.

Jerome. Yes, yes; his aunt always called him little Solomon.

Isaac. Why, the plagues of Egypt upon you all! But do you think I'll submit to such an imposition?

Ant. Isaac, one serious word; you'd better be content as you are; for, believe me, you will find that, in the opinion of the world, there is not a fairer subject for contempt and ridicule, than a knave become the dupe of his own art.

Isaac. I don't care; I'll not endure this. Don Jerome, 'tis you have done this; you would be so cursed positive about the beauty of her you locked up, and all the time I told you she was as old as my mother, and as ugly as the devil.

Duenna. Why, you little insignificant reptile!

Jerome. That's right; attack him, Margaret.

Duenna. Dare such a thing as you pretend to talk of beauty? A walking rouleau! a body that seems to owe all its consequence to the dropsy! a pair of eyes like two dead beetles in a wad of brown dough! a beard like an artichoke, with dry shrivelled jaws, that would disgrace the mummy of a monkey!

Jerome. Well done, Margaret!

Duenna. But you shall know that I have a brother, who wears a sword; and if you don't do me justice——

Isaac. Fire seize your brother, and you too! I'll fly to Jerusalem, to avoid you!

Duenna. Fly where you will, I'll follow you.

Jerome. Throw your snowy arms about him, Margaret. [*Exeunt* ISAAC *and* DUENNA.] But, Louisa, are you really married to this modest gentleman?

Louisa. Sir, in obedience to your commands, I gave him my hand within this hour.

Jerome. My commands!

Ant. Yes, sir; here is your consent, under your own hand.

Jerome. How! would you rob me of my child by a trick, a false pretence? and do you think to get her fortune by the same means? Why, 'slife, you are as great a rogue as Isaac!

Ant. No, Don Jerome; though I have profited by this paper, in gaining your daughter's hand, I scorn to obtain her fortune by deceit. There, sir. [*Gives a letter.*] Now give her your blessing for a dower, and all the little I possess shall be settled on her in return. Had you wedded her to a prince, he could do no more.

Jerome. Why, gad take me, but you are a very extraordinary fellow! But have you the impudence to suppose no one can do a generous action but yourself? Here, Louisa, tell this proud fool of yours that he's the only man I know that would renounce your fortune; and, by my soul, he's the only man in Spain that's worthy of it. There, bless you both. I'm an obstinate old fellow when I'm in the wrong; but you shall now find me as steady in the right.

Enter FERDINAND *and* CLARA.

Another wonder still! Why, sirrah! Ferdinand, you have not stole a nun, have you?

Ferd. She is a nun in nothing but her habit, sir; look nearer, and you will perceive 'tis Clara D'Almanza, Don Guzman's daughter; and, with pardon for stealing a wedding, she is also my wife.

Jerome. Gadsbud, and a great fortune. Ferdinand, you are a prudent young rogue, and I forgive you; and, ifecks, you are a pretty little damsel. Give your father-in-law a kiss, you smiling rogue.

Clara. There, old gentleman; and now mind you behave well to us.

Jerome. Ifecks, those lips ha'n't been chilled by kissing beads. Egad, I believe I shall grow the best humoured fellow in Spain. Lewis! Sancho! Carlos! d'ye here? are all my doors thrown open? Our children's weddings are the only holidays our age can boast; and then we drain, with pleasure, the little stock of spirits time has left us. [*Music within.*] But see, here come our friends and neighbours!

Enter MASQUERADERS.

And, 'ifaith, we'll make a night on't, with wine, and dance, and catches—then old and young shall join us.

FINALE.

Jerome. Come now for jest and smiling,
  Both old and young beguiling,
   Let us laugh and play, so blithe and gay,
  Till we banish care away.

Louisa. Thus crown'd with dance and song,
　　　　　The hours shall glide along,
　　　　　　With a heart at ease, merry, merry glees
　　　　　　Can never fail to please.

Ferd. Each bride with blushes glowing,
　　　　Our wine as rosy flowing,
　　　　　Let us laugh and play, so blithe and gay,
　　　　　Till we banish care away.

Ant. Then healths to every friend,
　　　　The night's repast shall end,
　　　　　With a heart at ease, merry, merry glees
　　　　　Can never fail to please.

Clara. Nor, while we are so joyous,
　　　　　Shall anxious fear annoy us;
　　　　　　Let us laugh and play, so blithe and gay
　　　　　　Till we banish care away.

Jerome. For generous guests like these
　　　　　Accept the wish to please;
　　　　　　So we'll laugh and play, so blithe and gay,
　　　　　　Your smiles drive care away.
　　　　　　　　　　　　　　　　　　[*Exeunt.*

A TRIP TO SCARBOROUGH:

A COMEDY.

DRAMATIS PERSONÆ.

AS ORIGINALLY ACTED AT DRURY LANE THEATRE, FEBRUARY 24, 1777.

Lord Foppington	Mr. Dodd.
Sir Tunbelly Clumsy . .	Mr. Moody.
Colonel Townly	Mr. Brereton.
Loveless	Mr. Smith.
Young Fashion	Mr. J. Palmer.
Probe	Mr. Parsons.
Jeweller	Mr. Lamash.
Shoemaker	Mr. Carpenter.
La'Varole	Mr. Burton.
Tailor	Mr. Parker.
Mendlegs	Mr. Norris.
Lory	Mr. Baddeley.
Amanda	Mrs. Robinson.
Berinthia	Miss Farren.
Miss Hoyden	Mrs. Abington.
Mrs. Coupler	Mrs. Booth.
Nurse	Mrs. Bradshaw.

PROLOGUE.

SPOKEN BY MR. KING.

WHAT various transformations we remark,
From east Whitechapel, to the west Hyde Park!
Men, women, children, houses, signs, and fashions,
State, stage, trade, taste, the humours, and the passions;
Th' Exchange, 'Change Alley, wheresoe'er you're ranging,
Court, city, country, all are changed or changing:
The streets, some time ago, were paved with stones,
Which, aided by a hackney-coach, half broke your bones.
The purest lovers then indulged no bliss;
They run great hazard if they stole a kiss.
One chaste salute—the damsel cried—*O fie!*
As they approach'd—slap went the coach awry—
Poor Sylvia got a bump, and Damon a black eye.

But now weak nerves in hackney-coaches roam,
And the cramm'd glutton snores, unjolted, home:
Of former times, that polish'd thing, a beau,
Is metamorphosed now, from top to toe;
Then the full flaxen wig, spread o'er the shoulders,
Conceal'd the shallow head from the beholders!

But *now* the whole's reversed—each fop appears,
Cropp'd, and trimm'd up, exposing head and ears:
The buckle then its modest limits knew,
Now, like the ocean, dreadful to the view,
Hath broke its bounds, and swallows up the shoe;
The wearer's foot, like his once fine estate,
Is almost lost, th' encumbrance is so great.

Ladies may smile—are *they* not in the plot?
The bounds of nature have not they forgot?
Were they design'd to be, when put together,
Made up, like shuttlecocks, of cork and feather?
Their pale-faced grandmammas appear'd with grace,
When dawning blushes rose upon the face;
No blushes now their once-loved station seek;
The foe is in possession of the cheek!
No heads, of old, too high in feather'd state,
Hinder'd the fair to pass the lowest gate;
A church to enter now, they must be bent,
If ever they should try th' experiment.

   As change thus circulates throughout the nation,
Some plays may justly call for alteration;
At least to draw some slender cov'ring o'er
That *graceless wit*° which was too bare before:
Those writers well and wisely use their pens,
Who turn our wantons into Magdalens;
And howsoever wicked wits revile 'em,
We hope to find in you their stage asylum.

    * And *Van* wants grace, who never wanted wit.—POPE

A TRIP TO SCARBOROUGH.

ACT I.—SCENE I.

The Hall of an Inn.

Enter Young Fashion *and* Lory, Postillion *following with a Portmanteau.*

Young F. Lory, pay the postboy, and take the portmanteau.

Lory. Faith, sir, we had better let the postboy take the portmanteau and pay himself.

Young F. Why sure there's something left in it.

Lory. Not a rag, upon my honour, sir. We eat the last of your wardrobe at Newmalton; and if we had had twenty miles farther to go, our next meal must have been of the cloak-bag.

Young F. Why, 'sdeath, it appears full.

Lory. Yes, sir. I made bold to stuff it with hay, to save appearances, and look like baggage.

Young F. What the devil shall I do? Harkee, boy, what's the chaise?

Post. Thirteen shillings, please your honour.

Young F. Can you give me change for a guinea?

Post. O yes, sir.

Lory. Soh, what will he do now? Lord, sir, you had better let the boy be paid below.

Young F. Why, as you say, Lory, I believe it will be as well.

Lory. Yes, yes; I'll tell them to discharge you below, honest friend.

Post. Please your honour, there are the turnpikes too.

Young F. Ay, ay, the turnpikes by all means.

Post. And I hope your honour will order me something for myself.

Young F. To be sure; bid them give you a crown.

Lory. Yes, yes. My master doesn't care what you charge them. So get along, you——

Post. And there's the hostler, your honour.

Lory. Pshaw! d—n the hostler. Would you impose upon the gentleman's generosity. [*Pushes him out.*] A rascal, to be so curst ready with his change!

Young F. Why, faith, Lory, he had nearly posed me.

Lory. Well, sir, we are arrived at Scarborough, not worth a guinea! I hope you'll own yourself a happy man; you have outlived all your cares.

Young F. How so, sir.

Lory. Why you have nothing left to take care of.

Young F. Yes, sirrah, I have myself and you to take care of still.

Lory. Sir, if you could prevail with somebody else to do that for you, I fancy we might both fare the better for it. But now, sir, for my Lord Foppington, your elder brother.

Young F. D—n my eldest brother.

Lory. With all my heart; but get him to redeem your annuity, however. Look you, sir, you must wheedle him, or you must starve.

Young F. Look you, sir, I will neither wheedle him nor starve.

Lory. Why, what will you do, then?

Young F. Cut his throat, or get some one to do it for me.

Lory. 'Gad so, sir, I'm glad to find I was not so well acquainted with the strength of your conscience as with the weakness of your purse.

Young F. Why, art thou so impenetrable a blockhead as to believe he'll help me with a farthing?

Lory. Not if you treat him *de haut en bas*, as you used to do.

Young F. Why, how wouldst have me treat him?

Lory. Like a trout; tickle him.

Young F. I can't flatter.

Lory. Can you starve?

Young F. Yes.

Lory. I can't; good-bye t'ye, sir.

Young F. Stay; thou'lt distract me. But who comes here; my old friend, Colonel Townly.

Enter Colonel Townly.

My dear colonel, I am rejoiced to meet you here.

Col. T. Dear Tom, this is an unexpected pleasure. What, are you come to Scarborough to be present at your brother's wedding?

Lory. Ah, sir, if it had been his funeral, we should have come with pleasure.

Col. T. What, honest Lory, are you with your master still?

Lory. Yes, sir, I have been starving with him ever since I saw your honour last.

Young F. Why, Lory is an attach'd rogue; there's no getting rid of him.

Lory. True, sir, as my master says, there's no

seducing me from his service—till he's able to pay me my wages. [*Aside.*

Young F. Go, go, sir; and take care of the baggage.

Lory. Yes, sir; the baggage! O Lord! I suppose, sir, I must charge the landlord to be very particular where he stows this?

Young F. Get along, you rascal. [*Exit* LORY, *with the portmanteau.*] But, colonel, are you acquainted with my proposed sister-in-law?

Col. T. Only by character; her father, Sir Tunbelly Clumsy, lives within a quarter of a mile of this place, in a lonely old house, which nobody comes near. She never goes abroad, nor sees company at home; to prevent all misfortunes, she has her breeding within doors; the parson of the parish teaches her to play upon the dulcimer, the clerk to sing, her nurse to dress, and her father to dance; in short, nobody has free admission there but our old acquaintance, Mother Coupler, who has procured your brother this match, and is, I believe, a distant relation of Sir Tunbelly.

Young F. But is her fortune so considerable?

Col. T. Three thousand a year, and a good sum of money, independent of her father, beside.

Young F. 'Sdeath! that my old acquaintance, Dame Coupler, could not have thought of me, as well as my brother, for such a prize.

Col. T. Egad, I wouldn't swear that you are too late; his lordship, I know, hasn't yet seen the lady; and, I believe, has quarrelled with his patroness.

Young F. My dear colonel, what an idea have you started!

Col. T. Pursue it, if you can, and I promise you you shall have my assistance; for besides my natural contempt for his lordship, I have at present the enmity of a rival towards him.

Young F. What, has he been addressing your old flame, the widow Berinthia?

Col. T. Faith, Tom, I am at present most whimsically circumstanced. I came here a month ago to meet the lady you mention; but she failing in her promise, I, partly from pique and partly from idleness, have been diverting my chagrin by offering up incense to the beauties of Amanda, our friend Loveless's wife.

Young F. I never have seen her, but have heard her spoken of as a youthful wonder of beauty and prudence.

Col. T. She is so indeed; and Loveless being too careless and insensible of the treasure he possesses, my lodging in the same house has given me a thousand opportunities of making my assiduities acceptable; so that, in less than a fortnight, I began to bear my disappointment from the widow with the most Christian resignation.

Young F. And Berinthia has never appeared?

Col. T. Oh, there's the perplexity; for just as I began not to care whether ever I saw her again or not, last night she arrived.

Young F. And instantly reassumed her empire?

Col. T. No, faith—we met; but the lady not condescending to give me any serious reasons for having fool'd me for a month, I left her in a huff.

Young F. Well, well, I'll answer for it she'll soon resume her power, especially as friendship will prevent your pursuing the other too far, but my coxcomb of a brother is an admirer of Amanda's too, is he?

Col. T. Yes, and I believe is most heartily despised by her. But come with me, and you shall see her and your old friend Loveless.

Young F. I must pay my respects to his lordship. Perhaps you can direct me to his lodgings?

Col. T. Come with me; I shall pass by it.

Young F. I wish you could pay this visit for me, or could tell me what I should say to him.

Col. T. Say nothing to him: apply yourself to his bag, his sword, his feather, his snuff-box; and when you are well with them, desire him to lend you a thousand pounds, and I'll engage you prosper.

Young F. 'Sdeath and furies! why was that coxcomb thrust into the world before me? O fortune, fortune, thou art a jilt, by Gad. [*Exeunt.*

SCENE II.

A Dressing-room.

Enter Lord Foppington, *in his Nightgown, and* La Varole.

Lord F. Well, 'tis an unspeakable pleasure to be a man of quality—strike me dumb! Even the boors of this northern spa have learn'd the respect due to a title. [*Aside.*] La Varole!

La Var. Mi lor——

Lord F. You ha'n't yet been at Muddymoat Hall, to announce my arrival, have you?

La Var. Not yet, mi lor.

Lord F. Then you need not go till Saturday [*Exit* La Varole], as I am in no particular haste to view my intended sposa. I shall sacrifice a day or two more to the pursuit of my friend Loveless's wife. Amanda is a charming creature, strike me ugly! and if I have any discernment in the world, she thinks no less of my Lord Foppington.

Re-enter LA VAROLE.

La Val. Mi lor, de shoemaker, de tailor, de hosier, de sempstress, de peru, be all ready, if your lordship please to dress.
Lord F. 'Tis well; admit them.
La Val. Hey, messieurs, entrez.

Enter TAILOR, SHOEMAKER, &c.

Lord F. So, gentlemen, I hope you have all taken pains to show yourselves masters in your professions?
Tai. I think I may presume to say, sir——
La Var. My lor, you clown you!
Tai. My lord—I ask your lordship's pardon, my lord. I hope, my lord, your lordship will be pleased to own I have brought your lordship as accomplished a suit of clothes as ever peer of England wore, my lord. Will your lordship please to view 'em now?
Lord F. Ay; but let my people dispose the glasses so that I may see myself before and behind; for I love to see myself all round.

Whilst he puts on his clothes, enter YOUNG FASHION *and* LORY.

Young F. Hey-day! What the devil have we here? Sure my gentleman's grown a favourite at court, he has got so many people at his levee. [*Apart.*
Lory. Sir, these people come in order to make him a favourite at court: they are to establish him with the ladies. [*Apart.*
Young F. Good heaven to what an ebb of taste are women fallen, that it should be in the power of a laced coat to recommend a gallant to them! [*Apart.*
Lory. Sir, tailors and hairdressers debauch all the women. [*Apart.*

Young F. Thou say'st true. But now for my reception. [*Apart.*

Lord F. Death and eternal tortures! Sir, I say the coat is too wide here by a foot.

Tai. My lord, if it had been tighter, 'twould neither have hook'd nor button'd.

Lord F. Rat the hooks and buttons, sir! Can anything be worse than this? As Gad shall jedge me, it hangs on my shoulders like a chairman's surtout.

Tai. 'Tis not for me to dispute your lordship's fancy.

Lory. There, sir, observe what respect does. [*Apart.*

Young F. Respect! D—n him for a coxcomb. But let's accost him. [*Apart.*] Brother, I'm your humble servant.

Lord F. O Lard, Tam, I did not expect you in England. Brother, I am glad to see you; but what has brought you to Scarborough, Tam? Look you, sir [*To the Tailor*], I shall never be reconciled to this nauseous wrapping gown, therefore pray get me another suit with all possible expedition, for this is my eternal aversion. [*Exit Tailor.*] Well but, Tam, you don't tell me what has driven you to Scarborough. Mrs. Calico, are not you of my mind?

Semp. Directly, my lord. I hope your lordship is pleased with your ruffles?

Lord F. In love with them, stap my vitals! Bring my bill, you shall be paid to-morrow.

Semp. I humbly thank your lordship. [*Exit.*

Lord F. Hark thee, shoemaker, these shoes ar'n't ugly, but they don't fit me.

Shoe. My lord, I think they fit you very well.

Lord F. They hurt me just below the instep.

Shoe. [*Feels his foot*]. No, my lord, they don't hurt you there.

Lord F. I tell thee they pinch me execrably.

Shoe. Why then, my lord, if those shoes pinch you, I'll be d—n'd.

Lord F. Why, wilt thou undertake to persuade me I cannot feel?

Shoe. Your lordship may please to feel what you think fit, but that shoe does not hurt you. I think I understand my trade.

Lord F. Now, by all that's good and powerful, thou art an incomprehensive coxcomb; but thou makest good shoes, and so I'll bear with thee.

Shoe. My lord, I have work'd for half the people of quality in this town these twenty years, and 'tis very hard I shouldn't know when a shoe hurts, and when it don't.

Lord F. Well, pr'ythee begone about thy business. [*Exit Shoemaker.*] Mr. Mendlegs, a word with you. The calves of these stockings are thicken'd a little too much; they make my legs look like a porter's.

Mend. My lord, methinks they look mighty well.

Lord F. Ay, but you are not so good a judge of those things as I am. I have studied them all my life; therefore pray let the next be the thickness of a crown piece less.

Mend. Indeed, my lord, they are the same kind I had the honour to furnish your lordship with in town.

Lord F. Very possibly, Mr. Mendlegs; but that was in the beginning of the winter, and you should always remember, Mr. Hosier, that if you make a nobleman's spring legs as robust as his autumnal calves, you commit a monstrous impropriety, and make no allowance for the fatigues of the winter. [*Exit Hosier.*

Jewel. I hope, my lord, those buckles have had the unspeakable satisfaction of being honoured with your lordship's approbation?

Lord F. Why, they are of a pretty fancy; but don't you think them rather of the smallest?

Jewel. My lord, they could not be well larger, to keep on your lordship's shoe.

Lord F. My good sir, you forget that these matters are not as they used to be: formerly, indeed, the buckle was a sort of machine, intended to keep on the shoe; but the case is now quite reversed, and the shoe is of no earthly use but to keep on the buckle. Now give me my watches, and the business of the morning will be pretty well over. [*Exit Jeweller.*

Young F. Well, Lory, what dost think on't? A very friendly reception from a brother, after three years' absence! [*Apart.*

Lory. Why, sir, 'tis your own fault; here you have stood ever since you came in, and have not commended any one thing that belongs to him. [*Apart.*

Young F. Nor ever shall, while they belong to a coxcomb. [*Apart.*] Now your people of business are gone, brother, I hope I may obtain a quarter of an hour's audience of you.

Lord F. Faith, Tam, I must beg you'll excuse me at this time, for I have an engagement which I would not break for the salvation of mankind. Hey! there! Is my carriage at the door? You'll excuse me, brother.
[*Going.*

Young F. Shall you be back to dinner?

Lord F. As Gad shall jedge me, I can't tell; for it is passible I may dine with some friends at Donner's.

Young F. Shall I meet you there? for I must needs talk with you.

Lord F. That I'm afraid mayn't be quite so praper; for those I commonly eat with are a people of nice conversation; and you know, Tam, your education has been a little at large. But there are other ordinaries in town—very good beef ordinaries. I suppose, Tam, you can eat beef? However, dear Tam, I'm glad to see thee in England, stap my vitals! [*Exit*

Young F. Hell and furies! Is this to be borne?

Lory. Faith, sir, I could almost have given him a knock o'the pate myself.

Young F. 'Tis enough. I will now show you the excess of my passion, by being very calm. Come, Lory, lay your loggerhead to mine, and, in cold blood, let us contrive his destruction.

Lory. Here comes a head, sir, would contrive it better than both our loggerheads, if she would but join in the confederacy.

Young F. By this light, Madam Coupler; she seems dissatisfied at something. Let us observe her.

Enter Mrs. Coupler.

Mrs. C. Soh! I am likely to be well rewarded for my services, truly; my suspicions, I find, were but too just. What! refuse to advance me a petty sum, when I am upon the point of making him master of a galleon! But let him look to the consequences, an ungrateful, narrow-minded coxcomb.

Young F. So he is, upon my soul, old lady; it must be my brother you speak of.

Mrs. C. Ha! stripling, how came you here? What, hast spent, all, eh? And art thou come to dun his lordship for assistance?

Young F. No; I want somebody's assistance to cut his lordship's throat, without the risk of being hanged for him.

Mrs. C. Egad, sirrah, I could help thee to do him almost as good a turn, without the danger of being burn'd in the hand for't.

Young F. How—how, old Mischief?

Mrs. C. Why, you must know I have done you the kindness to make up a match for your brother.

Young F. I'm very much beholden to you, truly!

Mrs. C. You may before the wedding-day yet; the lady is a great heiress, the match is concluded, the writings are drawn, and his lordship has come hither to put the finishing hand to the business.

Young F. I understand as much.

Mrs. C. Now you must know, stripling, your brother's a knave.

Young F. Good.

Mrs. C. He has given me a bond of a thousand pounds for helping him to this fortune, and has promised me as much more, in ready money, upon the day of the marriage; which, I understand by a friend, he never designs to pay me; and his just now refusing to pay me a part is a proof of it. If, therefore, you will be a generous young rogue, and secure me five thousand pounds, I'll help you to the lady.

Young F. And how the devil wilt thou do that?

Mrs. C. Without the devil's aid, I warrant thee. Thy brother's face not one of the family ever saw; the whole business has been managed by me, and all his letters go through my hands. Sir Tunbelly Clumsy, my relation—for that's the old gentleman's name—is apprised of his lordship being down here, and expects him to-morrow to receive his daughter's hand; but the peer, I find, means to bait here a few days longer, to recover the fatigue of his journey, I suppose. Now you shall go to Muddymoat Hall in his place. I'll give you a letter of introduction; and if you don't marry the girl before sunset, you deserve to be hanged before morning.

Young F. Agreed, agreed; and for thy reward——

Mrs. C. Well, well; though I warrant thou hast not a farthing of money in thy pocket now—no, one may see it in thy face.

Young F. Not a sous, by Jupiter.

Mrs. C. Must I advance then? Well, be at my lodgings, next door, this evening, and I'll see what may be done; we'll sign and seal; and when I have given thee some further instructions, thou shalt hoist sail and be gone. [*Exit.*

Young F. So, Lory, fortune, thou seest, at last takes care of merit; we are in a fair way to be a great people.

Lory. Ay, sir, if the devil don't step between the cup and the lip, as he used to do.

Young F. Why, faith, he has played me many a d—d trick to spoil my fortune; and, egad, I am almost afraid he's at work about it again now; but if I should tell thee how, thou'dst wonder at me.

Lory. Indeed, sir, I should not.

Young F. How dost know?

Lory. Because, sir, I have wondered at you so often, I can wonder at you no more.

Young F. No! What wouldst thou say, if a qualm of conscience should spoil my design?

Lory. I would eat my words, and wonder more than ever.

Young F. Why, faith, Lory, though I have played many a roguish trick, this is so full-grown a cheat, I find I must take pains to come up to't——I have scruples.

Lory. They are strong symptoms of death. If you find them increase, sir, pray make your will.

Young F. No, my conscience sha'n't starve me neither; but thus far I'll listen to it. Before I execute this project, I'll try my brother to the bottom. If he has yet so much humanity about him as to assist me, though with a moderate aid, I'll drop my project at his feet, and show him how I can do for him much more than what I'd ask he'd do for me. This one conclusive trial of him I resolve to make.

> Succeed or fail, still vict'ry is my lot;
> If I subdue his heart, 'tis well—if not,
> I will subdue my conscience to my plot.
>
> [*Exeunt.*

ACT II.—SCENE I.

Enter LOVELESS *and* AMANDA.

Love. How do you like these lodgings, my dear? For my part, I am so pleas'd with them, I shall hardly remove whilst we stay here, if you are satisfied.

Aman. I am satisfied with everything that pleases you, else I had not come to Scarborough at all.

Love. O! a little of the noise and folly of this place will sweeten the pleasures of our retreat; we shall find the charms of our retirement doubled when we return to it.

Aman. That pleasing prospect will be my chiefest entertainment, whilst, much against my will, I engage in those empty pleasures which 'tis so much the fashion to be fond of.

Love. I own most of them are, indeed, but empty; yet there are delights of which a private life is destitute, which may divert an honest man, and be a harmless entertainment to a virtuous woman; good music is one; and truly (with some small allowance) the plays, I think, may be esteemed another.

Aman. Plays, I must confess, have some small charms. What do you think of that you saw last night?

Love. To say truth, I did not mind it much; my attention was for some time taken off to admire the workmanship of nature, in the face of a young lady who sat some distance from me, she was so exquisitely handsome.

Aman. So exquisitely handsome!

Love. Why do you repeat my words, my dear?

Aman. Because you seem'd to speak them with such pleasure, I thought I might oblige you with their echo.

Love. Then you are alarmed, Amanda?

Aman. It is my duty to be so when you are in danger.

Love. You are too quick in apprehending for me. I view'd her with a world of admiration, but not one glance of love.

Aman. Take heed of trusting to such nice distinctions. But were your eyes the only things that were inquisitive? Had I been in your place, my tongue, I fancy, had been curious too. I should have ask'd her where she lived; yet still without design. Who was she, pray?

Love. Indeed I cannot tell.

Aman. You will not tell.

Love. Upon my honour then, I did not ask.

Aman. Nor do you know what company was with her?

Love. I do not. But why are you so earnest?

Aman. I thought I had cause.

Love. But you thought wrong, Amanda; for turn the case, and let it be your story; should you come home and tell me you had seen a handsome man, should I grow jealous because you had eyes?

Aman. But should I tell you he was exquisitely so, and that I had gazed on him with admiration, should you not think 'twere possible I might go one step farther, and inquire his name?

Love. She has reason on her side; I have talk'd too much; but I must turn off another way. [*Aside.*] Will you then make no difference, Amanda, between the language of our sex and yours? There is a modesty restrains your tongues, which makes you speak by halves when you commend; but roving flattery gives a loose to ours, which makes us still speak double what we think.

Enter a SERVANT.

Serv. Madam, there is a lady at the door in a chair desires to know whether your ladyship sees company; her name is Berinthia.

Aman. Oh dear! 'tis a relation I have not seen these five years; pray her to walk in. [*Exit* SERVANT.] Here's another beauty for you; she was, when I saw her last, reckoned extremely handsome.

Love. Don't be jealous now; for I shall gaze upon her too.

Enter BERINTHIA.

Ha! by heavens, the very woman! [*Aside.*

Ber. [*Salutes* AMANDA.] Dear Amanda, I did not expect to meet you in Scarborough.

Aman. Sweet cousin, I'm overjoyed to see you. Mr. Loveless, here's a relation and a friend of mine, I desire you'll be better acquainted with.

Love. [*Salutes* BERINTHIA.] If my wife never desires a harder thing, madam, her request will be easily granted.

Re-enter SERVANT.

Serv. Sir, my Lord Foppington presents his humble service to you, and desires to know how you do. He's at the next door; and if it be not inconvenient to you, he'll come and wait upon you.

Love. Give my compliments to his lordship, and I shall be glad to see him. [*Exit* SERVANT.] If you are not acquainted with his lordship, madam, you will be entertained with his character.

Aman. Now it moves my pity more than my mirth to see a man, whom nature has made no fool, be so very industrious to pass for an ass.

Love. No, there you are wrong, Amanda; you should never bestow your pity upon those who take pains for your contempt: pity those whom nature abuses, never those who abuse nature.

Enter Lord FOPPINGTON.

Lord F. Dear Loveless, I am your most humble servant.

Love. My lord, I'm yours.

Lord F. Madam, your ladyship's very obedient slave.

Love. My lord, this lady is a relation of my wife's.

Lord F. [*Salutes her.*] The beautifullest race of people upon earth, rat me. Dear Loveless, I am overjoyed that you think of continuing here. I am, stap my vitals! For Gad's sake, madam, how has your ladyship been able to subsist thus long, under the fatigue of a country life? [*To* AMANDA.

Aman. My life has been very far from that, my lord; it has been a very quiet one.

Lord F. Why that's the fatigue I speak of, madam; for 'tis impossible to be quiet, without thinking: now thinking is to me the greatest fatigue in the world.

Aman. Does not your lordship love reading then?

Lord F. Oh, passionately, madam; but I never think of what I read. For example, madam, my life is a perpetual stream of pleasure, that glides through with such a variety of entertainments, I believe the wisest of our ancestors never had the least conception of any of 'em. I rise, madam, when in tawn, about twelve o'clock. I don't rise sooner, because it is the worst thing in the world for the complexion: nat that I pretend to be a beau; but a man must endeavour to look decent, lest he makes so odious a figure in the side-bax, the ladies should be compelled to turn their eyes upon the play. So at twelve o'clock, I say, I rise. Naw, if I find it is a good day, I resalve to take the exercise of riding; so drink my chocolate, and draw on my boots, by two. On my return, I dress; and after dinner, lounge perhaps to the opera.

Ber. Your lordship, I suppose, is fond of music?

Lord F. Oh, passionately, on Tuesdays and Saturdays; for then there is always the best company, and one is not expected to undergo the fatigue of listening.

Aman. Does your lordship think that the case at the opera?

Lord F. Most certainly, madam. There is my Lady Tattle, my Lady Prate, my Lady Titter, my Lady Sneer, my Lady Giggle, and my Lady Grin: these have boxes in the front, and while any favourite air is singing, are the prettiest company in the waurld, stap my vitals! Mayn't we hope for the honour to see you added to our society, madam?

Aman. Alas! my lord, I am the worst company in the world at a concert, I'm so apt to attend to the music.

Lord F. Why, madam, that is very pardonable in the country or at church, but a monstrous inattention in a polite assembly. But I am afraid I tire the company?

Love. Not at all. Pray go on.

Lord F. Why then, ladies, there only remains to add, that I generally conclude the evening at one or other of the clubs; nat that I ever play deep: indeed I have been for some time tied up from losing above five thousand paunds at a sitting.

Love. But isn't your lordship sometimes obliged to attend the weighty affairs of the nation?

Lord F. Sir, as to weighty affairs, I leave them to weighty heads; I never intend mine shall be a burden to my body.

Ber. Nay, my lord, but you are a pillar of the state.

Lord F. An ornamental pillar, madam; for sooner than undergo any part of the fatigue, rat me, but the whole building should fall plump to the ground.

Aman. But, my lord, a fine gentleman spends a great deal of his time in his intrigues; you have given us no account of them yet.

Lord F. Soh! She would inquire into my amours; that's jealousy, poor soul! I see she's in love with me [*Aside*]. O Lord, madam, I had like to have forgot a secret I must needs tell your ladyship. Ned, you must not be so jealous now as to listen.

Love. Not I, my lord; I am too fashionable a husband to pry into the secrets of my wife.

Lord F. [*Squeezing* AMANDA's *hand.*] I am in love with you to desperation, strike me speechless! [*Apart.*

Aman. [*Strikes him on the ear.*] Then thus I return your passion, an impudent fool!

Lord F. Gad's curse, madam, I am a peer of the realm.

Love. Hey! what the devil, do you affront my wife, sir? Nay then—— [*Draws. They fight.*

Aman. What has my folly done? Help! murder! help! Part them, for heaven's sake.

Lord F. [*Falls back and leans on his sword.*] Ah! quite through the body, stap my vitals!

Enter SERVANTS.

Love. [*Runs to* Lord FOPPINGTON.] I hope I han't killed the fool, however. Bear him up. Call a surgeon there.

Lord F. Ay, pray make haste.

Love. This mischief you may thank yourself for.

Lord F. I may so; love's the devil indeed, Ned.

Enter PROBE *and* SERVANT.

Serv. Here's Mr. Probe, sir, was just going by the door.

Lord F. He's the welcomest man alive.

Probe. Stand by, stand by, stand by; pray, gentlemen, stand by. Lord have mercy upon us, did you never see a man run through the body before? Pray stand by.

Lord F. Ah, Mr. Probe, I'm a dead man.

Probe. A dead man, and I by! I should laugh to see that, egad.

Love. Pr'ythee, don't stand prating, but look upon his wound.

Probe. Why, what if I won't look upon his wound this hour, sir?

Love. Why then he'll bleed to death, sir.

Probe. Why then I'll fetch him to life again, sir.

Love. 'Slife! He's run through the body, I tell thee.

Probe. I wish he was run through the heart, and I should get the more credit by his cure. Now I hope you are satisfied? Come, now let me come at him—now let me come at him. [*Viewing his wound.*] Oons! What a gash is here! Why, sir, a man may drive a coach and six horses into your body.

Lord F. Oh!

Probe. Why, what the devil, have you run the

gentleman through with a scythe? A little scratch between the skin and the ribs, that's all. [*Aside.*

Love. Let me see his wound.

Probe. Then you shall dress it, sir; for if anybody looks upon it I won't.

Love. Why thou art the veriest coxcomb I ever saw.

Probe. Sir, I am not master of my trade for nothing.

Lord F. Surgeon!

Probe. Sir.

Lord F. Are there any hopes?

Probe. Hopes! I can't tell. What are you willing to give for a cure?

Lord F. Five hundred paunds with pleasure.

Probe. Why then perhaps there may be hopes; but we must avoid a further delay. Here, help the gentleman into a chair, and carry him to my house presently—that's the properest place—to bubble him out of his money [*Aside*]. Come, a chair; a chair quickly. There, in with him. [*They put him into a chair.*

Lord F. Dear Loveless, adieu: if I die, I forgive thee; and if I live, I hope thou wilt do as much by me. I am sorry you and I should quarrel, but I hope here's an end on't; for if you are satisfied, I am.

Love. I shall hardly think it worth my prosecuting any further, so you may be at rest, sir.

Lord F. Thou art a generous fellow, strike me dumb! But thou hast an impertinent wife, stap my vitals! [*Aside.*

Probe. So, carry him off—carry him off; we shall have him prate himself into a fever by-and-bye; carry him off. [*Exit, with* Lord Poppington.

Enter Colonel Townly.

Col. T. So, so, I'm glad to find you all alive. I

met a wounded peer carrying off. For heaven's sake, what was the matter?

Love. O, a trifle; he would have made love to my wife before my face, so she obliged him with a box o'the ear, and I run him through the body, that was all.

Col. T. Bagatelle on all sides. But pray, madam, how long has this noble lord been a humble servant of yours?

Aman. This is the first I have heard on't; so I suppose 'tis his quality more than his love has brought him into this adventure. He thinks his title an authentic passport to every woman's heart below the degree of a peeress.

Col. T. He's coxcomb enough to think anything; but I would not have you brought into trouble for him. I hope there's no danger of his life?

Love. None at all; he's fallen into the hands of a roguish surgeon, who, I perceive, designs to frighten a little money out of him; but I saw his wound—'tis nothing; he may go to the ball to-night if he pleases.

Col. T. I am glad you have corrected him without further mischief, or you might have deprived me of the pleasure of executing a plot against his lordship, which I have been contriving with an old acquaintance of yours.

Love. Explain——

Col. T. His brother, Tom Fashion, is come down here, and we have it in contemplation to save him the trouble of his intended wedding; but we want your assistance. Tom would have called, but he is preparing for his enterprise, so I promised to bring you to him; so, sir, if these ladies can spare you——

Love. I'll go with you with all my heart [*Aside*] —though I could wish, methinks, to stay and gaze a little longer on that creature. Good gods, how engaging she is! But what have I to do with beauty? I have already had my portion, and must not covet more.

Aman. Mr. Loveless, pray one word with you before you go. [*Exit* Colonel TOWNLY.

Love. What would my dear?

Aman. Only a woman's foolish question. How do you like my cousin here?

Love. Jealous already, Amanda?

Aman. Not at all. I ask you for another reason.

Love. Whate'er her reason be, I must not tell her true. [*Aside.*] Why, I confess she's handsome; but you must not think I slight your kinswoman, if I own to you, of all the women who may claim that character, she is the last that would triumph in my heart.

Aman. I'm satisfied.

Love. Now tell me why you asked?

Aman. At night I will. Adieu.

Love. I'm yours. [*Kissing her. Exit.*

Aman. I'm glad to find he does not like her, for I have a great mind to persuade her to come and live with me. [*Aside.*

Ber. So! I find my colonel continues in his airs; there must be something more at the bottom of this than the provocation he pretends from me. [*Aside.*

Aman. For heaven's sake, Berinthia, tell me what way I shall take to persuade you to come and live with me?

Ber. Why one way in the world there is; and but one.

Aman. And pray what is that?

Ber. It is to assure me, I shall be very welcome.

Aman. If that be all, you shall e'en sleep here tonight.

Ber. To-night!

Aman. Yes, to-night.

Ber. Why, the people where I lodge will think me mad.

Aman. Let 'em think what they please.

Ber. Say you so, Amanda? Why then they shall think what they please; for I'm a young widow, and I care not what anybody thinks. Ah, Amanda, it's a delicious thing to be a young widow.

Aman. You'll hardly make me think so.

Ber. Poh! because you are in love with your husband.

Aman. Pray, 'tis with a world of innocence I would inquire whether you think those we call women of reputation do really escape all other men as they do those shadows of beaus?

Ber. Oh no, Amanda; there are a sort of men make dreadful work amongst 'em; men that may be called the beau's antipathy; for they agree in nothing but walking upon two legs. These have brains; the beau has none. These are in love with their mistress; the beau with himself. They take care of their reputation; the beau is industrious to destroy it. They are decent; he's a fop; in short, they are men—he's an ass.

Aman. If this be their character, I fancy we had here, e'en now, a pattern of 'em both.

Ber. His lordship and Colonel Townly?

Aman. The same.

Ber. As for the lord, he is eminently so; and for the other, I can assure you there's not a man in town who has a better interest with the women, that are worth having an interest with.

Aman. He answers the opinion I had ever of him. [*Takes her hand.*] I must acquaint you with a secret—

'tis not that fool alone has talked to me of love. Townly has been tampering too.

Ber. So, so! here the mystery comes out! [*Aside.*] Colonel Townly! Impossible, my dear!

Aman. 'Tis true, indeed; though he has done it in vain; nor do I think that all the merit of mankind combined could shake the tender love I bear my husband; yet I will own to you, Berinthia, I did not start at his addresses, as when they came from one whom I contemned.

Ber. O this is better and better. [*Aside.*] Well said, innocence! and you really think, my dear, that nothing could abate your constancy and attachment to your husband?

Aman. Nothing, I am convinced.

Ber. What if you found he loved another woman better?

Aman. Well!

Ber. Well! why were I that thing they call a slighted wife, somebody should run the risk of being that thing they call—a husband. Don't I talk madly?

Aman. Madly indeed!

Ber. Yet I'm very innocent.

Aman. That I dare swear you are. I know how to make allowances for your humour; but you resolve, then, never to marry again?

Ber. Oh no! I resolve I will.

Aman. How so?

Ber. That I never may.

Aman. You banter me.

Ber. Indeed I don't; but I consider I'm a woman, and form my resolutions accordingly.

Aman. Well, my opinion is, form what resolution you will, matrimony will be the end on't.

Ber. I doubt it; but a——Heavens! I have business at home, and am half an hour too late.

Aman. As you are to return with me, I'll just give some orders, and walk with you.

Ber. Well, make haste, and we'll finish this subject as we go. [*Exit* AMANDA.] Ah, poor Amanda, you have led a country life. Well, this discovery is lucky! Base Townly! at once false to me and treacherous to his friend! and my innocent and demure cousin too! I have it in my power to be revenged on her however. Her husband, if I have any skill in countenance, would be as happy in my smiles as Townly can hope to be in hers. I'll make the experiment, come what will on't. The woman who can forgive the being robb'd of a favoured lover must be either an idiot or a wanton.

[*Exit.*

ACT III.—SCENE I.

Enter Lord FOPPINGTON *and* LA VAROLE.

Lord F. Hey, fellow, let my vis-a-vis come to the door.

La Var. Will your lordship venture so soon to expose yourself to the weather?

Lord F. Sir, I will venture as soon as I can to expose myself to the ladies.

La Var. I wish your lordship would please to keep house a little longer. I am afraid your honour does not well consider your wound.

Lord F. My wound! I would not be in eclipse another day, though I had as many wounds in my body as I have had in my heart. So mind, Varole, let these cards be left as directed; for this evening I shall wait on my father-in-law, Sir Tunbelly, and I mean to commence my devoirs to the lady, by giving an entertainment at her father's expense; and hark thee, tell Mr. Lovelace I request he and his company will honour me with their presence, or I shall think we are not friends.

La Var. I will be sure, mi lor.   [*Exit.*

Enter Young FASHION.

Young F. Brother, your servant; how do you find yourself to-day?

Lord F. So well that I have ardered my coach to the door; so there's no danger of death this baut, Tam.

Young F. I'm very glad of it.

Lord F. That I believe's a lie. [*Aside.*] Pr'ythee, Tam, tell me one thing; did not your heart cut a caper up to your mauth when you heard I was run through the bady?

Young F. Why do you think it should?

Lord F. Because I remember mine did so, when I heard my uncle was shot through the head.

Young F. It then did very ill.

Lord F. Pr'ythee, why so?

Young F. Because he used you very well.

Lord F. Well! Naw, strike me dumb! he starved me; he has let me want a thousand women, for want of a thousand paund.

Young F. Then he hindered you from making a great many ill bargains; for I think no woman worth money that will take money.

Lord F. If I was a younger brother I should think so too.

Young F. Then you are seldom much in love?

Lord F. Never, stap my vitals!

Young F. Why then did you make all this bustle about Amanda?

Lord F. Because she's a woman of an insolent virtue, and I thought myself piqued, in honour, to debauch her.

Young F. Very well. Here's a rare fellow for you, to have the spending of ten thousand pounds a year. But now for my business with him. [*Aside.*] Brother, though I know to talk of business (especially of money) is a theme not quite so entertaining to you as that of the ladies, my necessities are such, I hope you'll have patience to hear me.

Lord F. The greatness of your necessities, Tam, is the worst argument in the waurld for your being patiently heard. I do believe you are going to make a very good speech, but, strike me dumb! it has the worst beginning of any speech I have heard this twelvemonth.

Young F. I'm sorry you think so.

Lord F. I do believe thou art; but come, let's know the affair quickly.

Young F. Why then, my case, in a word, is this. The necessary expenses of my travels have so much exceeded the wretched income of my annuity, that I have been forced to mortgage it for five hundred pounds, which is spent. So, unless you are so kind as to assist me in redeeming it, I know no remedy but to take a purse.

Lord F. Why faith, Tam, to give you my sense of the thing, I do think taking a purse the best remedy in the waurld; for if you succeed, you are relieved that way; and if you are taken, you are relieved t'other.

Young F. I'm glad to see you are in so pleasant a humour; I hope I shall find the effects on't.

Lord F. Why, do you then really think it a reasonable thing, that I should give you five hundred pawnds?

Young F. I do not ask it as a due, brother; I am willing to receive it as a favour.

Lord F. Then thou art willing to receive it any how, strike me speechless! But these are d—d times to give money in; taxes are so great, repairs so exorbitant, tenants such rogues, and boquets so dear, that the devil take me, I am reduced to that extremity in my cash, I have been forced to retrench in that one article of sweet pawder, till I have brought it dawn to five guineas a maunth; now judge, Tam, whether I can spare you five hundred pawnds?

Young F. If you can't, I must starve, that's all. D—n him. [*Aside.*

Lord F. All I can say is, you should have been a better husband.

Young F. Ouns! If you can't live upon ten thousand a year, how do you think I should do't upon two hundred?

Lord F. Don't be in a passion, Tam, for passion is the most unbecoming thing in the waurld—to the face. Look you, I don't love to say anything to you to make you melancholy, but upon this occasion I must take leave to put you in mind, that a running horse does require more attendance than a coach-horse. Nature has made some difference 'twixt you and me.

Young F. Yes. She has made you older.—Plague take her! [*Aside.*

Lord F. That is not all, Tam.

Young F. Why, what is there else?

Lord F. [*Looks first on himself and then on his brother.*] Ask the ladies.

Young F. Why, thou essence-bottle, thou musk-cat! dost thou then think thou hast any advantage over me but what fortune has given thee?

Lord F. I do, stap my vitals!

Young F. Now, by all that's great and powerful, thou art the prince of coxcombs.

Lord F. Sir, I am proud at being at the head of so prevailing a party.

Young F. Will nothing provoke thee? Draw, coward!

Lord F. Look you, Tam, you know I have always taken you for a mighty dull fellow, and here is one of the foolishest plats broke out that I have seen a lang time. Your poverty makes life so burdensome to you, you would provoke me to a quarrel, in hopes either to slip through my lungs into my estate, or to get yourself run through the guts, to put an end to your pain; but I will disappoint you in both your designs; far with the temper of a philasapher, and the discretion of a statesman, I shall leave the room with my sword in the scabbard. [*Exit.*

Young F. So! farewell, brother; and now, conscience, I defy thee. Lory!

Enter LORY.

Lory. Sir.

Young F. Here's rare news, Lory; his lordship has given me a pill has purged off all my scruples.

Lory. Then my heart's at ease again; for I have been in a lamentable fright, sir, ever since your conscience had the impudence to intrude into your company.

Young F. Be at peace; it will come there no more;

my brother has given it a wring by the nose, and I have kick'd it downstairs. So run away to the inn, get the chaise ready quickly, and bring it to Dame Coupler's without a moment's delay.

Lory. Then, sir, you are going straight about the fortune?

Young F. I am. Away; fly, Lory.

Lory. The happiest day I ever saw. I'm upon the wing already. Now then I shall get my wages.

[*Exeunt.*

SCENE II.

A Garden.

Enter LOVELESS *and* SERVANT.

Love. Is my wife within?

Serv. No, sir, she has gone out this half hour.

Love. Well, leave me. [*Exit* SERVANT.] How strangely does my mind run on this widow; never was my heart so suddenly seized on before; that my wife should pick out her, of all womankind, to be her playfellow. But what fate does, let fate answer for. I sought it not; soh! by heav'ns! here she comes.

Enter BERINTHIA.

Ber. What makes you look so thoughtful, sir? I hope you are not ill.

Love. I was debating, madam, whether I was so or not, and that was it which made me look so thoughtful.

Ber. Is it then so hard a matter to decide? I thought all people were acquainted with their own bodies, though few people know their own minds.

Love. What if the distemper I suspect be in the mind?

Ber. Why then I'll undertake to prescribe you a cure.

Love. Alas! you undertake you know not what.

Ber. So far at least then you allow me to be a physician.

Love. Nay, I'll allow you to be so yet further; for I have reason to believe, should I put myself into your hand, you would increase my distemper.

Ber. How?

Love. Oh, you might betray me to my wife.

Ber. And so lose all my practice.

Love. Will you then keep my secret?

Ber. I will.

Love. Well; but swear it.

Ber. I swear by woman.

Love. Nay, that's swearing by my deity; swear by your own, and I shall believe you.

Ber. Well then, I swear by man!

Love. I'm satisfied. Now hear my symptoms, and give me your advice. The first were these; when I saw you at the play, a random glance you threw at first alarmed me. I could not turn my eyes from whence the danger came. I gaz'd upon you till my heart began to pant; nay, even now on your approaching me, my illness is so increased, that if you do not help me I shall, whilst you look on, consume to ashes.

[*Takes her hand.*

Ber. O Lord, let me go; 'tis the plague, and we shall be infected. [*Breaking from him.*

Love. Then we'll die together, my charming angel.

Ber. O 'gad! the devil's in you. Lord, let me go; here's somebody coming.

Enter a SERVANT.

Serv. Sir, my lady's come home, and desires to speak with you.

Love. Tell her I'm coming. [*Exit* SERVANT.] But before I go, one glass of nectar to drink her health.

[*To* BERINTHIA.

Ber. Stand off, or I shall hate you, by heavens.

Love. [*Kissing her.*] In matters of love, a woman's oath is no more to be minded than a man's. [*Exit.*

Ber. Um!

Enter Colonel TOWNLY.

Col. T. Soh! what's here—Berinthia and Loveless, and in such close conversation. I cannot now wonder at her indifference in excusing herself to me! O rare woman; well, then, let Lovelace look to his wife, 'twill be but the retort courteous on both sides. Your servant, madam. I need not ask you how you do, you have got so good a colour.

Ber. No better than I used to have, I suppose.

Col. T. A little more blood in your cheeks.

Ber. I have been walking!

Col. T. Is that all? Pray was it Mr. Loveless went from here just now?

Ber. O yes, he has been walking with me.

Col. T. He has!

Ber. Upon my word I think he is a very agreeable man; and there is certainly something particularly insinuating in his address!

Col. T. So, so! she hasn't even the modesty to dissemble! [*Aside.*] Pray, madam, may I, without impertinence, trouble you with a few serious questions?

Ber. As many as you please; but pray let them be as little serious as possible.

Col. T. Is it not near two years since I have presumed to address you?

Ber. I don't know exactly—but it has been a tedious long time.

Col. T. Have I not, during that period, had every reason to believe that my assiduities were far from being unacceptable?

Ber. Why, to do you justice, you have been extremely troublesome; and I confess I have been more civil to you than you deserved.

Col. T. Did I not come to this place at your express desire, and for no purpose but the honour of meeting you? And after waiting a month in disappointment, have you condescended to explain, or in the slightest way apologize for your conduct?

Ber. O heavens! apologize for my conduct!—apologize to you! O you barbarian! But pray now, my good, serious colonel, have you anything more to add?

Col. T. Nothing, madam, but that after such behaviour I am less surprised at what I saw just now; it is not very wonderful that the woman who can trifle with the delicate addresses of an honourable lover should be found coquetting with the husband of her friend.

Ber. Very true, no more wonderful than it was for this honourable lover to divert himself in the absence of this coquette, with endeavouring to seduce his friend's wife! O colonel, colonel, don't talk of honour or your friend, for heaven's sake.

Col. T. 'Sdeath! how came she to suspect this! [*Aside.*] Really, madam, I don't understand you.

Ber. Nay, nay, you saw I did not pretend to misunderstand you. But here comes the lady; perhaps you would be glad to be left with her for an explanation.

Col. T. O madam, this recrimination is a poor resource; and to convince you how much you are mistaken, I beg leave to decline the happiness you propose me. Madam, your servant.

Enter AMANDA. *Colonel* TOWNLY *whispers* AMANDA, *and exit.*

Ber. He carries it off well, however. Upon my word, very well. How tenderly they part! [*Aside.*] So, cousin, I hope you have not been chiding your admirer for being with me. I assure you we have been talking of you.

Aman. Fie, Berinthia!—my admirer. Will you never learn to talk in earnest of anything?

Ber. Why this shall be in earnest, if you please; for my part I only tell you matter of fact.

Aman. I'm sure there's so much jest and earnest in what you say to me on this subject, I scarce know how to take it. I have just parted with Mr. Lovelace; perhaps it is fancy, but I think there is an alteration in his manner which alarms me.

Ber. And so you are jealous? Is that all?

Aman. That all! Is jealousy, then, nothing?

Ber. It should be nothing, if I were in your case.

Aman. Why, what would you do?

Ber. I'd cure myself.

Aman. How?

Ber. Care as little for my husband as he did for me. Look you, Amanda, you may build castles in the air, and fume, and fret, and grow thin, and lean, and pale, and ugly, if you please; but I tell you, no man worth having is true to his wife, or ever was, or ever will be so.

Aman. Do you then really think he's false to me? for I did not suspect him.

Ber. Think so! I am sure of it.

Aman. You are sure on't?

Ber. Positively; he fell in love at the play.

Aman. Right, the very same; but who could have told you this?

Ber. Um. O, Townly! I suppose your husband has made him his confidant.

Aman. O base Loveless! And what did Townly say on't?

Ber. So, so, why should she ask that? [*Aside.*] Say! Why he abused Loveless extremely, and said all the tender things of you in the world.

Aman. Did he? Oh! my heart! I'm very ill. Dear Berinthia, don't leave me a moment. [*Exeunt.*

SCENE III.

Outside of Sir TUNBELLY'S *House.*

Enter Young FASHION *and* LORY.

Young F. So, here's our inheritance, Lory, if we can but get into possession; but methinks the seat of our family looks like Noah's ark, as if the chief part on't were designed for the fowls of the air, and the beasts of the field.

Lory. Pray, sir, don't let your head run upon the orders of building here; get but the heiress, let the devil take the house.

Young F. Get but the house! Let the devil take the heiress, I say. But come, we have no time to squander; knock at the door [LORY *knocks two or three times*]. What the devil, have they got no ears in this house? Knock harder.

Lory. Egad, sir, this will prove some enchanted castle; we shall have the giant come out, by-and-by, with his club, and beat our brains out. [*Knocks again.*

Young F. Hush, they come.

Serv. [*Within.*] Who is there?

Lory. Open the door and see. Is that your country breeding?

Serv. Ay, but two words to that bargain. Tummas, is the blunderbuss prim'd?

Young F. Ouns! Give 'em good words, Lory, or we shall be shot here a fortune catching.

Lory. Egad, sir, I think you're in the right on't. Ho! Mr. What-d'ye-call-'um, will you please to let us in? Or are we to be left to grow like willows by your moat side?

SERVANT *appears at the window with a blunderbuss.*

Serv. Well naw, what's ya're business?

Young F. Nothing, sir, but to wait upon Sir Tunbelly, with your leave.

Serv. To weat upon Sir Tunbelly? Why you'll find that's just as Sir Tunbelly pleases.

Young F. But will you do me the favour, sir, to know whether Sir Tunbelly pleases or not?

Serv. Why, look you, d'ye see, with good words much may be done. Ralph, go thy ways, and ask Sir Tunbelly if he pleases to be waited upon; and, dost hear, call to nurse, that she may lock up Miss Hoyden before the gates open.

Young F. D'ye hear that, Lory?

Enter Sir TUNBELLY CLUMSY, *with Servants, armed with Guns, Clubs, Pitchforks, &c.*

Lory. O! [*Runs behind his master.*] O Lord, O Lord, Lord, we are both dead men!

17—2

Young F. Fool! thy fear will ruin us.

[*Apart to* LORY.

Lory. My fear, sir? 'Sdeath, sir, I fear nothing. [*Apart.*] Would I were well up to the chin in a horsepond! [*Aside.*

Sir T. Who is it here hath any business with me?

Young F. Sir, 'tis I, if your name be Sir Tunbelly Clumsy.

Sir T. Sir, my name is Sir Tunbelly Clumsy, whether you have any business with me or not. So you see I am not ashamed of my name, nor my face either.

Young F. Sir, you have no cause, that I know of.

Sir T. Sir, if you have no cause either, I desire to know who you are; for, till I know your name, I sha'n't ask you to come into my house; and when I do know your name, 'tis six to four I don't ask you then.

Young F. Sir, I hope you'll find this letter an authentic passport. [*Gives him a letter.*

Sir T. Cod's my life, from Mrs. Coupler! I ask your lordship's pardon ten thousand times. [*To his Servant.*] Here, run in a-doors quickly; get a Scotch coal fire in the parlour, set all the Turkey-work chairs in their places, get the brass candlesticks out, and be sure stick the socket full of laurel—run. [*Turns to* Young FASHION.] My lord, I ask your lordship's pardon. [*To the Servant.*] And, do you hear, run away to nurse; bid her let Miss Hoyden loose again. [*Exit Servant.*] I hope your honour will excuse the disorder of my family. We are not used to receive men of your lordship's great quality every day. Pray, where are your coaches and servants, my lord?

Young F. Sir, that I might give you and your daughter a proof how impatient I am to be nearer akin to you, I left my equipage to follow me, and came away post with only one servant.

Sir T. Your lordship does me too much honour; it was exposing your person to too much fatigue and danger, I protest it was; but my daughter shall endeavour to make you what amends she can; and though I say it, that should not say it, Hoyden has charms.

Young F. Sir, I am not a stranger to them, though I am to her; common fame has done her justice.

Sir T. My lord, I am common fame's very grateful, humble servant. My lord, my girl's young—Hoyden is young, my lord; but this I must say for her, what she wants in art she has in breeding; and what's wanting in her age, is made good in her constitution. So pray, my lord, walk in; pray, my lord, walk in.

Young F. Sir, I wait upon you. [*Exeunt.*

SCENE IV.

An Apartment in Sir TUNBELLY CLUMSY's *House.*

Miss HOYDEN *discovered.*

Miss H. Sure nobody was ever used as I am. I know well enough what other girls do, for all they think to make a fool o'me. It's well I have a husband a coming, or 'ecod I'd marry the baker, I would so. Nobody can knock at the gate, but presently I must be locked up; and here's the young greyhound can run loose about the house all the day long, so she can. 'Tis very well——

Nurse [*Without, opening the door.*] Miss Hoyden! Miss, miss, miss! Miss Hoyden!

Enter NURSE.

Miss H. Well, what do you make such a noise for, ha? What do you din a body's ears for? Can't one be at quiet for you?

Nurse. What do I din your ears for? Here's one come will din your ears for you.

Miss H. What care I who's come? I care not a fig who comes, or who goes, as long as I must be locked up like the ale-cellar.

Nurse. That, miss, is for fear you should be drank before you are ripe.

Miss H. Oh, don't trouble your head about that; I'm as ripe as you, though not so mellow.

Nurse. Very well. Now I have a good mind to lock you up again, and not let you see my lord to-night.

Miss H. My lord! Why, is my husband come?

Nurse. Yes, marry, is he; and a goodly person too.

Miss H. [*Hugs* NURSE.] Oh, my dear nurse, forgive me this once, and I'll never misuse you again; no, if I do, you shall give me three thumps on the back, and a great pinch by the cheek.

Nurse. Ah, the poor thing! see now it melts; it's as full of good nature as an egg's full of meat.

Miss H. But, my dear nurse, don't lie now; is he come, by your troth?

Nurse. Yes, by my truly, is he.

Miss H. O Lord! I'll go and put on my laced tucker, though I'm locked up for a month for't.

[*Exeunt.*

ACT IV.—SCENE I.

An Apartment at Sir Tunbelly Clumsy's.

Enter Miss Hoyden *and* Nurse.

Nurse. Well, miss, how do you like your husband that is to be?

Miss H. O Lord, nurse, I'm so overjoyed I can scarce contain myself.

Nurse. Oh, but you must have a care of being too fond; for men, now-a-days, hate a woman that loves 'em.

Miss H. Love him! why, do you think I love him, nurse? 'Ecod, I would not care if he was hanged, so I were but once married to him. No, that which pleases me is to think what work I'll make when I get to London; for when I am a wife and a lady both, 'ecod, I'll flaunt it with the best of 'em. Ay, and I shall have money enough to do so too, nurse.

Nurse. Ah, there's no knowing that, miss; for though these lords have a power of wealth indeed, yet, as I have heard say, they give it all to their sluts and their trulls, who joggle it about in their coaches, with a murrain to 'em, whilst poor madam sits sighing and wishing, and has not a spare half-crown to buy her a Practice of Piety.

Miss H. Oh, but for that, don't deceive yourself, nurse; for this I must say of my lord, he's as free as an open house at Christmas; for this very morning he told me I should have six hundred a year to buy pins. Now if he gives me six hundred a year to buy pins, what do you think he'll give me to buy petticoats?

Nurse. Ah, my dearest, he deceives thee foully, and he's no better than a rogue for his pains. These Londoners have got a gibberish with 'em would confound a gipsy. That which they call pin-money, is to buy everything in the 'versal world, down to their very shoe-knots. Nay, I have heard some folks say that some ladies, if they'll have gallants as they call 'em, are forced to find them out of their pin-money too. But look, look, if his honour be not coming to you! Now, if I were sure you would behave yourself handsomely, and not disgrace me that have brought you up, I'd leave you alone altogether.

Miss H. That's my best nurse; do as you'd be done by. Trust us together this once, and if I don't show my breeding, I wish I may never be married, but die an old maid.

Nurse. Well, this once I'll venture you. But if you disparage me—— [*Exit.*

Miss H. Never fear.

Enter Young Fashion.

Young F. Your servant, madam. I'm glad to find you alone, for I have something of importance to speak to you about.

Miss H. Sir (my lord I meant), you may speak to me about what you please, I shall give you a civil answer.

Young F. You give so obliging a one, it encourages me to tell you in a few words what I think, both for your interest and mine. Your father, I suppose you know, has resolved to make me happy in being your husband; and I hope I may obtain your consent to perform what he desires?

Miss H. Sir, I never disobey my father in anything but eating green gooseberries.

Young F. So good a daughter must needs be an admirable wife. I am therefore impatient till you are mine, and hope you will so far consider the violence of my love, that you won't have the cruelty to defer my happiness so long as your father designs it.

Miss H. Pray, my lord, how long is that?

Young F. Madam, a thousand years—a whole week.

Miss H. Why, I thought it was to be to-morrow morning, as soon as I was up. I'm sure nurse told me so.

Young F. And it shall be to-morrow morning, if you'll consent.

Miss H. If I'll consent? Why I thought I was to obey you as my husband?

Young F. That's when we are married. Till then, I'm to obey you.

Miss H. Why then, if we are to take it by turns, it's the same thing. I'll obey you now, and when we are married, you shall obey me.

Young F. With all my heart. But I doubt we must get nurse on our side, or we shall hardly prevail with the chaplain.

Miss H. No more we sha'n't, indeed; for he loves her better than he loves his pulpit, and would always be a preaching to her by his good will.

Young F. Why then, my dear, if you'll call her hither, we'll persuade her presently.

Miss H. O lud, I'll tell you a way how to persuade her to anything.

Young F. How's that?

Miss H. Why tell her she's a handsome, comely woman, and give her half-a-crown.

Young F. Nay, if that will do, she shall have half a score of them.

Miss H. O gemini! for half that she'd marry you herself. I'll run and call her. [*Exit.*

Young F. Soh! matters go on swimmingly. This is a rare girl, i'faith. I shall have a fine time on't with her at London.

Enter LORY.

So Lory, what's the matter?

Lory. Here, sir — an intercepted packet from the enemy; your brother's postillion brought it. I knew the livery, pretended to be a servant of Sir Tunbelly's, and so got possession of the letter.

Young F. [*Looks at the letter.*] Ouns! he tells Sir Tunbelly here that he will be with him this evening, with a large party to supper. Egad, I must marry the girl directly.

Lory. Oh, z—ds, sir, directly to be sure. Here she comes. [*Exit.*

Young F. And the old Jezabel with her.

Re-enter Miss HOYDEN *and* NURSE.

How do you do, good Mrs. Nurse? I desired your young lady would give me leave to see you, that I might thank you for your extraordinary care and kind conduct in her education. Pray accept of this small acknowledgment for it at present, and depend upon my further kindness when I shall be that happy thing, her husband. [*Gives her money.*

Nurse. Gold, by the maakins! [*Aside.*] Your honour's goodness is too great. Alas! all I can boast of is, I gave her pure good milk, and so your honour would have said, and you had seen how the poor thing thrived—and how it would look up in my face—and crow and laugh, it would

Miss H. [*To* NURSE, *taking her angrily aside.*] Pray one word with you. Pr'ythee, nurse, don't stand ripping up old stories, to make one ashamed before one's love. Do you think such a fine proper gentleman as he is cares for a fiddle-come tale of a child? If you have a mind to make him have a good opinion of a woman, don't tell him what one did then, tell him what one can do now.—I hope your honour will excuse my miss-manners to whisper before you; it was only to give some orders about the family.

Young F. Oh, everything, madam, is to give way to business; besides, good housewifery is a very commendable quality in a young lady.

Miss H. Pray, sir, are young ladies good housewives at London-town? Do they darn their own linen?

Young F. Oh, no, they study how to spend money, not to save.

Miss H. 'Ecod, I don't know but that may be better sport, ha, nurse?

Young F. Well, you shall have your choice when you come there.

Miss H. Shall I? then, by my troth, I'll get there as fast as I can. His honour desires you'll be so kind as to let us be married to-morrow. [*To* NURSE.

Nurse. To-morrow, my dear madam?

Young F. Ay, faith, nurse, you may well be surprised at miss's wanting to put it off so long. To-morrow! no, no; 'tis now, this very hour, I would have the ceremony performed.

Miss H. 'Ecod, with all my heart.

Nurse. Oh, mercy! worse and worse!

Young F. Yes, sweet nurse, now and privately; for all things being signed and sealed, why should Sir Tunbelly make us stay a week for a wedding dinner?

Nurse. But if you should be married now, what will you do when Sir Tunbelly calls for you to be married?

Miss H. Why then we will be married again.

Nurse. What twice, my child?

Miss H. 'Ecod, I don't care how often I'm married, not I.

Nurse. Well I'm such a tender-hearted fool, I find I can refuse you nothing. So you shall e'en follow your own inventions.

Miss H. Shall I? O Lord, I could leap over the moon.

Young F. Dear nurse, this goodness of yours shall be still more rewarded. But now you must employ your power with the chaplain, that he may do his friendly office too, and then we shall be all happy. Do you think you can prevail with him?

Nurse. Prevail with him; or he shall never prevail with me, I can tell him that.

Young F. I'm glad to hear it; however, to strengthen your interest with him, you may let him know I have several fat livings in my gift, and that the first that falls shall be in your disposal.

Nurse. Nay, then I'll make him marry more folks than one, I'll promise him.

Miss H. Faith, do, nurse, make him marry you too; I'm sure he'll do't for a fat living.

Young F. Well, nurse, while you go and settle matters with him, your lady and I will go and take a walk in the garden. [*Exit* NURSE.] Come, madam, dare you venture yourself alone with me?

[*Takes* Miss HOYDEN *by the hand.*

Miss H. Oh dear, yes, sir; I don't think you'll do anything to me I need be afraid on. [*Exeunt.*

SCENE II.

AMANDA's *Dressing-room.*

Enter AMANDA, *followed by her* MAID.

Maid. If you please, madam, only to say whether you'll have me buy them or not?

Aman. Yes—no. Go, teaser; I care not what you do. Pr'ythee leave me. [*Exit* MAID.

Enter BERINTHIA.

Ber. What, in the name of Jove, is the matter with you?

Aman. The matter, Berinthia? I'm almost mad; I'm plagued to death.

Ber. Who is it that plagued you?

Aman. Who do you think should plague a wife, but her husband?

Ber. O, ho! is it come to that? We shall have you wish yourself a widow, by-and-by.

Aman. Would I were anything but what I am! A base, ungrateful man, to use me thus!

Ber. What, has he given you fresh reason to suspect his wandering?

Aman. Every hour gives me reason.

Ber. And yet, Amanda, you perhaps at this moment cause in another's breast the same tormenting doubts and jealousies which you feel so sensibly yourself.

Aman. Heaven knows I would not.

Ber. Why, you can't tell but there may be some one

as tenderly attach'd to Townly, whom you boast of as your conquest, as you can be to your husband.

Aman. I'm sure I never encouraged his pretensions.

Ber. Pshaw! pshaw! No sensible man ever perseveres to love without encouragement. Why have you not treated him as you have Lord Foppington?

Aman. Because he presumed not so far. But let us drop the subject. Men, not women, are riddles. Mr. Loveless now follows some flirt for variety, whom I'm sure he does not like so well as he does me.

Ber. That's more than you know, madam.

Aman. Why, do you know the ugly thing?

Ber. I think I can guess at the person; but she's no such ugly thing neither.

Aman. Is she very handsome?

Ber. Truly I think so.

Aman. Whate'er she be, I'm sure he does not like her well enough to bestow anything more than a little outward gallantry upon her.

Ber. Outward gallantry! I can't bear this. [*Aside.*] Come, come, don't you be too secure, Amanda; while you suffer Townly to imagine that you do not detest him for his designs on you, you have no right to complain that your husband is engaged elsewhere. But here comes the person we were speaking of.

Enter Colonel TOWNLY.

Col. T. Ladies, as I come uninvited, I beg, if I intrude, you will use the same freedom in turning me out again.

Aman. I believe it is near the time Loveless said he would be at home. He talked of accepting of Lord Foppington's invitation to sup at Sir Tunbelly Clumsy's.

Col. T. His lordship has done me the honour to invite me also. If you'll let me escort you, I'll let you into a mystery as we go, in which you must play a part when we arrive.

Aman. But we have two hours yet to spare; the carriages are not ordered till eight, and it is not a five minutes' drive. So, cousin, let us keep the colonel to play at piquet with us, till Mr. Loveless comes home.

Ber. As you please, madam; but you know I have a letter to write.

Col. T. Madam, you know you may command me, though I am a very wretched gamester.

Aman. Oh, you play well enough to lose your money, and that's all the ladies require; and so, without any more ceremony, let us go into the next room, and call for cards and candles. [*Exeunt.*

SCENE III.

BERINTHIA'S *Dressing-room.*

Enter LOVELESS.

Love. So; thus far all's well; I have got into her dressing-room, and it being dusk, I think nobody has perceived me steal into the house. I heard Berinthia tell my wife she had some particular letters to write this evening, before she went to Sir Tunbelly's, and here are the implements of correspondence. How shall I muster up assurance to show myself when she comes? I think she has given me encouragement; and to do my impudence justice, I have made the most of it. I hear a door open, and some one coming. If it should be my wife, what the devil should I say? I believe she mistrusts me, and by my life, I don't deserve her tenderness; however, I am determined to reform, though not yet. Ha! Berinthia! So I'll step in here, till I see what sort of humour she is in. [*Goes into the closet.*

Enter BERINTHIA.

Ber. Was ever so provoking a situation! To think I should sit and hear him compliment Amanda to my face! I have lost all patience with them both. I would not for something have Loveless know what temper of mind they have piqued me into; yet I can't bear to leave them together. No; I'll put my papers away, and return to disappoint them. [*Goes to the closet.*] O Lord! a ghost! a ghost! a ghost!

Re-enter LOVELESS.

Love. Peace, my angel; it's no ghost, but one worth a hundred spirits.
Ber. How, sir, have you had the insolence to presume to——run in again—here's somebody coming.
[LOVELESS *goes into the closet.*

Enter MAID.

Maid. O Lord, ma'am, what's the matter?
Ber. O heavens! I'm almost frightened out of my wits! I thought verily I had seen a ghost, and 'twas nothing but a black hood, pinn'd against the wall. You may go again: I am the fearfullest fool.
[*Exit* MAID.

Re-enter LOVELESS.

Love. Is the coast clear?

Ber. The coast clear? Upon my word, I wonder at your assurance!

Love. Why then you wonder before I have given you a proof of it. But where's my wife?

Ber. At cards.

Love. With whom?

Ber. With Townly.

Love. Then we are safe enough.

Ber. You are so? Some husbands would be of another mind, were he at cards with their wives.

Love. And they'd be in the right on't too; but I dare trust mine.

Ber. Indeed! and she, I doubt not, has the same confidence in you. Yet do you think she'd be content to come and find you here?

Love. Egad, as you say, that's true; then, for fear she should come, hadn't we better go into the next room, out of her way?

Ber. What, in the dark?

Love. Ay, or with a light, which you please.

Ber. You are certainly very impudent.

Love. Nay then, let me conduct you, my angel.

Ber. Hold, hold, you are mistaken in your angel, I assure you.

Love. I hope not; for by this hand I swear.

Ber. Come, come, let go my hand, or I shall hate you. I'll cry out, as I live.

Love. Impossible! You cannot be so cruel.

Ber. Ha! here's some one coming. Be gone instantly.

Love. Will you promise to return, if I remain here?

Ber. Never trust myself in a room again with you while I live.

Love. But I have something particular to communicate to you.

Ber. Well, well, before we go to Sir Tunbelly's, I'll walk upon the lawn. If you are fond of a moonlight evening, you'll find me there.

Love. I'faith, they're coming here now. I take you at your word. [*Exit* LOVELESS *into the closet.*

Ber. 'Tis Amanda, as I live. I hope she has not heard his voice; though I mean she should have her share of jealousy in her turn.

Enter AMANDA.

Aman. Berinthia, why did you leave me?

Ber. I thought I only spoiled your party.

Aman. Since you have been gone, Townly has attempted to renew his importunities. I must break with him, for I cannot venture to acquaint Mr. Loveless with his conduct.

Ber. Oh, no! Mr. Loveless mustn't know of it by any means.

Aman. Oh, not for the world. I wish, Berinthia, you would undertake to speak to Townly on the subject.

Ber. Upon my word, it would be a very pleasant subject for me to talk upon. But come, let us go back; and you may depend on't I'll not leave you together again, if I can help it. [*Exeunt.*

Re-enter LOVELESS.

Love. Soh, so! a pretty piece of business I have overheard! Townly makes love to my wife, and I am not to know it for all the world. I must inquire into this, and, by heav'n, if I find that Amanda has, in the smallest degree——Yet what have I been at here! O, 'sdeath! that's no rule.

That wife alone unsullied credit wins,
Whose virtues can atone her husband's sins.
Thus, while the man has other nymphs in view,
It suits the woman to be doubly true.

[Exit.

ACT. V.—SCENE I.

A Garden. Moonlight.

Enter LOVELESS.

Love. Now, does she mean to make a fool of me, or not? I sha'n't wait much longer, for my wife will soon be inquiring for me to set out on our supping-party. Suspense is at all times the devil; but of all modes of suspense, the watching for a loitering mistress is the worst. But let me accuse her no longer; she approaches with one smile, to o'erpay the anxieties of a year.

Enter BERINTHIA.

O, Berinthia, what a world of kindness are you in my debt! Had you stayed five minutes longer——

Ber. You would have gone, I suppose?

Love. Egad, she's right enough. *[Aside.*

Ber. And I assure you 'twas ten to one that I came at all. In short, I begin to think you are too dangerous a being to trifle with; and as I shall probably only make a fool of you at last, I believe we had better let matters rest as they are.

Love. You cannot mean it, sure?

Ber. What more would you have me give to a married man?

Love. How doubly cruel to remind me of my misfortunes!

Ber. A misfortune to be married to so charming a woman as Amanda?

Love. I grant all her merit, but——'Sdeath! now see what you have done by talking of her—she's here, by all that's unlucky, and Townly with her. I'll observe them.

Ber. O Ged, we had better get out of the way; for I should feel as awkward to meet her as you.

Love. Ay, if I mistake not, I see Townly coming this way also. I must see a little into this matter.

[*Steps aside.*

Ber. Oh, if that's your intention, I am no woman, if I suffer myself to be outdone in curiosity.

[*Goes on the other side.*

Enter AMANDA.

Aman. Mr. Loveless come home, and walking on the lawn! I will not suffer him to walk so late, though perhaps it is to show his neglect of me. Mr. Loveless, I must speak with you. Ha! Townly again! How I am persecuted!

Enter Colonel TOWNLY.

Col. T. Madam, you seem disturbed.

Aman. Sir, I have reason.

Col. T. Whatever be the cause, I would to heaven it were in my power to bear the pain, or to remove the malady.

Aman. Your interference can only add to my distress.

Col. T. Ah, madam, if it be the sting of unrequited love you suffer from, seek for your remedy in revenge; weigh well the strength and beauty of your charms, and rouse up that spirit a woman ought to bear. Disdain the false embraces of a husband. See at your feet a real lover; his zeal may give him title to your pity, although his merit cannot claim your love.

Love. So, so, very fine, i'faith. [*Aside.*

Aman. Why do you presume to talk to me thus? Is this your friendship to Mr. Loveless? I perceive you will compel me at last to acquaint him with your treachery.

Col. T. He could not upbraid me if you were—he deserves it from me; for he has not been more false to you, than faithless to me.

Aman. To you?

Col. T. Yes, madam; the lady for whom he now deserts those charms which he was never worthy of was mine by right; and I imagined too, by inclination. Yes, madam, Berinthia, who now——

Aman. Berinthia! Impossible!

Col. T. 'Tis true, or may I never merit your attention. She is the deceitful sorceress who now holds your husband's heart in bondage.

Aman. I will not believe it.

Col. T. By the faith of a true lover, I speak from conviction. This very day I saw them together, and overheard——

Aman. Peace, sir, I will not even listen to such slander; this is a poor device to work on my resentment, to listen to your insidious addresses. No, sir, though Mr. Loveless may be capable of error, I am convinced I cannot be deceived so grossly in him, as to believe what you now report; and for Berinthia, you should have fixed on some more probable person for my rival, than she who is my relation and my friend: for while I am myself free from guilt, I will never believe that love can beget injury, or confidence create ingratitude.

Col. T. If I do not prove to you——

Aman. You never shall have an opportunity. From the artful manner in which you first showed yourself to me, I might have been led, as far as virtue permitted, to have thought you less criminal than unhappy; but this last unmanly artifice merits at once my resentment and contempt. [*Exit.*

Col. T. Sure there's divinity about her; and she has dispensed some portion of honour's light to me; yet can I bear to lose Berinthia without revenge or compensation? Perhaps she is not so culpable as I thought her. I was mistaken when I began to think lightly of Amanda's virtue, and may be in my censure of my Berinthia. Surely I love her still, for I feel I should be happy to find myself in the wrong. [*Exit.*

Re-enter LOVELESS *and* BERINTHIA.

Ber. Your servant, Mr. Loveless.

Love. Your servant, madam.

Ber. Pray what do you think of this?

Love. Truly, I don't know what to say.

Ber. Don't you think we steal forth two contemptible creatures!

Love. Why, tolerably so, I must confess.

Ber. And do you conceive it possible for you ever to give Amanda the least uneasiness again?

Love. No, I think we never should, indeed.

Ber. We! Why, monster, you don't pretend that I ever entertained a thought?

Love. Why then, sincerely and honestly, Berinthia,

there is something in my wife's conduct which strikes me so forcibly, that if it were not for shame, and the fear of hurting you in her opinion, I swear I would follow her, confess my error, and trust to her generosity for forgiveness——

Ber. Nay, pr'ythee, don't let your respect for me prevent you; for as my object in trifling with you was nothing more than to pique Townly, and as I perceive he has been actuated by a similar motive, you may depend on't I shall make no mystery of the matter to him.

Love. By no means inform him; for though I may choose to pass by his conduct without resentment, how will he presume to look me in the face again?

Ber. How will you presume to look him in the face again?

Love. He, who has dared to attempt the honour of my wife!

Ber. You, who have dared to attempt the honour of his mistress! Come, come, be ruled by me, who affect more levity than I have, and don't think of anger in this cause. A readiness to resent injuries is a virtue only in those who are slow to injure.

Love. Then I will be ruled by you; and when you shall think proper to undeceive Townly, may your good qualities make as sincere a convert of him as Amanda's have of me. When truth's extorted from us, then we own the robe of virtue is a sacred habit.

> Could women but our secret counsels scan—
> Could they but reach the deep reserve of man—
> To keep our love they'd rate their virtue high,
> They live together, and together die.
>
> [*Exeunt.*

SCENE II.

Sir TUNBELLY CLUMSY'S *House*.

Enter Miss HOYDEN, NURSE, *and* Young FASHION.

Young F. This quick despatch of the chaplain I take so kindly, it shall give him claim to my favour as long as I live, I assure you.

Miss H. And to mine too, I promise you.

Nurse. I most humbly thank your honours; and may your children swarm about you like bees about a honeycomb!

Miss H. 'Ecod, with all my heart; the more the merrier, I say—ha, nurse?

Enter LORY.

Lory. One word with you, for heaven's sake.
[*Taking* Young FASHION *hastily aside.*

Young F. What the devil's the matter?

Lory. Sir, your fortune's ruined if you are not married. Yonder's your brother arrived, with two coaches and six horses, twenty footmen, and a coat worth fourscore pounds; so judge what will become of your lady's heart.

Young F. Is he in the house yet?

Lory. No, they are capitulating with him at the gate. Sir Tunbelly luckily takes him for an impostor; and I have told him that we had heard of this plot before.

Young F. That's right. [*Turning to* Miss HOYDEN.] My dear, here's a troublesome business my man tells me of, but don't be frightened; we shall be too hard for the rogue. Here's an impudent fellow at the gate (not knowing I was come hither incognito) has taken my name upon him, in hopes to run away with you.

Miss H. Oh, the brazen-faced varlet; it's well we are married, or may be we might never have been so.

Young F. Egad, like enough. [*Aside.*] Pr'ythee, nurse, run to Sir Tunbelly, and stop him from going to the gate before I speak with him.

Nurse. An't please your honour, my lady and I had best lock ourselves up till the danger be over.

Young F. Do so, if you please.

Miss H. Not so fast; I won't be locked up any more, now I'm married.

Young F. Yes, pray, my dear, do, till we have seized this rascal.

Miss H. Nay, if you'll pray me, I'll do anything.

[*Exit* Miss HOYDEN *and* NURSE.

Young F. [*To* LORY.] Hark you, sirrah, things are better than you imagine. The wedding's over.

Lory. The devil it is, sir!

Young F. Not a word—all's safe; but Sir Tunbelly don't know it, nor must not yet. So I am resolved to brazen the brunt of the business out, and have the pleasure of turning the impostor upon his lordship, which I believe may easily be done.

Enter Sir TUNBELLY CLUMSY.

Did you ever hear, sir, of so impudent an undertaking?

Sir T. Never, by the mass; but we'll tickle him, I'll warrant you.

Young F. They tell me, sir, he has a great many people with him, disguised like servants.

Sir T. Ay, ay, rogues enow, but we have mastered them. We only fired a few shot over their heads, and the regiment scowered in an instant. Here, Tummas, bring in your prisoner.

Young F. If you please, Sir Tunbelly, it will be best for me not to confront the fellow yet, till you have heard how far his impudence will carry him.

Sir T. Egad, your lordship is an ingenious person. Your lordship then will please to step aside.

Lory. 'Fore heaven, I applaud my master's modesty.
[*Exit with* Young FASHION.

Enter SERVANTS, *with* Lord FOPPINGTON *disarmed.*

Sir T. Come, bring him along, bring him along.

Lord F. What the plague do you mean, gentlemen? Is it fair time, that you are all drunk before supper?

Sir T. Drunk, sirrah! here's an impudent rogue for you now. Drunk or sober, bully, I'm a justice o' the peace, and know how to deal with strollers.

Lord F. Strollers!

Sir T. Ay, strollers. Come, give an account of yourself. What's your name? Where do you live? Do you pay scot and lot? Come, are you a freeholder or a copyholder?

Lord F. And why dost thou ask me so many impertinent questions?

Sir T. Because I'll make you answer 'em before I have done with you, you rascal you.

Lord F. Before Gad, all the answers I can make to 'em is, that you are a very extraordinary old fellow, stap my vitals!

Sir T. Nay, if thou art joking deputy lieutenants, we know how to deal with you. Here, draw a warrant for him immediately.

Lord F. A warrant! What the devil is't thou wouldst be at, old gentleman?

Sir T. I would be at you, sirrah (if my hands were not tied as a magistrate), and with these two double fists beat your teeth down your throat, you dog you.

Lord F. And why wouldst thou spoil my face at that rate?

Sir T. For your design to rob me of my daughter, villain.

Lord F. Rob thee of thy daughter! Now do I begin to believe I am in bed and asleep, and that all this is but a dream. Pr'ythee, old father, wilt thou give me leave to ask thee one question?

Sir T. I can't tell whether I will or not, till I know what it is.

Lord F. Why, then, it is, whether thou didst not write to my Lord Foppington, to come down and marry thy daughter?

Sir T. Yes, marry, did I, and my Lord Foppington is come down, and shall marry my daughter before she's a day older.

Lord F. Now give me thy hand, old dad; I thought we should understand one another at last.

Sir T. The fellow's mad. Here, bind him hand and foot. [*They bind him.*

Lord F. Nay, pr'ythee, knight, leave fooling; thy jest begins to grow dull.

Sir T. Bind him, I say—he's mad. Bread and water, a dark room, and a whip, may bring him to his senses again.

Lord F. Pr'ythee, Sir Tunbelly, why should you take such an aversion to the freedom of my address, as to suffer the rascals thus to skewer down my arms like a rabbit? Egad, if I don't awake, by all that I can see, this is like to prove one of the most impertinent dreams that ever I dreamt in my life. [*Aside.*

Re-enter Miss HOYDEN *and* NURSE.

Miss H. [*Going up to him.*] Is this he that would have run—Fough, how he stinks of sweets! Pray, father, let him be dragged through the horse-pond.

Lord F. This must be my wife, by her natural inclination to her husband. [*Aside.*

Miss H. Pray, father, what do you intend to do with him—hang him?

Sir T. That at least, child.

Nurse. Ay, and it's e'en too good for him too.

Lord F. Madame la gouvernante, I presume: hitherto this appears to me to be one of the most extraordinary families that ever man of quality marched into. [*Aside.*

Sir T. What's become of my lord, daughter?

Miss H. He's just coming, sir.

Lord F. My lord, what does he mean by that, now? [*Aside.*

Re-enter Young FASHION *and* LORY.

Stap my vitals, Tam, now the dream's out.

Young F. Is this the fellow, sir, that designed to trick me of your daughter?

Sir T. This is he, my lord; how do you like him? Is not he a pretty fellow to get a fortune?

Young F. I find by his dress he thought your daughter might be taken with a beau.

Miss H. Oh, gemini! Is this a beau? Let me see him again. Ha! I find a beau is no such ugly thing, neither.

Young F. Egad, she'll be in love with him presently. I'll e'en have him sent away to gaol. [*Aside.*] Sir, though your undertaking shows you a person of no extraordinary modesty, I suppose you ha'n't confidence enough to expect much favour from me? [*To* Lord FOPPINGTON.

Lord F. Strike me dumb, Tam, thou art a very impudent fellow.

Nurse. Look, if the varlet has not the effrontery to call his lordship plain Thomas.

Lord F. My Lord Foppington, shall I beg one word with your lordship?

Nurse. Ho, ho, it's my lord with him now. See how afflictions will humble folks.

Miss H. Pray, my lord, don't let him whisper too close, lest he bite your ear off.

Lord F. I am not altogether so hungry as your ladyship is pleased to imagine.—Look you, Tam, I am sensible I have not been so kind to you as I ought, but I hope you'll forgive what's past, and accept of the five thousand pounds I offer. Thou mayst live in extreme splendour with it, stap my vitals!
[*Apart to* Young FASHION.

Young F. It's a much easier matter to prevent a disease than to cure it. A quarter of that sum would have secured your mistress, twice as much cannot redeem her. [*Apart. Leaving him.*

Sir T. Well, what says he?

Young F. Only the rascal offered me a bribe to let him go.

Sir T. Ay, he shall go, with a plague to him. Lead on, constable.

Enter a SERVANT.

Serv. Sir, here is Muster Loveless, and Muster Colonel Townly, and some ladies, to wait on you.
[*To* Young FASHION.

Lory. So, sir, what will you do now? [*Aside.*

Young F. Be quiet; they are in the plot [*Aside to*

Lory.] Only a few friends, Sir Tunbelly, whom I wished to introduce to you.

Lord F. Thou art the most impudent fellow, Tam, that ever nature yet brought into the world. Sir Tunbelly, strike me speechless; but these are my friends and acquaintance, and my guests, and they will soon inform thee whether I am the true Lord Foppington or not.

Enter Loveless, Colonel Townly, Amanda, *and* Berinthia.

Young F. So, gentlemen, this is friendly; I rejoice to see you.

Col. T. My lord, we are fortunate to be the witnesses of your lordship's happiness.

Love. But your lordship will do us the honour to introduce us to Sir Tunbelly Clumsy?

Aman. And us to your lady?

Lord F. Ged take me, but they are all in a story.

Sir T. Gentlemen, you do me much honour; my Lord Foppington's friends will ever be welcome to me and mine.

Young F. My love, let me introduce you to these ladies.

Miss H. By goles, they look so fine and so stiff, I am almost ashamed to come nigh 'em.

Aman. A most engaging lady, indeed!

Miss H. Thank ye, ma'am.

Ber. And I doubt not will soon distinguish herself in the beau monde.

Miss H. Where is that?

Young F. You'll soon learn, my dear.

Love. But, Lord Foppington——

Lord F. Sir!

Love. Sir! I was not addressing myself to you, sir! Pray who is this gentleman? He seems rather in a singular predicament——

Col. T. For so well-dressed a person, a little oddly circumstanced, indeed.

Sir T. Ha, ha, ha! So, these are your friends and your guests, ha, my adventurer?

Lord F. I am struck dumb with their impudence, and cannot positively say whether I shall ever speak again or not.

Sir T. Why, sir, this modest gentleman wanted to pass himself upon me as Lord Foppington, and carry off my daughter.

Love. A likely plot to succeed, truly, ha, ha!

Lord F. As Gad shall judge me, Loveless, I did not expect this from thee. Come, pr'ythee confess the joke; tell Sir Tunbelly that I am the real Lord Foppington, who yesterday made love to thy wife; was honoured by her with a slap on the face, and afterwards pinked through the body by thee.

Sir T. A likely story, truly, that a peer would behave thus?

Love. A pretty fellow, indeed, that would scandalize the character he wants to assume; but what will you do with him, Sir Tunbelly?

Sir T. Commit him, certainly, unless the bride and bridegroom choose to pardon him.

Lord F. Bride and bridegroom! For Gad's sake, Sir Tunbelly, 'tis tarture to me to hear you call 'em so.

Miss H. Why, you ugly thing, what would you have him call us, dog and cat?

Lord F. By no means, miss; for that sounds ten times more like man and wife than t'other.

Sir T. A precious rogue this to come a wooing!

Re-enter a SERVANT.

Serv. There are some gentlefolks below to wait upon Lord Foppington.

Col. T. 'Sdeath, Tom, what will you do now?
[*Apart to* Young FASHION.

Lord F. Now, Sir Tunbelly, here are witnesses, who I believe are not corrupted.

Sir T. Peace, fellow! Would your lordship choose to have your guests shown here, or shall they wait till we come to 'em?

Young F. I believe, Sir Tunbelly, we had better not have these visitors here yet. Egad, all must out.
[*Aside.*

Love. Confess, confess; we'll stand by you.
[*Apart to* Young FASHION.

Lord F. Nay, Sir Tunbelly, I insist on your calling evidence on both sides, and if I do not prove that fellow an impostor——

Young F. Brother, I will save you the trouble, by now confessing that I am not what I have passed myself for. Sir Tunbelly, I am a gentleman, and I flatter myself a man of character; but 'tis with great pride I assure you I am not Lord Foppington.

Sir T. Ouns! what's this? an impostor? a cheat? Fire and faggots, if you are not Lord Foppington, who the d—l are you?

Young F. Sir, the best of my condition is, I am your son-in-law; and the worst of it is, I am brother to that noble peer.

Lord F. Impudent to the last, Gad dem me.

Sir T. My son-in-law! Not yet, I hope.

Young F. Pardon me, sir; thanks to the goodness of your chaplain, and the kind offices of this old gentlewoman.

Lory. 'Tis true, indeed, sir; I gave your daughter away, and Mrs. Nurse, here, was clerk.

Sir T. Knock that rascal down! But speak, Jezabel, how's this?

Nurse. Alas! your honour, forgive me! I have been overreached in this business as well as you. Your worship knows, if the wedding-dinner had been ready you would have given her away with your own hands.

Sir T. But how durst you do this without acquainting me?

Nurse. Alas! if your worship had seen how the poor thing begged and prayed, and clung and twined about me like ivy round an old wall, you would say, I, who had nursed it, and reared it, must have had a heart like stone to refuse it.

Sir T. Ouns! I shall go mad! Unloose my lord there, you scoundrels!

Lord F. Why, when these gentlemen are at leisure, I should be glad to congratulate you on your son-in-law, with a little more freedom of address.

Miss H.. Egad, though, I don't see which is to be my husband after all.

Love. Come, come, Sir Tunbelly, a man of your understanding must perceive that an affair of this kind is not to be mended by anger and reproaches.

Col. T. Take my word for it, Sir Tunbelly, you are only tricked into a son-in-law you may be proud of; my friend, Tom Fashion, is as honest a fellow as ever breathed.

Love. That he is, depend on't; and will hunt or drink with you most affectionately; be generous, old boy, and forgive them——

Sir T. Never. The hussy! when I had set my heart on getting her a title.

Lord F. Now, Sir Tunbelly, that I am untrussed, give me leave to thank thee for the very extraordinary reception I have met with in thy d—d, execrable mansion; and at the same time to assure you, that, of all the bumpkins and blockheads I have had the misfortune to meet with, thou art the most obstinate and egregious, strike me ugly!

Sir T. What's this? I believe you are both rogues alike.

Lord F. No, Sir Tunbelly, thou wilt find, to thy unspeakable mortification, that I am the real Lord Foppington, who was to have disgraced myself by an alliance with a clod; and that thou hast matched thy girl to a beggarly younger brother of mine, whose title-deeds might be contained in thy tobacco-box.

Sir T. Puppy! puppy! I might prevent their being beggars, if I chose it; for I could give 'em as good a rent-roll as your lordship.

Lord F. Ay, old fellow, but you will not do that, for that would be acting like a Christian, and thou art a barbarian, stap my vitals!

Sir T. Udzookers! Now six such words more, and I'll forgive them directly.

Love. 'Slife, Sir Tunbelly, you should do it, and bless yourself. Ladies, what say you?

Aman. Good Sir Tunbelly, you must consent.

Ber. Come, you have been young yourself, Sir Tunbelly.

Sir T. Well, then, if I must, I must; but turn—turn that sneering lord out however, and let me be revenged on somebody. But first look whether I am a barbarian or not; there, children, I join your hands; and when I'm in a better humour I'll give you my blessing.

Love. Nobly done, Sir Tunbelly; and we shall see you dance at a grandson's christening yet.

Miss H. By goles though, I don't understand this. What, an't I to be a lady after all? only plain Mrs. ——What's my husband's name, nurse?

Nurse. Squire Fashion.

Miss H. Squire, is he? Well, that's better than nothing.

Lord F. Now I will put on a philosophic air, and show these people, that it is not possible to put a man of my quality out of countenance. [*Aside.*] Dear Tam, since things are fallen out, pr'ythee give me leave to wish thee joy; I do it *de bon cœur*, strike me dumb! You have married into a family of great politeness and uncommon elegance of manners, and your bride appears to be a lady beautiful in person, modest in her deportment, refined in her sentiments, and of nice morality, split my windpipe!

Miss H. By goles, husband, break his bones, if he calls me names.

Young F. Your lordship may keep up your spirits with your grimace, if you please; I shall support mine by Sir Tunbelly's favour, with this lady and three thousand pounds a year.

Lord F. Well, adieu, Tam. Ladies, I kiss your hands. Sir Tunbelly, I shall now quit this thy den; but while I retain the use of my arms, I shall ever remember thou art a demn'd, horrid savage; Ged demn me! [*Exit.*

Sir T. By the mass, 'tis well he's gone, for I should ha' been provoked, by-and-by, to ha' dun un a mischief. Well, if this is a lord, I think Hoyden has luck o'her side, in troth.

Col. T. She has indeed, Sir Tunbelly——but I hear the fiddles; his lordship, I know, had provided 'em.

Love. O, a dance and a bottle, Sir Tunbelly, by all means.

Sir. T. I had forgot the company below; well—

what—we must be merry then, ha? and dance and drink, ha? Well, 'fore George, you sha'n't say I do these things by halves. Son-in-law there looks like a hearty rogue, so we'll have a night on't: and which of these ladies will be the old man's partner, ha? 'Ecod, I don't know how I came to be in so good a humour.

Ber. Well, Sir Tunbelly, my friend and I both will endeavour to keep you so: you have done a generous action, and are entitled to our attention. If you should be at a loss to divert your new guests, we will assist you to relate to them the plot of your daughter's marriage, and his lordship's deserved mortification; a subject which perhaps may afford no bad evening's entertainment.

Sir T. 'Ecod, with all my heart; though I am a main bungler at a long story.

Ber. Never fear; we will assist you, if the tale is judged worth being repeated; but of this you may be assured, that while the intention is evidently to please, British auditors will ever be indulgent to the errors of the performance. [*Exeunt.*

END OF VOL. I.

PRINTED BY BALLANTYNE, HANSON AND CO.
LONDON AND EDINBURGH

www.ingramcontent.com/pod-product-compliance
Lightning Source LLC
Chambersburg PA
CBHW030315240426
43673CB00040B/1174